IMAGINOMICON

Mardukite Research Library Catalogue No. "Liber-3D"
Cover Graphics and Systemology Logos by Kyra Kaos
Published from
Mardukite Borsippa HQ, San Luis Valley, Colorado

A MARDUKITE SYSTEMOLOGY PUBLICATION

IMAGINOMICON
THE GATEWAY TO HIGHER UNIVERSES

A GRIMOIRE FOR THE HUMAN SPIRIT

BY JOSHUA FREE

© 2021, JOSHUA FREE

ISBN : 978-0-578-91362-9

A MARDUKITE SYSTEMOLOGY PUBLICATION

Mardukite Research Library Catalogue No. "Liber-3D"

Published by the *Joshua Free Imprint* for the *Mardukite Academy of Systemology*
A division of the *Founding Church of Mardukite Zuism & Systemology Society*

cum superiorum privilegio veniaque

FIRST EDITION

First Printing — June 2021

The Way Out. Hidden for 6000 Years.
But now we have the Key.

IMAGINOMICON

A Grimoire to Summon and Invoke,
Command and Control, the
Most Powerful Spirit to Ever Exist.

* YOUR SELF *

Ascend Beyond Physical Existence,
Fly Across All Gateways Freely,
Go Back to When it All Began and
Reclaim that Personal Universe
Where the Spirit once called Home.

All Creation, Space, Life, Universes and Everything in between -- whether apparent in physical existence or not -- operates as "Systems."

These subjects often give the impression of being too vast, complex or irrelevant to daily life to really "know" about; or else we are told they cannot be known with certainty, remaining matters of opinion, such as *alternate realities, cosmic evolution, metahuman,* the *Mind* -- and yes, contemporary traditional methods in present society still have no handle on the *Spirit*, the only "thing" which *every one* of us actually *is*.

The truth is that we *can know* about these things; and not because of advancements in physical sciences, but because we all play a role *creating things* to *know about* for any Universe we are present. We simply agree to forget, then assign all responsibility for creation (and power to be at cause) to some "unknown source"; and now we *have* something to "think on" and "figure out" again, as is the standard way Humans "earn" their knowledge.

A true understanding of this "Systemology" reveals a basic underlying pattern back of *all* existence:

—Whether a *Cell* - or a *Solar System*;

—Whether an *Atom* - or a *Galaxy*;

—Whether a single *Life* – or entire *Dimensions*; and

—Whether a product *created* by unlimited *Imagination* of an individuated *Self*, as a point of *Awareness* operating from an original native "Alpha" state in a personal "Home Universe" – or an *Effort* applied by *Force* from a *genetic-body* "interior" to this Physical Universe, operating from an implanted "internal" viewpoint, existing to entrap considerations and focused *Awareness* of a *Spiritual Being* to "believe" itself so strongly *identified* "as" a "material body" that care and protection of a "body" and its survival occupy most of our attention in a lifetime.

Examining systems -- in Self-Honesty -- for its parts, we certify that "*bodies*" and "*minds*" exist, but are also separable from each other; and neither one is the *Spirit*. "I" as *Self* is only "I-AM" and not actually identifiable as a *Body* or a *Mind.* Yet, no matter what is said religiously or philosophically in passing, an individual still tends to "believe" that they *are* one-- thinking, acting, even "looking" out in the world while identifying *Self* exclusively with a viewpoint and its "lens" of perception; and additional fragmentation ensues.

IMAGINOMICON demonstrates true actualized command of a Mind-System, and control of a Body, as operated from "outside of" those Systems, not from an interior viewpoint. This is an optimum position, not only to better handle the Human Condition in this Physical Universe, but also as a Master Key to unlock realizations that make experience of "Higher Universes" potentially possible.

During this transitional period of Human history, returning an individual's *Awareness* to its true "Alpha" state is the primary goal. Wizardry of the IMAGINOMICON goes beyond New Age ideas of "astral work" or "mental travel" and even techniques dependent on "energetic" bodies. A Seeker gains certainty on conscious abilities to knowingly separate *Self* (as *Spirit*) from the Human Condition and Physical Universe and experience existence independent of *any* Mind-Body System.

IMAGINOMICON provides training necessary to recognize the *Gateway* bridging Physical and Spiritual Universes; and exercises to practice ability to manage freely crossing the threshold between existences -- succeeding here, where other paths have failed to reach beyond the boundaries of their paradigms of traditional mysticism and conventional spirituality; libraries filled with magical correspondences, obscure symbols and outdated methods carrying poorly duplicated messages -- none of which have actually brought Seekers any closer to truly *"breaking free from the Matrix."*

Creation and experience of "Higher Universes" *condensed* into more rigidly solid environments; each time imposing more barriers, reducing freedoms and narrowing considerations for what *Self* is willing (and able) to *be, know, do,* and *have.* The IMAGINOMICON brings a *Seeker* from being, in effect, a victim of the Physical Universe, up to a certainty of ability to knowingly create from within their own Personal Universe.

The *Spirit* never stopped existing or creating in a Home Universe; but it *agreed* to superimpose other creations and considerations as their own. Fragmentation simply causes this unknowing continuous compulsive creation to persist on automatic. Systemology techniques decrease the intensity and energetic charge of *"imprints"* and *"implants"* that *anchor* an individual's point-of-view and considerations for their own existence to the Physical Universe. After countless lifetimes spent with Awareness scattered in fragmentation, isn't it time someone demonstrated how to clean up the pieces and pull your *Self* back together in wholeness?

Rather than rely on cultural mythologies, cosmologies and imperfect kabbalahs, Mardukite Systemology goes straight to the source, using *Arcane Tablets* of Mesopotamia as inspiration to chart an effectively workable course for *The Pathway to Self-Honesty.* This required several former volumes in this series to detail appropriately, including *"Tablets of Destiny,"* *"Crystal Clear"* and *"Metahuman Destinations,"* while we waited patiently to finally begin delivering the "Wizard Grade" work.

IMAGINOMICON demonstrates a realization of goals achieved with the very first complete defragmentation procedure outline. Precise instructions and references guide a Seeker *up* the *Pathway* and *through* the *Gates.* This special premiere edition also includes two supplemental Basic Courses, providing newcomers and returning Seekers with a concise summary of Systemology to date, vocabulary, diagrams and advice for effective use as an applied spiritual philosophy.

Released to the Mardukite Academy and Systemology Society as *Liber-3D,* completing *Wizard Level-0, Grade-IV Metahuman Systemology.*

TABLET OF CONTENTS

DEDICATION

to those on the Pathway
and climbing the Ladder
and to Next Generations
of rising Metahumans

—

Love unto the
uttermost generation
is higher than
the love of one's
neighbor.
What should be
loved about
humanity,
is that it is in
transition.
—F. NIETZSCHE

∞

EDITOR'S NOTE

"The Self does not actualize Awareness
past a point not understood."
—*Tablets of Destiny*

While preparing this book for publication, the editors
have made every effort to present this material in a
straightforward manner—using clear, easy to read and
understand language.

Wherever appropriate, ambiguous and archaic terms
are described in the text, defined as numbered footnotes
and/or found in the glossary.

A clear understanding of this material is critical for
achieving actual realizations and personal benefit from
applying philosophies of *Mardukite Zuism* and
NexGen Systemology spiritual technology.

The *Seeker* should be especially certain not to simply
"read through" this book without attaining proper
comprehension as "knowledge." Even when the
information continues to be "interesting"—if at any point
you find yourself feeling lost or confused while reading,
trace your steps back. Return to the point of
misunderstanding and go through it again.

It is expected that a *Seeker* will work through this material
multiple times to achieve optimum results.

And *now* responsibility for this power and its actualization
is passed on to you, the *Seeker*.

Take nothing within this book on faith.
Apply the information directly to your life.
Decide for yourself.

∞

IMAGINATION
is more important
than knowledge.
For knowledge is limited
to all we now know
and understand,
while imagination embraces
the entire world and
all there ever will be to
know and understand.

—A. EINSTEIN

Woe! Woe!
Thou hast destroyed it!
The Beautiful World!
The demigod crushed it!
Destroyed!

We carry its fragments
into the void.

Create! Create!
Build it again,
The Beautiful World!
Stronger! Brighter!
Build it again,
Build, in your heart
with senses washed clean,
Begin Life's new start.
Create! Create!
Create!

—GOETHE, "FAUST"

IMAGINOMICON

— FIRST STEPS —

A MARDUKITE SYSTEMOLOGY
BASIC INTRODUCTION COURSE

:: General Introduction to Mardukite Systemology ::

THIS IS SYSTEMOLOGY—A HISTORY & OVERVIEW
[Summation Presented by David Zibert]
REVISED INTRODUCTION FOR GRADE-III

Since the inception of the Mardukite NexGen Systemology Society a decade ago, many things have been brewing quietly and unseen in the underground; but, fear not, as slowly but surely, everything will be brought to light... as a "New Babylon" *is rising*—and the Grade-III work is now complete.

Original literary presentations of NexGen Systemology occurred underground in 2011 and continued through 2013. Essential materials from this period were reissued as "*Systemology: The Original Thesis.*" These materials first began to appear in 2011 as a series of booklets by Joshua Free, which at first glance were actually quite different from anything he had really presented before. The booklets were the first to present "Systemology"—or else, the work of the "Systemological Society"—as an offshoot of the Mardukite Research Organization and extension of the Mardukite Chamberlains group, which previously participated in development of our former Grade-II "Mardukite Core" research library, now collected in its entirety within the anthology: "*Necronomicon: The Complete Anunnaki Legacy.*"

Of course, "Systemology" stands for "system logics"—or else, "the logics behind the systems," which is also to say, in more esoteric terms: "the magic behind the magic."

In 2011, several booklets were released in the original Systemology "thesis" series; the first titled "*Human, More Than Human: Awakening to the Next Evolution.*" It was really a down to earth approach; a simple user-friendly booklet about how, quite literally, "Humans are more than Human"—that we are more than our physical body and that there are actual "worlds" out there that most individuals are unaware of in their daily lives. It was really just taking the reader by the hands and saying in a rather basic and gentle way how *"we are more than human."*

The original underground release and presentation of Systemology was quite peculiar at the time. Even I wasn't sure what the goal was behind all this. But in the end, it made sense—and there was a brief follow-up published soon after: *"Systemology Defragmentation: Self-Honesty for the Next Evolution."* This title delved into the core of the matter and explained the basic theory behind "defragmentation" processes; which is the same as *ascent* up the *"Ladder of Light"* as we know it from our *Grade-II* presentation of the Babylonian *"Spiritual Star-Gate"* paradigm.

Systemology presented a new approach to the core *Pathway*; the same *Pathway* represented by the previous "Mardukite Core" and our explorations into the Babylonian paradigm proper—but these new booklets presented main tenets of this core without the more esoteric, magical or religious semantic trappings that we commonly find with other literal interpretations of the *Arcane Tablets*.

Then, a third booklet continued this original thesis series, arriving in 2012 as *"Transhuman Generations: The Next Evolution of a Species."* It relates how worldviews are programmed in the generational cycles that repeat over an over—and, of course, when most individuals are unaware of that taking place, such as we see today in the world that we live in, a cyclic history is bound to simply repeat itself. Although the material is quite basic, it is an important consideration for Self-Actualization.

Another installment appeared in 2013, titled *"Systemology For Life: Patterns and Cycles."* This one continued in the spirit of *"Transhuman Generations,"* but emphasized personal cycles— and about cycles repeating themselves—yes, through the generations, but more specifically, cycles repeating themselves as we experience them as individuals: how to notice them, and go beyond them, of course, toward the goal of *Self-Honesty* which is, again, achieved via "defragmentation."

These booklets described above are now gathered together for a small anthology reissued officially as *"Systemology: The Original Thesis."* They also appear in the complete Grade-III anthology: *"The Systemology Handbook."* In addition to these, a few other small underground releases were not as widely circulated. One of these being *"The Games: Portals of Self-Transformation & The Underground Occult Initiation."* It was a very controversial booklet when it was first published; relating some of Joshua Free's adventures in the West Coast Occult Underground. Excepts continue to be reprinted in various volumes.

It became apparent in 2013 that many individuals, even those among the Mardukite network still studying the *Grade-II* "Mardukite Core," were not ready for Joshua Free's new "Systemology" developments at face value. Very few outside our elite close-knit membership of the original "NexGen Systemological Society" really took notice of what we working toward from 2011 to 2013—and we continued to work even more quietly and unnoticed thereafter. Of course, this was all about to change with the public reboot that is presently going on now as we enter the 2020's.

There is also an interesting aspect of "Mardukite Systemology" uniquely experienced by an individual that follows the work of Joshua Free chronologically from its beginning—and seeing how "Systemology" *was* the goal; seeing how it was always the *unspoken goal* standing in the center of everything since the very beginning of Mardukite Ministries and the Mardukite Research Organization in 2008. An individual sequentially studying the materials for our complete "Master Course Grades" may still experience this development personally for themselves. Anyone who has read certain introductory material from *"Necronomicon: The Anunnaki Bible"* or *"The Complete Anunnaki Bible"* by Joshua Free—even those individuals that read *"The Great Magickal Arcanum"*—will notice that the "logic of systems" *and* an aim toward applied spiritual technology of "Systemology" is what has been there all along, underlying the journey, driving the work forward.

Δ Δ Δ Δ Δ Δ

In October 2019, the Systemology Society experienced a new public debut with an arrival of the first true core textbook for Grade-III, catalogued as *Mardukite Systemology "Liber-One,"* released globally as *"The Tablets of Destiny: Using Ancient Wisdom to Unlock Human Potential"* and published from the new *Joshua Free Imprint*. It concisely presents the entire fundamental foundation for "Mardukite Systemology" itself—and upon which a series of further Systemology publications are now based upon.

Great care has been taken with *"Tablets of Destiny"* (*Liber-One*) so that everything in the book is as clear a message as possible—particularly for a novice of this paradigm—including concise definitions of each word that could be problematic or misunderstood during solitary studies. Care is also taken in clearly defining vocabulary newly introduced for our Systemology. Furthermore, *Liber-One* includes a summary of each lesson, given at the end of a chapter for optimal clarity. I also found that these summaries are great for just a quick second reading and review.

"The Tablets of Destiny" (*Liber-One*) is actually *not* a rehash of what was done before (with *"Systemology: The Original Thesis"*) —it is a completely new presentation. It presents, for example, the logics behind the systems, and of what "Mardukite Chamberlains" had discovered concerning Babylon. We had once been like: "Okay, we found *that*. Now, *what* do we *do* with it?—And how does everyone get *benefit* from it?" But now, *this* is where we are. This is what we *do*.

And *this is* Grade-III "*Mardukite Systemology.*"

At its most basic core: Mardukite Systemology is an applied spiritual technology of the 21st century AD, based on the spiritual wisdom from the 21st century BC; which were compiled in their rawest tablet forms and presented for the *Grade-II* Mardukite Core—"*Complete Anunnaki Bible,*" "*Sumerian Religion,*" "*Novem Portis*" and so on.

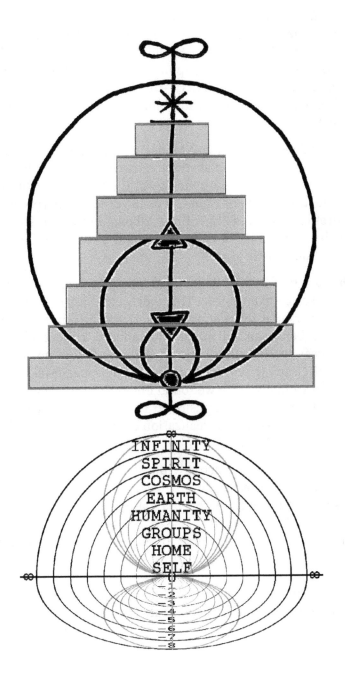

Grade-III launches with *Liber-One*, introducing what we have termed the "Standard Model" (of Systemology), otherwise known as the "*ZU-Line*" (in Mardukite Zuism). This, in itself, is a workable, non-dogmatic, applied spiritual technology of the same *Babili* "Ladder of Lights"—the StarGates of this Universe —of which a *Seeker* is already familiar with by first working through *Grade-II*.

So, how does the "Standard Model" or "ZU-Line" work? Well, first of all, these are an abstract construct, graphically defining parameters for a Systemology of the Human Condition. It is divided as *seven*—or *eight*—steps for practical purposes, but theoretically extends to Infinity, above and below its scale; just like the Ladder of Lights paradigm of *Gates*, or any such similar Kabbalistic Model.

"*The Tablets of Destiny*" (*Liber-One*) focuses on the lower levels of the scale—from *0-to-4*. This work emphasizes building a strong personal foundation of emotional health and mental strength before an individual is introduced to more advanced practices—such as those included in its follow up manual, "*Crystal Clear*" (*Liber-2B*) and the other upper-level Grades. But, most importantly, we found out that a sane "Mind-Body Connection" is a prerequisite to experiencing a *Self-Honest*, clear and unfragmented realization of Self as "I-AM" ("Alpha-Spirit") in this lifetime.

This new approach is actually quite different from previous attempts and other traditions; even the most pious *Gnostic* paradigms still continue to *reject* material existence—what we refer to as "*beta-existence*"—as an "illusion." We are not rejecting the Physical Universe in Mardukite Systemology; no, rather we acknowledge that its existence is based on artificial agreements regarding an otherwise very real universe, in which a Human being—operating as a "*genetic vehicle*"—is the tool used to experience such a reality.

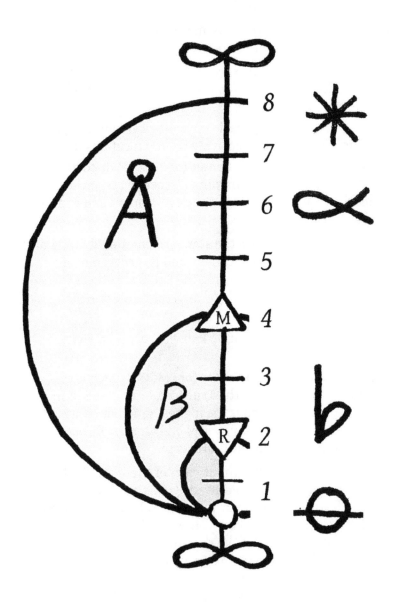

Lower gradients of the *ZU-line* (*Standard Model*) run as follows —but, be aware that these descriptions are something of an over simplification; there is more to it, though this should suffice for our present introductory review:

0 — Inert Matter (theoretical zero, since everything in existence is basically a motion), or else Body Death (for the "genetic vehicle");

1 — Physical Body (basic physiological functions/cellular "fight/flight") receiving communications from...

2 — Reactive Control Center (or "RCC") which includes survival programming ("reactive response mechanism") inherent to the development and experience of all physical life.

Between "1" and "2" lies the standard emotional range of the Human Condition, which can be, and is, programmed and encoded with *imprints* preventing the Self from access to its own experience of higher levels of *Awareness* in *Self-Honesty*. Then we have:

3 — Thought (associative knowledge) and activity communicated from...

4 — Master Control Center (or "MCC") which is the point of contact from the True Self, or Higher Self in some paradigms, and is the highest gradient relating to the genetic vehicle or physical body for the Human Condition in the Physical Universe.

Self-Honesty is to be sought at each of these gradients as one moves upward on the "Pathway." This means that, for example, if you are not at a point of Self-Honesty regarding gradient "1" and "2," then you won't be certain to have a Self-Honest command of the thoughts and programming beyond that, which is preventing you from experiencing the *knowingness* and *beingness* of your "Higher" or "Truest" expression of Self; which we refer to as the "Alpha Spirit"—the "I-AM"—a spiritual being which merely maintains *considerations* of experiencing a beta-existence.

In effect what is sought on this "Pathway" is a clear *communication* with the continuity of All Life—and that starts with your own—and when you have a Self-Honest experience of your own life, you practice the same for ALL Life at each Sphere of Existence, or else it isn't truly Self-Honesty. This systematic process—as we present it in our "Systemology"—begins with removal of emotional imprinting; all of which is coming from the *Reactive Control Center* (RCC) and so cannot be seen rationally and analytically by the *Master Control Center* (MCC). This means that most people live their life in a reactionary fashion, often under the control of their emotions without even knowing it.

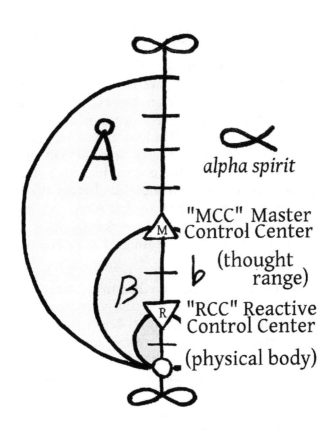

alpha spirit

"MCC" Master Control Center

(thought range)

"RCC" Reactive Control Center

(physical body)

Here, it is important to mention, that what is implied by references to "emotions" really concerns the negative states of the Human Condition—which are all reactionary in nature—such as hopelessness, fear, anger, lust, jealousy, and so forth. For example: usually when you are angry, you are operating as a reaction to something—and the encoded mechanisms are commanded by the *Reactive Control Center* or *RCC* (plotted at "2.0" on the Standard Model or ZU-line). This is quite different from experiences of more positive states, such as being "in love" or personal enthusiasm about *willingness* to act on something, *&tc.*, which puts the individual at *cause*, rather than as an *effect*, and which are commanded by the *Master Control Center* or *MCC* ("4.0").

Much of our Mardukite ("NexGen") Systemology paradigm could be summed up as returning the Self to the state of being Cause rather than the Effect. An individual should always be able to use the *Master Control System* to control their thoughts, noticing if the *Reactive Control Center* takes over with its emotion control, and even correct this condition with methods of *"Self-Processing."** Pre-programmed automated reactivity may eventually be dissolved altogether—and that's *Self-Honesty*; *that is* our "Systemology" in a nutshell. Of course, there is much more to this and our methodology of application; but the important part to understand about the "levels" is that *Self-Honesty* is still to be sought at each *gradient*—and a *Seeker* will quickly discover that these tiers of *true realization* act as *Gateways* to accessing increasingly higher points of "Actualized Awareness."

The first of our basic practical method to systematically process "emotional imprinting" effectively is described and outlined fully in *"Tablets of Destiny"* (*Liber-One*), referred to as "Route-1" in later Grades. And there are many other practical processes to assist a *Seeker* within *Grade-III* material as included in the follow up workbook style companion, *"Crystal*

---

* Details for "Self-Processing" are introduced in *"Crystal Clear"* (*Liber-2B*), also contained in the complete Grade-III anthology, *"Systemology Handbook."*

Clear" (*Liber-2B*), released in December 2019, just two months after "*Tablets of Destiny*."

The basic theory supporting the Standard Model and *ZU-line* is represented by a simple cosmology rooted in lore contained on *Arcane Tablets* from ancient *Mesopotamia*. To put it simply: you have "AN" which is the "*Spiritual*"; and "KI" which is the "*Physical*"—between which exists a *continuum* called "ZU," which manifests as "*Life*" or else "*Spiritual Life Awareness*." A more specific treatment og the nature of "ZU" became the subject of "*The Power of Zu*," a supplemental lecture series delivered by Joshua Free in December 2019, for the release of "*Crystal Clear*." Lecture transcripts were published in book form and also appear in the complete Grade-III anthology, "*Systemology Handbook*."

Yes, we are aware that some individuals will see "*Tablets of Destiny*" and "*Crystal Clear*" as merely just another "Self-Help" book series—which from a certain perspective this *is* a "Self-Help" series—but my take on this is that apparent these "Self-Help" books containing "deep esoteric occult wisdom" makes for a great change from all those books posing as "deep esoteric occult wisdom" and yet turn out to be mere Self-Help books that provide "no help."

But, as is generally written at the beginning of each volume of material: "Don't take anything from these books on faith. Apply these principles directly to your life..."—then confirm whether these principles and methodology are true for you, from the perspective of Self;

and thus not only discover,

but live, the *Life* you were meant to *live*,

Self-Honestly as a *Free Spirit*.

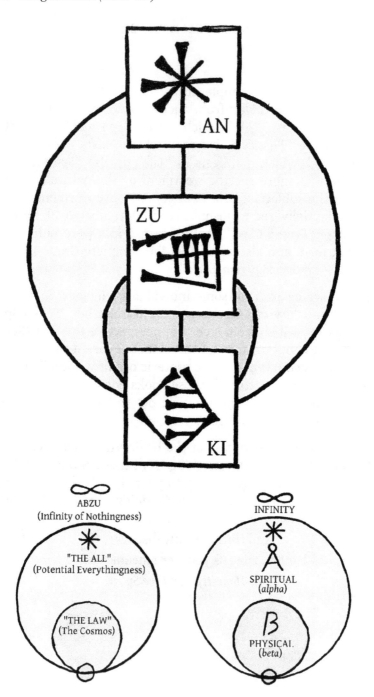

:: THIS IS GRADE-IV MARDUKITE SYSTEMOLOGY ::
PROFESSIONAL PILOTING PROCEDURES
COURSE INTRODUCTION
[Based on the lectures by Joshua Free]
REVISED VERSION

SYSTEMOLOGY is the practical application of "systems theory" to the study and spiritual experience of *Life, the Universe and Everything*. This "spiritual technology" may be referred to as "NexGen Systemology," "Mardukite Systemology" and/or "Metahuman Systemology" to distinguish it from other academic sciences and modern uses of the term.

MARDUKITE SYSTEMOLOGY is a developing product or result from intensive work conducted by an official extension of the "Mardukite Research Organization" in late 2010, as directed and recorded by mystic philosopher and underground esoteric author, Joshua Free. *Systemology* work is treated as the applied spiritual philosophy and practical technology accessible to us today (and for the future) from the oldest cuneiform writings and *Arcane Tablets* set down in ancient Babylon—from the heart of Mesopotamia and "Sumerian" civilization.

There are some *Seekers*—operating below the knowledge tier of Grade-III Mardukite Systemology—that treat the same *Arcane Tablets* with an exclusively religious or mystical appreciation. This is known as MARDUKITE ZUISM—though to be clear, the two movements are mutually *inclusive*. We now treat *Mardukite Systemology* as the "upper level" applied spiritual philosophy, techniques for spiritual counseling and methodology of spiritual evolution (Self-Actualization) methodology *for* the formerly established "religio-mystical" understanding of *Mardukite Zuism*, in any of its derivative forms found today, including "Mesopotamian Neopaganism."

Training at our Academy for Grade-IV "Metahuman Systemology" is treated as an "intermediate course." However, the book themselves are presented in a straightforward direct manner and may be "understood" by anyone—of course, to the extent or level an individual has actualized their "ledge" of understanding. For this reason, our Master Grades of Research and Discovery, which a Seeker may study separately, are structured to represent three "levels" of increasing understanding that lead toward a basic state of *Self-Honesty* and *Actualized Awareness*. The subject of each Grade always remains the same: *Life, Universes and Everything*. The only factor that differs is the "level" of understanding used to treat study and practice of the information.

"*Systemological Self-Processing*," as introduced in Grade-III ("*Crystal Clear*"), developed after a decade of additional experimental esoteric research privately conducted by remote members of an underground "Systemological Society." This ongoing exploration into "applied spiritual philosophy" is established in light of all collected wisdom from various mystical and spiritual pursuits during the last 6,000 years of record history—most of which is found to be either erroneous and/or unworkable in effectively producing consistent stable results for higher states of *Actualized Awareness*.

Whether performed alone using a workbook (like "*Crystal Clear*"), with assistance of a friend, counseling from a Minister of Mardukite Zuism or by a Professional "Pilot" of Systemology, the functional purpose of "*Systemology Processing*"—or "*systematic processing*"—is for a Seeker to effectively *actualize* true *realizations* that produce positive movement upward on the "Pathway to Self-Honesty."

During a twenty-five year engagement with the underground esoteric and "New Age" community, Joshua Free discovered that the majority of practitioners following the "Route of Magick and Mysticism"* or "Route of Druidism and Dragon Legacy"‡—and other esoteric traditions amalgamated from diverse "organizations," "orders" and "fellowships"—were

---

* Grade-I, Route-A; see "*The Great Magickal Arcanum*" by Joshua Free.
‡ Grade-I, Route-D; see "*Merlyn's Complete Book of Druidism.*"

not independently arriving at the intended *realizations* from these philosophies, much less an *actualization* of the same, that might lead an individual steadily *outside* of the "Human Condition." This is just one of the stumbling blocks Joshua Free discovered concerning most contemporary approaches to "enlightenment" and various metaphysical "Self-Help" regimens.

A primary goal of our Systemology—which should be evident by the techniques and training for *Grade III*—is raising an individual's state of *Actualized Awareness*. This requires, by definition, bringing what is hidden into the light, or else carrying those aspects of "consciousness" existing below a level of analytical surface thought up to such where they may be treated "consciously" or "knowingly" as *Self*—from the perspective of the true and actual *Spiritual Self*—which we call the "Alpha Spirit."

Raising a *Seeker's* "level" of *Awareness*—*Actualized Awareness*—means very simply bringing more of an individual's "actual present space-time" (beta)-*Awareness* in "phase" or "synch" with the "Alpha Spirit"—the True "I-AM"-*Self*. This brings power and attention of *Awareness* more under control of the *Seeker*, which is to say a "clear communication" of *actual* potential.

"It is my goal for NexGen Systemology that we can elevate the *Actualized Awareness* of all *Seekers*—all able *Humans*—on Earth and to provide a true vehicle for their spiritual evolution in Self-Honesty. It is an objective for all Systemology Pilots and Mardukite Ministers to bring conscious *Awareness* of *Humanity* up and out from the heavy sticky murky mud they are subjected to. By cumulatively shedding skin and layers of everything that is not the true I-AM Self, achieving greater realization in Self-Honesty and increased *Actualized Awareness*, a *Seeker* ascends through a sequence of Gates to Higher Understanding—and ultimately to experiencing the Higher Universes that we have merely forgotten about."

A *Seeker* is introduced to *Grade-IV* with the third professional volume in our series, *"Metahuman Destinations: Piloting the Course to Homo Novus"*—and therein discovers that they are at an intermediate stepping stone between two great planes of realization:

a.) what has come before—treated as the "Master" levels, including basic *Grades I-II*, and the *Grade-III* "Pathway to Self-Honesty" distinguishing "Mardukite Systemology"; and

b.) what we are leading into now—using *Grade-IV* as a stable reaching point toward our higher "Wizard" levels, distinguishing remaining Grades of "Actualized Technology" (*A.T.*) still forthcoming.

"Professional Piloting Procedure" is introduced in the *Grade-IV* volume, *"Metahuman Destinations"*; meaning we now can provide both the Pilot *and* Seeker with skill development, education and strengthening personal certainty of the "Alpha Spirit" as an "Actualized Technician" (*A.T.*) of this spiritual technology.

Joshua Free first announced an integration of "Systematic Self-Processing" and "Professional Piloting" into Mardukite Systemology during a lecture given on August 9, 2019.*

"There are many solitary methods of heightening Awareness and increasing mental skills necessary for 'processes,' but I bring up this example... because when engaged in [professional] processing, there are two people involved: one of them is going through the 'processing' toward Self-Honesty and one of them is assisting from a point of Self-Honesty. We identify the one receiving the service, or going through the 'processing,' as the Seeker. In order to differentiate a very specific role that the assistant has in this process, the individual administering the 'processes' is referred to as the Pilot. And let me make this point clear from the get

---

* Transcripts appear as an extended course published in the original edition of *"Tablets of Destiny" (Liber-One)* and reprinted in the complete *Grade-III* anthology, *"Systemology Handbook."*

go: the Pilot is specifically and exclusively responsible for Self-Honestly assisting the Seeker in reaching their chosen *destination*—nothing more or less. The Pilot is not a tour guide; not an interpreter; not a doctor; certainly not a therapist in the traditional sense—they are offering no actual advice toward or against anything that is uncovered as a result of systematic processing. Any and all realizations are meant for the Seeker to discover, determine and actualize on their own. The Seeker merely has the confidence now of knowing there is a safety net of travel by someone who has already been where they want to go!"

Based on this description, your first thoughts may be that *Grade-IV* course material must pertain exclusively to rigorous "procedures" and esoteric philosophies useful only to upper-level students of our unique underground brand and style of knowledge dissemination. But, this could not be any further from the truth. *Anyone* can benefit from the instruction and applied spiritual philosophies explained and demonstrated in every Mardukite Systemology publication.

Many believe that all respectable spiritual, mystical or philosophical "routes" regarding *Life, the Universe and Everything,* are headed in the "same direction" or considered in equal regard. If humanity's historical timeline and workable effectiveness of their methods are any indication, we can be certain the resulting "destination" for this plethora of "routes to knowledge" brewed within the intellectual labyrinths of the "human condition" are anything but equal to one another. In fact, what—if anything—could be truly identified as "equal" to anything else in this "physical universe" (which we refer to as *"beta existence"*). In fact, "associative knowledge" and the inability to properly *distinguish* "things" from other "things" in *beta-existence*, is one of the primary sources of "personal fragmentation"—resolution of which is a main priority of our Systemology.

The purpose of systemology and systematic piloting is to support responsibility of the Prime Directive in *beta-existence* of all *Life, Universes and Everything*—which is *to exist* and to act toward a continuation of *existence*—and for this purpose: to actualize the highest reach as "cause" on the Spheres of Existence. This is to say "defragmenting"—or clearing energetic channels—all the way up to to the highest states of knowing and being, or *Actualized Awareness*. At this higher truer point of *Self-Awareness* as an Alpha-Spirit—beyond compulsive and unknowing participation in the "Human Condition"—the original Alpha Prime Directive finally returns: *to create.*

Being high-level "cause" means *Self-directing* communication and control of energy and power consistently toward continuation of a higher and truer personal viewpoint from this "Alpha" state. This includes *Self-directing* effects that will promote the highest ideals of "ethical utility" as the individual reaches across the "Spheres of Existence."

Δ Δ Δ Δ Δ Δ Δ

In the professional *Grade-IV* installment published as *"Metahuman Destinations,"* a Systemologist learns the fastest route toward actualizing the highest extent of reach as "cause" is to act toward assisting all existence insofar as it mutually helps to maintain the Prime Directive at all levels; "help" being one of the highest forms of communication, which allows an individual to *be* at a position of *cause* and also increase energy frequencies on the Zu-line. The ability to extend our reach as "cause" is accelerated by the "help" and "assistance" of whatever we may take responsibility for, even if its only responsibility of being in communication with a Universe.

When we consider the role of "Pilots" in Systemology—they are helping and assisting a Seeker, which in turn is helping and assisting the Pilot's reach. A *Seeker* must be willing *to be* helped and assisted—and be willing to help and assist the Pilot—by providing a full "attention" (presence) for participation in the session and processing communications. The Pilot or Minister must also be willing and able to help and assist a *Seeker*.

The first part of *Grade IV* emphasizes defragmentation of *communication*—all personal communication systems—and proper command of the same. "Communication, Command and Control" is a particularly important stable orientation point for fully accessing further work. For experimental and training purposes, this part was originally released for the Academy as *"Liber-2C"* and *"Liber-2D"* in Spring 2020; revised as "Unit-1" and "Unit-2" within *"Metahuman Destinations"* released in October 2020.

The remainder of *Grade IV* introduces the systematic design of Bodies, Minds and Universes. Emphasis turns toward a new methodology of techniques to put personal power of consideration, creative ability and command of imagination back under full *Self-determination*. An extension of earlier work as it applied to newer goals composed an Academy draft of *"Liber-3C"* in Summer 2020, but reissued as "Unit-3" in *"Metahuman Destinations."* This development allowed a cross-over for Grade-IV—and the completion of its objectives and goals—as "Systemology Wizard Level-0" with publication of *"Imaginomicon"* (*Liber-3D*) a year later in Summer 2021.

"And when one truly realizes the full considerations that a combination of communication and imagination truly has upon the individual, an entirely new or previously unreachable universe of possibilities suddenly becomes real again; becomes a potential Reality again within the reach of Self as Alpha Spirit. Each an every one of us is a participant in the creation of universes and realities and we have the responsibility to our Self to permit the highest freedom of the Alpha Spirit to once again unfold as the present Awareness as Self. This is a state that is completely within reach of all individuals on planet Earth today; all we have to do is free ourselves to create a better world. So, let's get together and help one another create a better world."

:: AN INTRODUCTION TO METAHUMAN SYSTEMOLOGY ::

OBJECTIVES AND GOALS OF MARDUKITE GRADE-IV
[Based on a lecture by Joshua Free]
REVISED VERSION

Completion of the "Core" for *Grade-III Mardukite Systemology* allowed our work to move up to a new level of understanding and practicality; and now we are able to speak from an even greater, higher, more widely encompassing perspective with *Grade-IV Professional Piloting Procedure*—as presented in "*Metahuman Destinations*" (*Liber-Two*) compilation. We are still moving upward on the *Pathway* and not simply restricting this knowledge-to what applies exclusively to *Piloted* processing.

We are dealing with new vistas for our understanding and are achieving significant advancements toward our true end goals at an accelerated rate. But it is important that we do not miss any steps along the way—important for all *Seekers*, whether *Pilots* or otherwise. It is apparent to many working through this material that we have tapped into something that shifts us up and beyond what we find at the *Master Grades*, but it was always dependent on what realizations were in reach up to this point.

Grade-IV builds upon former instruction given as the *Grade-III* "Master" level of Mardukite work that precedes our present "Wizard" *Grades*. To make certain no stone has remained unturned, a Seeker is prompted systematically through the *Grade-III* work as an integral part of *Grade-IV,* and combined, the "whole package" is intended to yield very specific attainable goals. Before we move a *Seeker* beyond *Grade-IV* there are certain things we expect from the processing taking place and realizations held. There is no question that an adequate education of true knowledge can accelerate this journey—but this is only on an assumption that a *Seeker* is ready to receive and interpret the information. Otherwise, its just more data added to a heap.

We have all made decisions—however much they may seem influenced by external or other-determined sources—about what we are *willing* to be, *willing* to do, *willing* to have a communication with—and *Self* does not like to be wrong. So, here we are systematically unwrapping this mess of convoluted beliefs and confusing agreements we made as Self along the way. You would think it should be an easy task, but the Human Condition is very much tied to the "physical" way of things—and the more greatly an Alpha Spirit identifies *Self* or *"I"* with this "physical" way of things, it becomes that much harder to change considerations about anything; and I mean *real* "change." If an individual really could freely change their considerations about existence as freely as they might like to think they can, then states of strong fragmentation would not exist and persist. And yet they do.

The purpose of "systematic processing"—within the tradition of ministry in Mardukite Zuism and applied spiritual philosophy in Metahuman Systemology—is to increase free range of consideration available to an individual; regain command and control of their Human Condition *knowingly* as an Alpha Spirit. We have traveled down a long pathway to the present state of affairs in this Universe—and this journey has indeed left us in a state of severe fragmentation; has left us fragmented about the identity of *Self.* With absence of true knowingness, the true creative ability of the Spirit diminishes if fixedly stuck in *considering* that these conditions of the Physical Universe are the absolute. I am here to tell you that this entire Physical Universe—this *beta-existence*—that the Human Condition is presently anchored to, is but a speck of dust in the widest encompassing considerations of the ALL.

There is no reason for me to be unnecessarily esoteric here: each and every one of you carries a certain knowing that you have descended or "fallen" from some higher consideration of space-time energy and form—and just about every spiritual, philosophical and scientific methodology of the contemporary age seems to hint around a bit about this; but few of us are now content in waiting around to see what any further *agreement* with knowledge about the design of this Physical Universe (*beta-Existence*) is going to offer. Some of us have already peeked behind the screens and know what it is going to offer: a way of further dividing what is already here into another sub-level universe that the consideration of *I-as-Self* can get entrapped in.

The subject of *willingness* appears very frequently in our Systemology—and if we are going to think about things in terms of "magic" or "will" or "intention" and everything else along those lines, then this is the common meeting ground and a place to start; and it is why we consider this upper-route of Mardukite Metahuman Systemology as "Wizard" work; this position to be that some in our *Piloting* courses have referred to as "Actualized Technicians" and "Alpha Tech" and so on. Many have realized this is getting us where we want to be—and there is no question about this.

The questions, at least for me, have always returned to organization and delivery, the means of structuring research and way in which its discoveries are analyzed—all of which has occupied nearly a decade now of my current lifetime, just in regards to the Systemology that I have been involved in developing behind-the-scenes of the more publicly visible Mardukite *Grade-II* work and the "Routes" explored in *Grade-I*. But all of this contributed to our "Complete Mardukite Master Course"—these other "Routes" are excellent entrance points onto the *Pathway* so long as they are treated as such and not as the ends in themselves. That is too often the alluring trap, and why such methods are allowed to be so freely explored in contemporary society: they are just betting you will get trapped in them.

By its very definition, "fragmentation" implies separation and disconnection; or what some define as dissonance, disharmony and discontinuity... a lot of "dis" words in there. It is for this reason that we emphasize "communication" at the very start of *Grade-IV*, in *"Metahuman Destinations"*—because a *Seeker* is not going to get any further with their Master Grade material without some remedy of being very blatantly "out of communication" with *Life*, the *Universe* and whatever the individual is *unwilling* to "know," *unwilling* to "be" or "face" or "confront" and so on. A *Seeker* has narrowed their decisions of what is acceptable or conceivable to "know" or "be" within preexisting programming and thus has become an "effect" of the same—thereby giving up responsibility for Self-determinism of the Alpha state.

This isn't a "fire and brimstone" sermon; I'm not here saying all this to judge or condemn; you have actually already accomplished that part on your own for your Self—and there is more value in my working to remedy *that* condition than there is in my reinforcing it as others have done in their methods of using knowledge, religion and spirituality to further trap humanity in the lower systems. We are all here now because we suddenly found ourselves *unwilling*—or believe ourselves *unworthy*—to consider any *Higher Universe* to occupy —and that, in a nutshell, defines the actual present state of affairs we are treating in our Systemology.

Δ Δ Δ Δ Δ Δ Δ

The journey down a *Pathway of Fragmentation* that led us to this point did not happen all at once—nor is it important that we grasp a complete understanding of our full Cosmic History at this juncture of work in order to deliver or receive effective processing. We are most concerned with what a *Seeker* is able to relate to concerning *this* lifetime, before we begin to compound matters any further. We already demonstrate the significance of these principles with application to *this* lifetime using systematic methods of *Analytical Recall* ("Route-2") as introduced in our text, *"Crystal Clear"*; and newer methods linking circumstances and experiences to energetic flows referred to as "circuits" for of *Communication Processing* ("Route-3") in "Metahuman Destinations."

When a *Seeker* is brought to consider moments they have gone out of communication in their life experiences, the realizations that may occur can be startling—but they are what we are targeting to overcome. Of course, if we emphasize only the negative states and conditions, we would only be effective in validating the negatives—which is only one type of flow. So, we may, for example, have the *Seeker* recall a time when they were in "good" communication in alternation with those times when they had broken ties or "cut" communication lines with others and yes, even "things"—really any "form" with "mass" that we assign a label to and which can hold, carry or incite some kind of energetic charge; and this is referred to as a "terminal."

Another excellent example to demonstrate to *Seekers* is what *willingness* has been diminished in connection—or rather "disconnection"—to certain *facets* that are emotionally charged or otherwise imprinted to restrict considerations. Each and every one of us has certain "charged" *places*, or *people* or *ideas* that trigger something—some kind of "ping"—just by their being flashed into our view. Sometimes we do not even need a physical representation of this to be present in our physical environment. Merely the thought or *concept* of it—being formed in our Personal Universe, or as some consider, the "Mind's Eye"—puts us in a position to be "for" or "against" some mode of consideration. We are not even talking about "intuition" here, although it is sometimes mistaken as such when these channels aren't clear.

For example, an individual experiences some type of traumatic event or *Imprinting Incident* at such and such place and around such and such type of facets and suddenly the *willingness* for any later *duplication* of these is diminished. The individual doesn't even want to be around that physical area location any more and will even go to great lengths to avoid this "other-determined" restimulation that exposure incites. We've covered this stuff in *Grade-III* pretty well, especially in regards to the emotional encoding discussed in "*The Tablets of Destiny*" text. The point that was not necessarily driven home within that volume is that this successive validation of being "out of communication" with existence led *Self* down a dark spiral of intentional forgetfulness; and this is a state that we are only now discovering any real remedies for, after having swirled about within this murky mess for countless aeons.

When we talk about "communication," we often mean *willingness* to reach for *knowingness*. There is also the method of processing that we consider "objective," and this targets the *willingness* to reach for action and the command and control of *doing* things as cause. Yes, we want to understand Cosmic Law or Causal Law; but it is not hard and certainly not as convoluted as physical sciences make it out to be. The average *Grade-II Mardukite* or Hermetic philosopher "understands" Cosmic Law pretty well—they have a handle on some of the basic principles by which beta-existence has been Ordered. But we are not trying to get entrapped any further into this Physical Universe and therefore do not need to make our sole occupation a discovery of more intricacies to agree with. It is, for the most part, a closed system with the illusion of recursive infinity so that it may become the sole occupation of its inhabitants; infinitely divisible by "discovered knowledge"— which has to be created and forgotten just get a sense of being discovered again.

A 6,000 year legacy of secret and esoteric knowledge to mastering the worldly universe is what is "mastered" at the "Master" levels of our work, or rather the "*Master Grades.*" Most individuals who have come and gone never even reach the apex of *this* much during their lifetimes, then alone move past it. It is a quite enamoring study—and it has been concisely condensed within our series of Master Edition hardcover volumes including: *The Great Magickal Arcanum, Merlyn's Complete Book of Druidism, Necronomicon: The Complete Anunnaki Legacy* and especially our *Grade-III* compendium, *The Systemology Handbook.* Corresponding Mardukite Academy lectures and supplements are collected in an additional companion volume: *The Complete Mardukite Master Course.*

The *Pathway* that led us to this point is treacherous and tortuous. As much as we are set out to desensitize or discharge more commonly known implanted terminals of the Human Condition, it should be observed that there are just as many—

if not more—potential trappings when one crosses that first *Gate* and has stepped beyond exclusive considerations of mundane existence. This is when a lot of dissonance starts to occur and a ritual magician of the present age does not realize they are sitting in their circles talking to themselves, changing themselves or their considerations if effective; but more often than not, they are waiting for the *Books* and *Candles* to start talking *to them*, and well... we have already seen the personality effects that result from hanging suspended too long within that first sphere.

None of the lower Graded Routes are inherently wrong or bad in the moral or ethical sense. What they are—and what we have presented them as—are tiers on a very well-known *"Ladder"* of ascent that lead us through the same barriers of consideration that we contributed in setting up for ourselves on the way here. When this responsibility is dismissed, we have no actual authority or control over the matter. It is true we have given it up; have decided at one time or another that it would be better not to have it—but, now we know our mistake. The only issue, until fairly recently, is that there have been no successful demonstrations of a map to remedy this mistake. We've just sort of "lived with" it and agreed to it as a reality. They've just kept telling us to "suck it up" and "this is how it is" and we have agreed to be this effect via the very participation with this Game.

Handling of systematic processing—at Grade-IV—is codified by a schedule called: *Systemology Operating Procedure 2-C*, since it was introduced in *Liber-2C*, it is our second official outline of procedure, and is also a step toward basic restoration of the Alpha Spirit's ability "to see." *SOP-2C* is fully outlined in the text, *"Metahuman Destinations."* Its structure continues and incorporates what we already set out in *Grade-III*. For example, Resurfacing from *"Tablets of Destiny"* and Analytical Recall from *"Crystal Clear"* are still both retained and valid in *Grade-IV*.

Willingness to "recall" and "resurface" and "remember"—the consideration that it is acceptable to *do so* without reservation—is where the *Seeker* arrives directly in *Grade-III*. At least, this is where we should expect them to arrive. If they aren't getting there on their own—and we're not going to leave them behind as a result—we simply incorporate *Grade-III* work as a preliminary to approaching the full extent of *Grade-IV*, and development of *SOP-2C* allows for this. There is no reason that a *Seeker* cannot "self-process" themselves through the full extent of *Grade-III* work, either. The thing of it is: there is no short-cutting these processes and side-stepping realizations.

Without a free and total *willingness* for analytical recall on any aspect on an internal level, there can be no clear communication and certainly no demonstration of *Piloted* processing that will prove effective. We can process a *Seeker* to increase willingness for analytical recall and thereby improve their reach as communication, but until this whole matter is satisfactorily been resolved, there is no reason to even consider work of "higher" *Grades* and *Routes*. They will not prove to be as effective as they otherwise would be in the right hands or applications.

At *Grade-IV* we apply processing that directly targets energetic flow of communication and the *Seeker's* willingness to engage or reach as a *Self-directed* action—which again requires working through a whole host of energetic masses that have accumulated from heavily charged experiences; those that lay as a mass or resistance on an otherwise freely dispersing wire or energy current. If that seems too esoteric, let us just say that we must clear the obstacles that exist in the pathway of true *Self-honest* vision for the Alpha Spirit.

Fragmentation at this level of processing—particularly as it applies to the most readily available memory that we can resurface from this lifetime—is, at its core, entirely *analytical* or *mental* in nature. And by this, I mean that it is linked to the realm of "Thought." The fundamental inhibitions and excuses, the inabilities and hindrances we attach to our personality, the blocks and long lists of things we don't want to know or acknowledge—all of this accumulates over time, persisting to affect our range of present-time considerations and thoughts, based on fixed solidity of former considerations and thoughts; including those we have chosen to forget about and no longer take responsibility for.

All of this contributed to where we have considered *Self* to be; and all of this, once recognized and realized and accepted, becomes a map *out* of the mess we got ourselves into. All that is waiting, is for us to take the responsibility and resume command. That's it! That's all we have to do. But since we have so carefully and systematically arrived at this state we are at now, it seems it takes a bit more than a single moment of passive "positive thinking" to pull us completely out of its gravity. It shouldn't have to; though for the amount of fragmentation that most individuals are carrying around, it seems to take a little more work. But, I am pleased to say that: systematically, we *have* found a way, and that *is* the essence of our work now today.

::A Mardukite Academy Lecture by Joshua Free::
SYSTEMOLOGY—THE ORIGINAL THESIS
[Master Course Lecture #39]
INTRODUCTION COURSE EDIT

Grade-III "Mardukite Systemology" as it is presented now—and its continuing evolution—is a consequence subsequent to application of my *original thesis* on Systemology, itself a composition of multiple essays and various papers I presented to the underground "*Systemological Society*" nearly a decade ago.

During the past ten years, "Mardukite Chamberlains" Alumni and members of *Moroii ad Vitam* continued to assist and support the original "*NexGen Systemological Society*" even though very little had been published on the subject officially between 2013 and 2019. A combination of *those* individuals *and* incessant application of my "*Systemology: Original Thesis*" theory *to* Grade-II work resulted in, *finally*, "*The Tablets of Destiny*" nearly a year ago, which is "*Liber-One*"—really the public inception—of what took nearly a decade of underground work to establish officially as "Mardukite Systemology."

Although, it's not—it's something that's used for "posterity." We don't really require, for example, an individual to have read "*Systemology: The Original Thesis*" in order to understand "*The Tablets of Destiny*" or to apply the material in "*Crystal Clear*" to their life. However, for purposes of having a "Master" understanding of how this all developed and what this all entails, it *is* all included in the Grade-III Master Edition textbook, "*The Systemology Handbook*." It is also available as a stand-alone title.

"*Systemology: The Original Thesis*" applied a *philosophy* to a general universalist understanding of the Human Condition. It was definitely of a "Mardukite" flavor, because, of course, it incorporated the idea of the ancient Anunnaki, the establishment of civilization and its progression—as we've cover it

Grade-II and "*The Complete Mardukite Master Course.*" But, it was mainly a *philosophy.*

It wasn't until we *crossed* this philosophy numerous times with ancient cuneiform texts—which we refer to numerous times as the *Arcane Tablets*—that we were able to get any kind of *workable* effective systematic methodology out of this information. This, of course, spawned Mardukite Systemology. which has actually been able to develop at an exponential rate—as a result of finally breaking through with these *Keys.*

It's ironic, because what we are talking about in Grade-III is the "Ishtar Gate," and so, the level of—well, I've made jokes in the past about "getting beyond the Ishtar Gate"; that it was something that just didn't seem to have happened anywhere, as far as recorded traditions in history, and in the literary preservation of these systems—in regards to how "actualized" the various "initiates" and "followers" of these other "routes" really were.

The objective *goal* of Grade-III to complete the Master Grades, has always been about *breaking through* the Ishtar Gate; actually being able to surpass the point of initial "beta-fragmentation" as it concerns, for example, emotional reactivity and all of the "pre-patterned" forms of behavior that seem to override and take over our sensibilities, or an individual's ability to command experience as *Self*, and actually be *Self-Directed* and *Self-Determined* in totality. So, it was at *that* point—in delivering material to that point—that we finally capped off the "*The Complete Mardukite Master Course*" with three Master Grades; because, what else is it but, you know, a gradient of Self-Mastery. And so, that's where we're at.

In the original presentation of the thesis, the first booklet is referred to as "*Human, More Than Human.*" The catch phrase for this—and the pamphlet for it—and the way we've even re-introduced "*The Tablets of Destiny*" when we were promoting it a year ago was that:

"The Universe exists within a Sea of Infinity, an ocean of pure potentiality. Do you know your place? Sealed within the Human Condition is a unique life program special to you. Unlock the power of your true identity and live the life you were meant to, Self-honestly as a Free Spirit within NexGen Systemology."

"And what we discovered—or rediscovered—is not a *new* methodology, but the *first* one: the archetypal System of Systems known to the ancients. We used it. We applied the acid test of reality—and only the truth remained. We saw it first hand; beneath the veils and levels and layers of the systems... only the truth remained."

And therein, I began a series of booklets to compose "*Systemology: The Original Thesis*"—trying to drive in the direction of "metahuman" or *homo novus*, this next level of Awareness and Realization and Beingness, that seemed to be only scraped upon or alluded to in all these former spiritual systems and mystical traditions; but of which has never seemed to be obtained or never seemed to be able to be delivered—at least, never to *my* satisfaction.

There was always this allusion that "well, there might be something in the afterlife; or if you do good now, well good things will eventually happen to you" or something of this respect. But, other than this "morals and dogma" mentality, there didn't seem to be a delivery to any point; no one even seemed to be any *happier* or *better off* in the long run for the fact that they were actually working through whatever it is they were working through—they were always still lost in their own fragmentation and operating on various imprinting and so forth.

So, what I was really working to establish in "*Human, More Than Human*" is the idea that humans are *more than* human; I mean, it's kinda given in the title. And this has been kind of joked about in the past, by those that have commented on it, about how blatantly forthright some of this really was. Then again, it could still be taken kind of "tongue in cheek"—with a "Well, we've kind of all known *that*, but then we've been told we *have a soul* and there's spiritual forces at war over us and then we go to Heaven or we go to Hell" and so forth.

Well—[*sniffs*]—I really didn't find any of that to be the case within our Systemology. *But*, I did find that an individual *was* themselves this thing they had separated as "soul." The individual *was* "spirit," *was* "I-AM," *was* the "Alpha" of this other existence, and that any of this other stuff that had been attached to it *was* basically *that*: energies and masses and fragments, memories, different emotional encoding, implants, that had been *attached* to the individual by their own considerations and identification of "I-AM" *to* anything.

It was *those things* that were weighing down the quality of the Spirit, the quality of what they were considering "soul." *But*, it isn't like an individual "had" one; like, they were carrying it around in their pocket or something like that—but that it *is* what the individual actually *is*; and that is what we consider the "Alpha Spirit" in Systemology.

Another concept introduced at the very beginning of the thesis is this very idea of "fractioning" of reality—that there's separations—and that these separations are what an individual has a sense of. As separation of individuality and true knowingness takes greater hold—as more and more fragmentation is basically standing in the way of a clear view and a clear channel between Self and its own experience—that's when an individual begins to feel more *solemn*, they feel more *hollow*, there is a certain *sadness* that takes over; they become more *introverted*.

Now, when I say *introverted*, I don't mean someone that has the ability to, you know, "self-analyze" or "look within" or be able to observe their own behavior or correct patterns of the Mind and so forth—but an "introverted person" that's basically just *withdrawn* from their interaction and communication with energies, their interaction with flows and energies, the social environment and so forth. This is one of the things that seems to *dim* along with the decline of *Actualized Awareness*.

The other thing pointed out in *"Human, More Than Human"* regards the "standard issue" state of a Human being—and how they basically go about their everyday lives *believing* they're "Self-directed" and *believing* they're "Self-determined" and that they are actually experiencing life and everything with clarity, but that there is actually so much artificial programming and fragmentation and "conditioning" taking place— and control over the mental imagery, the associations of knowledge, all of the emotional responses that are attached to experience and former encounters with different facets of life—that really get in the way of that.

The purpose of *"Crystal Clear"*—because we knew it was going to take a while to establish any kind of "Piloting Program" or get a solid "Ministry" and elements of "clergy" and "Zuism" on the road—is that *"Crystal Clear"* is really meant to be a *"self-processing"* guide, although it can be used quite effectively along with Piloting. But it was really meant to be a self-processing guide that an individual could use on their own. Back when I was writing material for *"Systemology: The Original Thesis,"* we *didn't* even have a workable concept of "self-processing" available; we didn't have any kind of practical effective aspect to apply our philosophy until we really spent many more years with it.

When you start to look at what we've done with *"Tablets of Destiny"* and *"Crystal Clear,"* a lot of the stuff from *"The Thesis"* seems very *elementary* and basic; but the material from *"Systemology: The Original Thesis" is* a fairly accessible introduction to our work, if not using *"The Tablets of Destiny"* directly. Another, more recently released, publication of ours excerpts introductory material from all Grade-III sources—*"The Way Into The Future: A Handbook For Humanity"*—with selections from my writings edited by James Thomas, one of our Publication Staff Officers.

An individual that doesn't really have a background in Meso-potamia, that hasn't worked through Grade-II materials, might actually be able to *reach* a few of the realizations on their own, just by working through the material of "*The Thes-is*" prior to treating, for example, "*The Tablets of Destiny*" directly. It's for that reason that I bring this up, because although we treat Grade-III in a certain way now, my aspirations toward it may be even found in "*The Great Magick-al Arcanum.*" In fact, since the 1990's, I had always intended on this gradient of work being an upper-level of, for example, the "*Hermetic Order of the Crystal Dawn*" that I was operating underground in the "Merlyn Stone" days.

The whole purpose—or the actual reasoning behind the name "Crystal Dawn" had to do with this same "crystal clarity," the same "metaphors" that we apply all the way up to present day, you know, *twenty years* later with "*Crystal Clear.*" That was essentially the functional purpose of the establishment of the "Crystal Dawn" *project* back in the late 1990's. At the time, before "*Arcanum*" and the Mardukites, we didn't have a "Master Grade" system to actually bridge this kind of understanding.

I was primarily dealing with Grade-I type involvement in the 1990's and the first few years of the 21st century—and the individuals around me, the ones I was encountering, for example, in the "New Age" marketplaces and bookstores and so forth, were still primarily stuck still considering things only at that level. The rest of them, those that were considered "Lightworkers" or dealing in "Eastern Spirituality" and "chakras" and whatnot, they seemed to be pretty much, you know, attached to their own paradigms with that—but were still not *quite* breaking through to find effective means of *really releasing* from the Human Condition.

It's really that element—the idea of the Human Condition being something *separate* from *Self*, separate from I-AM, that is actually one of the pinnacles of Grade-III realizations. This is something that former levels of understanding (or former Grades) are not necessarily impressing fully. They kind of make it seem like, "Well, you're this being or an Awareness and when you die you just float around as this ghostly being and so forth" or "your shackled to one of these or another afterlives" or "you go off to happy hunting grounds." These are artificial spiritual beliefs; they're attached only to certain "religions" and so forth; they don't necessarily have any other basis in fact.

In the language of Grade-III, when we're talking about "*encoding,*" we're talking about the *emotional* level of "*imprinting.*" And this is what, in the past, or in psychology or in other philosophies, we might refer to as "conditioning." And then, when we're talking about "*thought,*" when we're talking about beliefs—when we're talking about the associative knowledge that an individual has with the actual understanding that they're maintaining with the world around them—we're talking about basic mental programing; we're talking about the Mind-System at that point.

Our Standard Model is not just spiritual puffery. It also demonstrates that in *beta-existence,* a "Mind" and a "Body" *communicate* through stimulation of biochemicals. So, again, what we find is that there are certain "push-button" mechanisms attached to the Human Condition, where it can be "conditioned" or "fragmented" or "controlled" or "manipulated" or given false knowledge based on sensory stimulation and *encoding* of essentially either "*pleasure*" or "*pain.*"

We see a lot of imprinting and fragmentation attached to points of, for example, *pain*, or in other elements, *loss*—any sense of suffering on the individual; because, you're talking about *that* individual's experience from *within* that Body, and the more that happens, the individual begins to *feel*, the individual begins to start *thinking as* identified with a Body.

The programming for parameters of *beta-existence* all come from within, *interior* to Mind-Systems and the Human Condition. The more an individual, for example, feels pain, and isn't really able to confront or face the nature of that—or maintain control over that experience and their *Mental Imag-*

ery and *imprinting* of that experience—they begin to become more and more the *effect* of, for example, their experience of and as the Human Condition. They begin to associate and then identify more and more of what they believe Self or I-AM *is* with the Human Condition.

In the past, this has been treated only loosely in some "regressive" techniques and certain forms of "creative psychology" and so forth; but, it's never really been brought into the level of "mysticism" or being treated at, for example: just last week at the Academy we were talking about "ritual magic," we were talking about "Anunnaki"—potentially "alien gods" and things, you know, for the last few days—and now we're talking about ways of basically relieving the suffering of the Human Condition enough to get an individual to *free* their considerations outside, the fact that they're not their body.

Now, when we talk about things like the "Matrix-System"—today, this is an example where we have certain pieces of *inspired* science-fiction media and so forth, which kind of demonstrate a certain understanding or at least give tangible *examples* for concepts—that many years ago would be harder to explain, and harder for individuals to understand. For example, now everyone has at least some kind of idea of a "Reality Matrix-System" now. But really, we consider a "matrix" like a "grid." The "grid" implies action in multiple directions, so we're talking about a *duality*—we're talking about systems that basically operate with energy flows due to considerations of polarity. This is even touched on in *"Liber-R,"* the final installment of Grade-II, *"Novem Portis"* or *"Necronomicon Revelations,"* which was written and released simultaneously with the first portion of *"The Thesis."*

But, we're talking about the "Matrix"—we're talking about a visible series of lights, the "array," the "light-matrix"—the System—that basically is what you can see; what is around, what is given substance. And an individual participates in this regularly. That is one of the functions of the Alpha Spirit: that they can *create*—if nothing else, they *create* the imagery

experienced within their own Universe. This is what is basically being "snap-shot" around us—we, you know, there is a
certain sense of newness or "novelty" when we discover
something or see something for the first time; and there is a
certain *imprint* that takes place, which kind of dulls our
Awareness thereafter, when we basically lead off the *imprint*
we carry as what is real.

So, let's say you've got a certain encounter taking place. It's
basically just energy and mass moving through space and giving a concept of time or duration. Then experience takes over
—the parameters of what the senses can experience; the Human Condition can take over; and then all of this is given a
classification and other associations for identification. And so
the next time an individual encounters the "same" thing,
there is a certain energy signature—key waves and frequencies that are picked up by sensory faculties of the body, since
the Spirit is no longer interested in handling it directly—and
rather than give it full attention, like as if it were new, we get
basically just a replay—we get basically just an experience of
the former snap-shots that have been taken, and thrown up
at us. That's basically all of what we are experiencing in *beta-
existence*; because the *Self* still has to *create* the *image* of the
form that is being treated, based on the energy signatures received. A lot of times, this is what causes the "world around
us" to kind of "cave in"—because we aren't really (consciously) participating in its creation anymore; we've just
basically passed on that responsibility. Although we are still
creating it, we're creating it just on basic pictures and imprints and snap-shots from the past that we are compulsively
still creating.

The second text that was developed—the second booklet that
was released for "*Systemology: The Original Thesis*"—was called:
"*Defragmentation.*" Again, a very self-explanatory title. After
establishing the nature of the Alpha Spirit in "*Human, More
Than Human*," the "*Defragmentation*" booklet was about, basically, getting back to that point. This is where Self as an
Awareness Point or Total Consciousness is treated as the

I-AM or the *"Alpha Free Spirit"* (as it was originally referred) and that a Self-Honest experience of the I-of-Self *is* the only *True Identity* of the *Individual* and the only *True Point-of-View* of the Observer; the most basic, prime—*Alpha*—state of Self.

Programming—and what some have called "conditioning"—or encoding, is what dictates fragmentation of the. And, of course, you have a material existence, since it is consciousness-created, it is fragmented and developed by these creative Alpha Spirits; and we are *all* participating in doing this. The stuff of Universes has been created, compacted, recycled, turned to dust, compacted again and made a bit more solid for the next condensed level of material Universes. Basically, these systems are composed of fragmented parts; and then, of course, they work and are interrelated to each other —and that's where we start to deal with this idea that what we're dealing with is called "Systemology." Because even when we're talking about traditions and different paradigms and all of the ways in which this ancient wisdom has been extended to us, you still have modern systems that are essentially fragments of an ancient wisdom.

Here we start to treat the nature of systems, systems operating within each other, larger systems operating upon smaller ones—kind of *"cog-wheel"* aspects and dynamics; and that's what it is—it is *"dynamic systems"* we are treating. But, this isn't—it's not the mechanistic "clockwork" universe as a lot of physics would have you believe; it's *dynamic systems*, where each one is—it's not just "billiard balls" hitting against "billiard balls." There's other considerations that work upon that. Other "unseen" forces that perturb what is apparent; all of which mainly relate to the individual.

I mean, the individual is the one that is basically able to tip the scale on that. Yeah, we would have a very "clockwork" mechanistic universe *were it not* for the fact that there is *Life* in this Universe—and *Life* has the ability to *change* things, to *create* things, to *destroy* things; and all of these are not parameters that are necessarily totally fixed.

> The individual—the Awareness—
> that is making these choices is
> not a part of this Physical Universe.

There's no mechanistic "cog" definition that applies to the individual; with the one exception that comes close, only because it acknowledges it at all, and that's "game theory." But this is what has separated, for example, *our* Systemology and what has kept "religion" and "science" at various odds: most material sciences can only really be concerned with a material *objective* universe as it applies *almost* free of the Observer; which is not actually the Universe we cohabit as a POV with other POV. So, material science is unable to do that since even it's *Point-of-View* is always impinging upon it its own expectations, its own observations and, of course, the limits that sensory organs or the perceptions or what have you are able to *view* and *define* its "observed" *causal effects.*

Because, that's what we're dealing with: *cause* and *effect*, pretty much at all points here; we're dealing with an individual trying to be as much at *cause* as possible over their experience of reality, over their creation and direction of energies and so forth—as opposed to becoming the *effect* and slowly *succumbing* to all of these forces of this material universe, which will definitely, if allowed to—you know, it's a *hungry* universe—it will definitely take over, if allowed.

When we talk about "programmed-identity-personas" or "*phases*," we're talking about these "*personalities*" that act as "filters" in which to view the world—more POVs. We're talking about, from the perspective of the "Mind-System," filters for the Human Condition that are embedded with *emotional* energies. They have their own harmonic *resonance*; they have their own *inclinations* as to what is considered attractive and what is considered repulsive for that "personality package."

And by putting one of them "on"—by having these filters "on"—you filter more of the experience and that actually *validates* function of the filters and basically makes things more solid. So, experience becomes reality and reality becomes experience; and then *emotional encoding* and the *memory imprinting* and all of that determine what the definitions or parameters of that reality experience are—as they are perceived and associated and assigned meaning.

This is basically what constitutes the experience of *Life*, the *Universe* and *Everything*; and at a "philosophical" level, this stuff all seems, you know, real *easy*... it all seems to make sense. But *still*, it took ten years to bring it to anything practical; primarily the best example of that for Grade-III being the material presented in *"Crystal Clear."* Even in that sense, we talk about distortions or fragmentation of an individual right *in* the text of *"Defragmentation"* in *"Systemology: The Original Thesis"* as "crystalline distortions"—distortions in the perception lens; basically, referring to pre-programmed *compulsions*, *obsessions*, *tendencies*, and what is ignorantly generalized as "disorders" and "phobias."

Unfortunately, most of psychology is no longer dealing with anything about "consciousness"—if it ever even did before. It's only concerned with "behaviors." And I have an academic background in that, but I don't find it helpful. If you ever take a look at the *"DSM-IV"*—it's this huge diagnostic manual used for psychology concerning mental health and mental behavior—really, it's just a bunch of classifications; it's just a bunch of definitions. Every little quirk that an individual has, or could potentially have, is somehow in there and classifiable as a "disorder" and so forth. But, they have no methodology behind actually *correcting* any of this—that's never been established; nor has there ever been, within that paradigm of "mental health," an establishment of what *"sanity"* actually is —or when an individual is finally *"done,"* for example, with their "therapy." Beingness never seems to get returned to the patient.

That's why we take this up in the sense of "spirituality" and even the "religion" of Mardukite Zuism *and* a pursuit of a *higher* level of "metaphysics" and so forth, because honestly, there's no reason for me to endeavor into the fields of "medicine" and "psychology" and interfere with the realms of "doctors" because, we're not even playing in the same realm. We're treating a *Spirit*, which they've no longer acknowledged even *exists*—as far as their practices are concerned. We're dealing with the *Mind*, which because it's not fixed strictly to the "brain" as an "organ" as far its actual existence —yeah, sure it uses the "brain organ"—but, because they were never able to find the "I-AM" or Alpha Spirit, because they were never able to find "consciousness" and put it under the microscope, because they've never been able to define the "Mind" and actually be able to determine what it is, for example, independent of the brain as a physical organ, *none* of that stuff exists in the realm of physical sciences and psychology. Our domain and their domain do not seem to overlap in any way shape or form, except for the fact that, well, you can kind of classify the knowledge in the same vicinity many times.

These "crystalline distortions" can become *crystal clear*, when this crystalline catalyst, for example, the "function machine" that I was referring to in an *earlier* lecture [of "*The Complete Mardukite Master Course*"]—whatever is being used by the Mind-System to process the energetic transmission of information; if this is crystal clear of fragmentation, then the experience can be.

You can see the *effects* in everyday life of just what external fragmentation programming actually—and the encoding— leads to, in terms of the Human Condition. You see a lot of people with irrational or erratic or completely chaotic thought; the inability to concentrate or focus—the kind of fatigue and irritability that seems to plague the Human Condition more and more everyday; and of course, this increased attention on ailments and diseases of the body. This all affects what we're treating or looking towards in Mardukite Systemology as a "Self-Honest" experience.

That's what we're trying to correct even within Grade-III and our application of the work and the milestones that we consider capped off with Grade-III, because as much as one uses the *nomenclature* or the concept of "Wizards" and what not, no real "Wizard" work can be done until we get a person back up to *zero*; back up to at least a point of—you know, even though they are occupying the Human Condition, they are not completely trapped by all of the "push–pull" mechanism that are attached to that.

And there are *mechanisms* that have been created along the way, affecting what they've been treating as an experience; and both the mechanisms and the experience they feel a real need to hold onto, because without holding onto that experience, they feel like they don't *have* something. And so, this concept of *loss*, the programmed conditioning about *loss*, it's really what keeps many people from letting things go—old ideas, old energetic masses, the inability to forgive, the inability to look at something new.

Like in "*objective processing*," we might have an object on the table—we get an individual to look at it as if practically for the first time with full awareness, over and over again, to be able to duplicate that action perfecting and without mental strain. We treat this kind of stuff at higher levels of "Systematic Processing" and it yields results, because we're looking at the highest-level application of all those old *rites* and *lores* and *rituals* and *pathways*—and all this stuff that's come before —we looked at the highest-level of what we could apply from that and what it might do, and therein we found Mardukite Systemology.

:: First Steps to Grade-IV Wizard Materials ::
THOUGHT PROCESSES, THOUGHTFORMS AND FRAGMENTATION OF MENTAL SYSTEMS
[A Summation by David Zibert]
REISSUED LIBER-3C VERSION

Although not exactly encouraged in our society—or formally trained in any way—I would like to tell you a bit about why it is not only interesting, but rather important, for you to inquire about the Mind; its various fragmentation and thought processes as a system. What I'm referring to here as "The Mind," is the human faculty of "reason," or "Awareness"— which, in part, differentiates humanity—and systems of the Human Condition—from other basic organic lifeforms.

Surely, all life has its own capacity for reasoning—within the limitation of its own species or genetic vehicle; its own "Mind-System" you could say—be it animal, insects, plants, even minerals are alive in their own ways and grow based on a crystalline pattern.[‡] But there is definitely something that sets operating as the "Human Condition" apart from all of these other forms of life—and that's what I am referring to here as the "Mind-System." It is our grand peculiarity as a species...

That being said: we sure have a lot in common with other life forms—"All-as-One" interconnected by "Spheres of Existence" in the Physical Universe—but if this "Mind" we are talking about is what sets us apart: *what* is unique to *our* current experience of life on Earth? Maybe that's worth exploring a bit; worth spending some time understanding—as human beings—what we have in common with, for example, dogs. What have we completely overlooked or dismissed in this existence. We might appreciate dogs more when living

---

‡ See Joshua Free's edition of John Toland's *"Pantheisticon"*—also reprinted in the Grade-I "Route of Druidism & Dragon Legacy" Master Edition anthology, *"Merlyn's Complete Book of Druidism."*

life as—or extending our point-of-view to experience life as—a dog, don't you think?

Command of the "Mind-System" is the key to a superior experience of life and reality, not just in this beta-existence, but as a key to unlocking potential to experience life and reality of *Higher Universes.*

When you're "thinking up" something, functions of the "Mind-System" appear to be quite straightforward. You just "do it"—and either ideas and/or memories seem to simply pop up in your "head"; often even in words for more abstract concepts—but also perceived as images, sounds, even smells or tastes. This is especially true when it comes to memory recall, since all information from the senses is associated and imprinted as ideas and mental images too.

What you might be unaware of, is that there is a systematic process going on in within and as the "Mind"—and, of course, at another level of activity, biochemically taking place throughout the brain as you "think up" stuff. This is all part of what I refer to as the "Thought Process." The brain is a biological machine used to process activities of the "Mind-System" (mental machinery) for a genetic vehicle in this Physical Universe. So, let us certainly not confuse ourselves here: the "Mind" is not the "brain"—the brain is an organic meat machine; the Mind is machinery composed of only energy.

Δ Δ Δ Δ Δ Δ

When you think up something, where does it come from? Basically, from nowhere—or what can be described as the "unmanifest reality," or else "infinite potentiality." In effect, *thinking* is simply a means to communicate with reality—solidifying it. Just thinking a thought instantly manifests it within the reality of your mental universe, engaging the "Mind-System," which is always comparing and evaluating thoughts and data with previous experience and former thoughts in order to have it "make sense."

Your Mind-System is always "on" and always computing right, correctly within itself; essentially incapable of a wrong computation. All of the errors come from erroneous data supplied and collected through experiences; the analytical functions of the Mind as an operating system simply calculate what it is given. *Self* assigned the value. But there are also labels, patterns of association and attribution of Identity. Every thought gets stored in some folder within the Mind-System, creating a memory-chain or track, associated together to create artificial structures and patterns. Each subsequent thought is compared to each file—and "processed" through each circuit—for each associated folder. This further validates classification and evaluation of these patterns as "memory."

Thought Processes operate like circuits and channels of a communication system, communicating the *reality* of a Universe; your own *Personal Universe* and the *Personal Universes* of others. The same thoughts and memories might be filed differently by different individuals and given quite a different consideration as reality. That's why, for example, different individuals might "recall" different *facets* from the same event, or associate the same *facets* in a unique way.

Paradigms and semantic systems are all approximations of reality. Each contributes to the creation of biased "thought-forms" ultimately leading the individual to a biased experience of reality—and thereafter, a reality and understanding limited by the experience. The same erroneous data is stored for future evaluations of perception. These biased or "rigidly fixed" paradigms—operating in exclusion to Self-Honesty—*are* the artificial illusion that philosophers chase after, first consciously and knowingly created and then maintained as compulsively created automatic mechanisms.

The true origin of all personal thought is Self, the Awareness that is monitoring the Mind-System. Energy is created at command of Self, in Alpha States, not from lower-level machinery restricted to material senses. When one is considers a "mental" *point-of-view* "interior" to the reactionary level of a physical body, the "brain" may independently operate as an organic machine that relays orders to other control centers related to the "body" functions and motions as a genetic vehicle, but these are all easily manipulated reactive stimulus-response mechanisms.

Δ Δ Δ Δ Δ Δ

One might notice how some individuals have a tendency to invoke accepted authorities in order to validate their own agreements and data association—such as in academia. Generally in the contemporary academia of any age, promoting original ideas is not only frowned upon, but mostly forbidden, whether by the "*laws*" of specially funded sciences or "forces" of organized religions. Both have their coffers to fill. The irony here being that these alleged "accepted" authorities go through the same thought process and are subject to the same fragmentation described by Joshua Free in the professional series of Systemology books: "*Metahuman Destinations,*" "*Crystal Clear*" and even "*Tablets of Destiny.*" Consensual reality is indeed both malleable and corruptible—and whomever controls the most agreed upon paradigm controls that reality.

If you are seeking an actual Self-Honest reality experience, the way is to free yourself and be able to think beyond the paradigms and semantic systems you have been formerly programmed with. Some esoteric mystics have called this "Crossing to the Abyss," or else "Antinomian Thinking." But whatever name given—the core material inspiring our Systemology and routes toward Self-Honesty is not a *new* discovery; for it has been long whispered of in select underground circles. It was, for example, acknowledged by early Christian Gnostics—and is reflected stronger in even older historical texts such as the "*Chaldean Oracles*" or the Babylonian "*Epic of Creation.*"*

---

* The Babylonian "*Epic of Creation*" or *Enuma Eliš* is a primary emphasis of Mardukite Zuism and Grade-II materials contained within "*The Complete Anunnaki Bible*" edited by Joshua Free, reissued in the

The QBL or *"Kabbalah"* (*"Cabala,"* etc.) is perhaps one of the more widely known mystical paradigms employed in Western esoterica and contemporary mysticism. It developed through Rabbinical Jewish lore based on knowledge first concealed as the "Gate" (or "Star-Gate") system of Babylon. I use the Semitic Kabbalah here only as an example, since it is not directly a part of Mardukite Zuism or Mardukite Systemology; but it is a way some *Seekers* will already be familiar with the more "esoteric" concepts explored in our Systemology.

In the example of QBL: When you "think up" something, it comes from AIN, the sea of infinite potentialities, then it manifests in the reality of Kether, the "Crown," and then *swoosh!* The whole "Tree of Life" manifests rather instantly in response, and the thought is computed to fit somewhere on this systematized model—largely based on associative semantic data within the paradigm—to make the content and evaluations of the thought compute with reality, preventing the individual's universe from collapsing on itself. And, of course, several different semantics and interpretations for the same Qabbalistic model exist to even fit *that* knowing into some predisposed category of knowing.

You, therefore, unknowingly—or even knowingly—place each and every thought and memory upon one or another "Sphere of Existence"—called *Sephiroth* in the QBL—and these get fixed and stored in your memory bank. And when thinking or recalling something else, the Mind-System takes into account everything that is already stored in this memory bank as a comparison in order to file the thought or memory once again into a "Sphere of Existence" and fix it upon a timeline, confirming it and having it make sense, thus once more preventing the mind from collapsing. We could just as well apply this to any version of the "Tree of Life" or "World Tree" or "Chakra Centers" or "Gate-System." They are all semantic

---

complete *Grade-II* Master Edition 2020 hardcover anthology, *"Necronomicon: The Complete Anunnaki Legacy."* As it applies to Grade-III, the Standard Model and cosmology of Systemology, refer to *"Tablets of Destiny"* or *"Systemology Handbook."*

paradigms for relaying some level of understanding concerning the circuits and channels of Thought Processes taking place in the Mind-System.

In this sense, thoughts confirm and feed other thoughts endlessly; keeping you busy in a "mental maze," never letting you see the actual thought or clear memory as it truly is in a defragmented state, outside of a paradigm system or other erroneous associations. This mental fragmentation is what defines how you experience the reality of your own Personal Universe, falsely measure against and superimposed by reality of other Universes.

Now, in regards to an individual trying to get out of this process: you can, of course, attempt to shift paradigms all you want; and this is pretty much what most of the mystical occult scene—and even the "New Thought" movement—is presently concerned with; with endless presentations of personal "gnosis," offering only a different paradigm for a different experience of reality semantics. But these, while interesting, have a tendency to only fragment and obscure one's understanding of reality and their personal universe even further. Hence these other paths are really akin to simply getting out of a cage just to enter a more alluring one. Do you see that?

What we have developed over the course of a decade for Mardukite Zuism and Systemology far surpasses attempts made by these former paradigms—each one reaching further and further away from its original source, never returning the Mind and its control back to the original state that it once maintained before its fragmentation into the various human systems. And perhaps for the first time, in a long time, there is a recognizable way out; solutions revealed to us now in the 21st century A.D. of what has only been touched upon in obscurity since the original cuneiform tablet renderings of the 21st century B.C.

We are ready to face these challenges now... *Are you?*

IMAGINOMICON

— ENTRY POINTS —

METAHUMAN SYSTEMOLOGY
GRADE-IV WIZARD LEVEL 0

:: I ::

THE GATES OF HIGHER UNDERSTANDING
《 UNIFYING MARDUKITE ZUISM & SYSTEMOLGY 》
INTRODUCTORY COURSE FUNDAMENTALS
VOCABULARY AND SEMANTICS
GRADE-IV WIZARD-0 IMAGINOMICON EDIT

Many esoteric[1] models of universal cosmology[2] and spiritual ascension appear on the timeline[3] of acutely recorded history over the past 6,000 years, and the most ancient of these records—the *Arcane Tablets*—reveal a simple account of *Cosmic History*, that which later inspired an entire planet of cultural mythologies and religious interpretations. Yet none of these further fragments and facets of the original *Crystal* ever brought a clearer experience or more perfect understanding[4] than what had come before. As a result, the truth inherent in the simplicity once shared became forgotten and lost to a sea of "symbols" and "representations" that reflected the poorest shadows of a former age—and the *Ancient Mystery School*[5] was born.

---

1 **esoteric** : hidden; secret; knowledge understood by a select few.

2 **cosmology** : a systematic philosophy defining origins and structure of an apparent Universe.

3 **timeline** : plotting out history in a linear (line) model to indicate instances (experiences) or demonstrate changes in state (space) as measured over time; a singular conception of continuation of observed time as marked by event-intervals and changes in energy and matter across space.

4 **understanding** : a clear 'A-for-A' duplication of a communication as 'knowledge', which may be comprehended and retained with its significance assigned in relation to other 'knowledge' treated as a 'significant understanding'; the "grade" or "level" that a knowledge base is collected and the manner in which the data is organized and evaluated.

5 **Ancient Mystery School** : the original arcane source of all esoteric knowledge on Earth, concentrated between the Middle East and modern-day Turkey and Transylvania c. 6000 B.C. and then dispersing south (Mesopotamia), west (Europe) and east (Asia) from that location.

Patterns demonstrated by this marked descent of civilization
are cyclic in nature and apply to all "systems"—including the
condensation[6] of "universes." Some have classified tendencies
of this "downward spiral" using terms for energy, such as
"entropy"[7]—whereas others think in terms of material "degradation." Regarding a relative direction between states or
conditions,[8] there are also those that refer to these motions
as "condensation" and "evaporation." In our Systemology, we
use a "Standard Model" (also treated[9] as the "ZU-line"[10] when

---

6   **condense (condensation)** : the transition of vapor to liquid; denoting a
    change in state to a more substantial or solid condition; leading to a
    more compact or solid form.

7   **entropy** : the reduction of organized physical systems back into chaos-
    continuity when their integrity is measured against space over time.

8   **condition** : an apparent or existing state; circumstances, situations and
    variable dynamics affecting the order and function of a system; a
    series of interconnected requirements, barriers and allowances that
    must be met; in "contemporary language," bringing a thing toward a
    specific, desired or intentional new state (such as in "conditioning"),
    though to minimize confusion about the word "condition" in our liter-
    ature, *NexGen Systemology* treats "contemporary conditioning"
    concepts as imprinting, encoding and programming.

9   **treat / treatment** : an act, manner or method of handling or dealing
    with someone, something or some type of situation; to apply a specific
    process, procedure or mode of action toward some person, thing or
    subject; use of a specific substance, regimen or procedure to make an
    existing condition less severe; also, a written presentation that handles
    a subject in a specific manner.

10 ***Zu*-line** : a theoretical construct in *Mardukite Zuism and Systemology*
    demonstrating *Spiritual Life Energy (ZU)* as a personal individual
    "continuum" of Awareness interacting with all Spheres of Existence on
    the Standard Model of Systemology; a spectrum of potential variations
    and interactions of a monistic continuum or singular *Spiritual Life
    Energy (ZU)* demonstrated on the Standard Model; an energetic
    channel of potential POV and "locations" of Beingness, demonstrated
    in early Systemology materials as an individual Alpha-Spirit's personal
    Identity-continuum, potentially connecting *Awareness (ZU)* of *Self*
    with "*Infinity*" simultaneous with all points considered in existence; a
    symbolic demonstration of the "*Life-line*" on which *Awareness (ZU)*
    extends from the direction of the "Spiritual Universe" (AN) in its true
    original *alpha state* through an entire possible range of activity
    resulting in its *beta state* and control of a *genetic-entity* occupying the

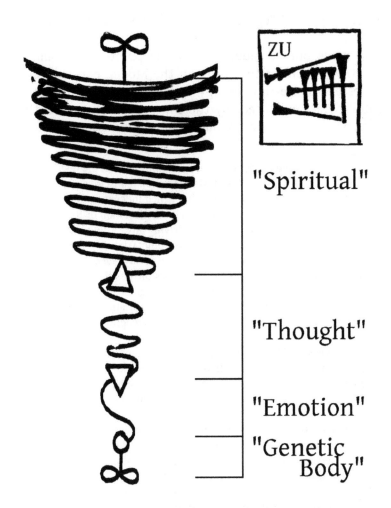

ZU

"Spiritual"

"Thought"

"Emotion"

"Genetic
Body"

it applies to the individual "*Self*") with a systematic continuum[11] between "zero" and "Infinity." We use this to easily
demonstrate understanding of varying gradients:[12] conditions

---

Physical Universe (KI).

11 **continuum** : a continuous enduring uninterrupted sequence or condition; observing all gradients on a *spectrum*; measuring quantitative
variation with gradual transition on a spectrum without demonstrating
discontinuity or separate parts.

12 **gradient** : a degree of partitioned ascent or descent along a scale, elevation or incline; "higher" and "lower" values in relation to one another.

of existence[13] and "degrees"[14] by which they are experienced.

As we move our consideration of viewpoint—the *"Point-of-View"* (*POV*)[15]—closer to "zero" on the Model, experience of manifested[16] space-time energy-matter is more greatly fragmented[17] and condensed. By the time we reach "0" on this model, we are at a basic singularity or continuity[18] of beta-ex-

---

13 **existence** : the *state* or fact of *apparent manifestation*; the resulting combination of the Principles of Manifestation: consciousness, motion and substance; continued *survival*; that which independently exists; the *'Prime Directive'* and sole purpose of all manifestation or Reality; the highest common intended motivation driving any *"Thing"* or *Life*.

14 **degree** : a physical or conceptual *unit* (or point) defining the variation present relative to a *scale* above and below it; any stage or extent to which something *is* in relation to other possible positions within a *set* of *"parameters"*; a point within a specific range or spectrum; in *Nex-Gen Systemology*, a *Seeker's* potential energy variations or fluctuations in thought, emotional reaction and physical perception are all treated as *"degrees."*

15 **point-of-view (POV)** : a point to view from; an opinion or attitude as expressed from a specific identity-phase; a specific standpoint or vantage-point; a definitive manner of consideration specific to an individual phase or identity; a place or position affording a specific view or vantage; circumstances and programming of an individual that is conducive to a particular response, consideration or belief-set (paradigm); a position (consideration) or place (location) that provides a specific view or perspective (subjective) on experience (of the objective).

16 **manifestation** : something brought into existence.

17 **fragmentation** : breaking into parts and scattering the pieces; the *fractioning* of wholeness or the *fracture* of a holistic interconnected *alpha* state, favoring observational *Awareness* of perceived connectivity between parts; *discontinuity*; separation of a totality into parts; in *NexGen Systemology*, a person outside a state of *Self-Honesty* is said to be *fragmented*.

18 **consideration** : careful analytical reflection of all aspects; deliberation; determining the significance of a "thing" in relation to similarity or dissimilarity to other "things"; evaluation of facts and importance of certain facts; thorough examination of all aspects related to, or important for, making a decision; the analysis of consequences and estimation of significance when making decisions; in *NexGen Systemology*, the postulate or Alpha-Thought that defines the state of beingness for what something *"is."*

istence,[19] or with the *stuff* of this "Physical Universe."

With each descent of a Universe, the same considerations[20] of existence that composed the first postulated[21] Universe are fragmented and then reformed and compressed into another "lower" more "solid" continuity. When we apply this model to the "beta"-*Awareness*[22] level[23] of an individual,[24] we say that

19 **beta (existence)** : all manifestation in the "Physical Universe" (KI); the "Physical" state of existence consisting of vibrations of physical energy and physical matter moving through physical space and experienced as "time"; the conditions of *Awareness* for the *Alpha-spirit* (*Self*) as a physical organic *Lifeform* or "*genetic vehicle*" in which it experiences causality in the *Physical Universe*.

20 **consideration** : careful analytical reflection of all aspects; deliberation; determining the significance of a "thing" in relation to similarity or dissimilarity to other "things"; evaluation of facts and importance of certain facts; thorough examination of all aspects related to, or important for, making a decision; the analysis of consequences and estimation of significance when making decisions; in *NexGen Systemology*, the postulate or Alpha-Thought that defines the state of beingness for what something "*is.*"

21 **postulate** : to put forward as truth; to suggest or assume an existence *to be*; to provide a basis of reasoning and belief; a basic theory accepted as fact; in *NexGen Systemology*, "Alpha-Thought"—the top-most decisions or considerations made by the Alpha-Spirit regarding the "*is-ness*" (what things "*are*") about energy-matter and space-time.

22 **beta (existence)** : all manifestation in the "Physical Universe" (KI); the "Physical" state of existence consisting of vibrations of physical energy and physical matter moving through physical space and experienced as "time"; the conditions of *Awareness* for the *Alpha-spirit* (*Self*) as a physical organic *Lifeform* or "*genetic vehicle*" in which it experiences causality in the *Physical Universe*.

23 **level** : a physical or conceptual *tier* (or plane) relative to a *scale* above and below it; a significant *gradient* observable as a *foundation* (or surface) built upon and subsequent to other levels of a totality or whole; a *set* of "*parameters*" with respect to other such *sets* along a *continuum*; in *NexGen Systemology*, a *Seeker's* understanding, *Awareness* as *Self* and the formal grades of material/instruction are all treated as "*levels.*"

24 **individual** : a person, lifeform, human entity or creature; a *Seeker* or potential *Seeker* is often referred to as an "individual" within Mardukite Zuism and Systemology materials.

they are "withdrawing" attention[25] and *Awareness*[26] and thus becoming more of the "effect" of the Physical Universe as their consideration of *Beingness* approaches "zero."

Our methodology[27] greatly differs from former manic-type spiritual philosophies seeking spiritual oneness with a continuity of *this* Physical Universe; because we seek a return to oneness as *Self* in a Spiritual Universe. Our systems logic demonstrates that occupying a POV at the zero-point of this Universe is the equivalent to occupying a "dead body" or a "rock"—because at the continuity point of a Universe, all matter is equally identified with all other matter.

Similarly, as we consider points further *away* from "zero," the same energetic patterns appear more "vapor-like" and "fluid" and increase in their "potentiality"[28] as an existence or potential beingness and as a POV. Likewise, an individual's *Awareness* increases along with their "reach" in an upward direction as "cause," which is to say true *Actualization*[29] and

---

25 **attention** : active use of *Awareness* toward a specific aspect or thing; the act of "attending" with the presence of *Self*; a direction of focus or concentration of *Awareness* along a particular channel or conduit or toward a particular terminal node or communication termination point; the Self-directed concentration of personal energy as a combination of observation, thought-waves and consideration; focused application of *Self-Directed Awareness*.

26 **attention** : active use of *Awareness* toward a specific aspect or thing; the act of "attending" with the presence of *Self*; a direction of focus or concentration of *Awareness* along a particular channel or conduit or toward a particular terminal node or communication termination point; the Self-directed concentration of personal energy as a combination of observation, thought-waves and consideration; focused application of *Self-Directed Awareness*.

27 **methodology** : a system of methods, principles and rules to compose a systematic paradigm of philosophy or science.

28 **potentiality** : the total "sum" (collective amount) of "latent" (dormant —present but not apparent) capable or possible realizations; used to describe a state or condition of what has not yet manifested, but which can be influenced and predicted based on observed patterns and, if referring to beta-existence, Cosmic Law.

29 **actualization** : to make actual, not just potential; to bring into full solid Reality; to realize fully in *Awareness* as a "thing."

Self-determinism[30] to the extent they may Self-Honestly project or extend their POV.

Although considerable discrepancy in semantics,[31] vocabulary and human understanding exists in regards to our Cosmic History[32] and the original *map* and *key* left to us on the *Arcane Tablets*, most of this "mythology" and "symbolism"[33] has previously only been used as a basis of lesser purposes—including the further solidification and fragmentation of an individual's considerations as they occupy this beta-existence. This is one of the primary concerns with basing our Systemology on the Standard Model or any fixed paradigm:[34] that its classification and demonstration of "divisions," "levels" and "layers" of existence will be over-identified as "symbols" that poorly substitute true understanding as a *knowing*.

Foundations for our higher graded work—including *Systemology Grade-IV*—is grounded firmly on the basis of research and discoveries presented in *Grade-III*; particularly as introduced in *"The Tablets of Destiny"* (*Liber-One*) and its companion manual *"Crystal Clear"* (*Liber-2B*). [These materials also appear in the complete Grade-III Master Edition text, *"The Systemology Handbook."*] The entire premise[35] of our "Standard Model" and "ZU-line" is established within those texts, supplemented

30 **Self-determinism** : the freedom to act, clear of external control or influence; the personal control of Will to direct intention.
31 **semantics** : the *meaning* carried in *language* as the *truth* of a "thing" represented, *A-for-A*; the *effect* of language on *thought* activity in the Mind and physical behavior; language as *symbols* used to represent a concept, "thing" or "solid."
32 **Cosmic History** : the entire continuous *Spiritual Timeline* of all existence, starting with the *Infinity of Nothingness* and individuation of Self and its Home Universe, running through various Games Universes and ultimately leading to condensation and solidification of this Physical Universe experienced in present-time.
33 **symbol** : a concentrated mass with associated meaning or significance.
34 **paradigm** : an all-encompassing *standard* by which to view the world and *communicate* Reality; a standard model of reality-systems used by the Mind to filter, organize and interpret experience of Reality.
35 **premise** : a basis/statement of fact from which conclusions are drawn.

by suggestions for practical systematic "processing"[36] that correlates with each installment of instruction. The subject of "processing" itself, and the complete course on "Communication, Control and Command" is what opens our present *Systemology Grade-IV*, with the publication, *"Metahuman Destinations" (Liber-Two)*

The most ancient recorded chronicle of our Cosmic History on Earth—that which includes cosmological information predating even the existence of *Life* on Earth—is best found on cuneiform[37] tablets; and among these, the *"Babylonian Epic of Creation"* known to scholars as the *Enuma Eliš*, so named for its opening lines. Unfortunately, even in ancient Babylon,[38] these and other *Arcane Tablets* functionally assisted those that sought further fragmentation and successive[39] programming of the Human Condition[40] rather than liberating it. This is another pattern that we have seen many times since whenever similarly derived paradigms sought to provide any aid to the spiritual "Rescue Mission" (via "defragmentation[41] of the Hu-

---

36 **processing, systematic** : the inner-workings or "through-put" result of systems; in *NexGen Systemology*, a methodology of applied spiritual technology used toward personal Self-Actualization; methods of selective directed attention, communicated language and associative imagery that targets an increase in personal control of the human condition.

37 **cuneiform** : the oldest extant writing system at the inception of modern civilization in Mesopotamia; a system of wedge-shaped script inscribed on clay tablets with a reed pen, allowing advancements in record keeping and communication no longer restricted to more literal graphic representations or pictures.

38 **Babylonian** : the ancient Mesopotamian civilization that evolved from *Sumer*; inception point for systematization, civic society and religion.

39 **successively** : what comes after; forward into the future.

40 **Human Condition** : a standard default state of Human experience that is generally accepted to be the extent of its potential identity (*beingness*)—currently *Homo Sapiens Sapiens,* but which is scheduled for replacement by *Homo Novus*.

41 **defragmentation** : the *reparation* of wholeness; collecting all dispersed parts to reform an original whole; a process of removing "*fragmentation*" in data or knowledge to provide a clear understanding; applying techniques and processes that promote a *holistic*

man Condition") presently taking place in the Physical Universe and on Earth.

In fact, these efforts have been going on for quite some time—so long, in fact, that it seems as if all the interested parties have already now arrived *here.*

In previous *Grade-III* instruction for *"The Tablets of Destiny,"* a basic systemological interpretation of themes and events for the *Enuma Eliš* are provided in order to demonstrate, describe and illustrate the Standard Model. This is of significant benefit to a Mardukite "Seeker"[42] continuing from the *Grade-II* "Mardukite Core."

At the completion of *Grade-III Mardukite Systemology*—or *"The Complete Mardukite Master Course"* at the Academy—a Seeker is expected to have mostly "flattened the waves"[43] that collapsed[44] around even those considerations fixed regarding

---

interconnected *alpha* state, favoring observational *Awareness* of continuity in all spiritual and physical systems; in *NexGen Systemology*, a *"Seeker"* achieving an actualized state of basic *"Self-Honest Awareness"* is said to be *beta-defragmented*, whereas *Alpha-defragmentation* is the rehabilitation of the *creative ability*, managing the *Spiritual Timeline* and the POV of *Self* as Alpha-Spirit (I-AM); see also *"Beta-defragmentation."*

42 **Seeker** : an individual on the *Pathway to Self-Honesty*; a practitioner of *Mardukite Systemology* or *NexGen Systemology Processing* that is working toward *Spiritual Ascension.*

43 **"flatten a wave" ("process out")** : to reduce *emotional encoding* of an *imprint* to zero; to dissolve a *wave-form* or *thought-formed* "solid" such as a *"belief"*; to completely run a *process* to its end, thereby *flattening* any previously *"collapsed-waves"* or *fragmentation* that is obstructing the *clear channel* of *Self-Awareness*; also referred to as "processing-out"; to discharge all previously held emotionally encoded imprinting and erroneous programming and beliefs that otherwise fix the free flow (wave) to a particular pattern, solid or concrete *"is"* form.

44 **collapsing a wave** : also, *"wave-function collapse"*; in *Quantum Physics*, the concept that an Observer is "collapsing" the wave-function to something "definite" by measuring it; defining or calculating a wave-function or interaction of potential interactions by an Observation; in *NexGen Systemology*, when a wave of potentiality or possibility because a finite fixed form; Consciousness or *Awareness* "collapses" a

ancient Mesopotamian[45] semantics, even though our System-ology is originally drawn from it. We accurately state that our applied Systemology is a progressive futurist development of what was discovered in our revival of "Mardukite Zuism." It directly prompted the discovery of an applied spiritual tech-nology for the 21st Century AD that is clearly present, but somehow lost, during the 21st Century BC—from the time of the "Age of Aries" (c. 2160 B.C.). Behind the scenes, an actual *Mardukite Babylonian systematization* has carried through to today, and it rests in our hands now—and for all those who wish to journey along up the *Pathway* with us.

Does this mean we are, in any way, rejecting the historical premise on which we first drew our knowledge?[46] ...certainly not. But, let us just say that it took thousands of years to un-cover (or recover, depending on your perspective) and translate the cuneiform source of global cosmologies, mytho-logies and creation myths from ancient Babylon—the *Enuma Eliš*—and in more than a century since its widespread aca-demic circulation in the late 1800's, it has still taken until *now* to develop any workable cohesion of its information for any effective spiritual ideal or application other than explor-ation of its cultural mythology as a series of esoteric symbols and traditions. This is very much akin to the understanding and knowledge that hovers around that *first* level or "Gate" of realizations; which we have markedly explored within *Grade-I Route of Magic & Mysticism* [see *"The Great Magickal Arcanum"*

---

wave-function of energy-matter as a necessary "third" Principle of Ap-parent Manifestation (first described in *"Tablets of Destiny"*);
potentiality as a wave is collapsed into an apparent *"is"*, the energy of which is freed up in systematic processing by *"flattening"* a "col-lapsed" wave back into its state of potentiality.

45 **Mesopotamia** : land between Tigris and Euphrates River; modern-day Iraq; the primary setting for ancient *Sumerian* and *Babylonian* tradi-tions thousands of years ago, including activities and records of the *Anunnaki.*

46 **knowledge** : clear personal processing of informed understanding; in-formation (data) that is actualized as effectively workable understand-ing; a demonstrable understanding on which we may 'set' our *Aware-ness*—or literally a "know-ledge."

by Joshua Free] with the intention that a Seeker will "flatten" programming that keeps them suspended as the "effect" of that level of understanding.

During personal investigations into evolutions of Western mysticism, which led to the formal 2008 launch of Mardukite Ministries (Mardukite Zuism), one key avenue from *Grade-I* served as a greater platform then any other for an early precursor to our NexGen Systemology, notably referred to as "Druidism." This information is explored directly in our material for the *Grade-I Route of Druidism & The Dragon Legacy*. [Refer to *"Merlyn's Complete Book of Druidism"* by Joshua Free.] It is actually on *this* very foundation, and explorations into the origins of ancient Druidism, that led the author to develop Mesopotamia (and specifically Babylon) as a "public" emphasis for further work continued underground, by the Mardukite Chamberlains (Mardukite Research Organization), primarily from 2009 until 2012, when the *Grade-II* "Mardukite Core" reached its apex; and the *second "Gate"* dislodged...

For the next eight years, "Mardukite Systemology" developed quietly in the underground as a futurist or "NexGen" movement dedicated to achieving the "next step" on this *Pathway* —one that would inevitably lead up and out of the "systems" laid out to entrap occupation and ensnare the attentions, willpower and spiritual energy of "Self" to this *beta-existence.* How then might we use the best of what we had found effective and workable to return the individual Seeker toward the direction that they *truly* occupy as an "Alpha"[47] condition in a higher spiritual plane? This was no simple task; requiring *eight* dedicated years to intensive underground research and experimentation.

A perceptive Seeker having followed the serpent trail through lower *Grades* will undoubtedly recognize many elem-

---

47 **alpha** : the first, primary, basic, superior or beginning of some form; in *NexGen Systemology,* referring to the state of existence operating on spiritual archetypes and postulates, will and intention "exterior" to the low-level condensation and solidarity of energy and matter as the 'physical universe'.

ents found in our Standard Model and "ZU-line" that are consistent in both the ancient Babylonian sources *and* those in Europe qualifying a "Druid's Cabala" (from Welsh sources) and the Druid Triads. The gradient distinction plotted as a "seven-plus-one" methodology is mirrored in throughout the globe and across the timeline of human tradition—from the Eastern *chakras*[48] to the *StarGates of Babylon.* An entire volume could be prepared exclusively on esoteric associations and correspondences—such as found in our Grade-I Master Library—information that an individual could otherwise spend their entire lifetime correlating and associating various symbols to things, but still not reach any greater level of *realization*[49] or higher point of *Actualized Awareness* that carries them on upward toward a more ideal state of *knowing* and *being.*

With the exception of a few semantics from Mesopotamia, we carry very little of the *"stuff"* along with us as we progress through higher gradients of understanding and personal *Awareness.* This has long been one of the shortcomings of previous attempts toward *Ascension,* whereby an initiate is not given tools to properly "let go" of the material programming and personal imprinting[50] along the way, and is instead app-

---

48 **chakra** : an archaic Sanskrit term for "wheel" or "spinning circle" used in *Eastern* wisdom traditions, spiritual systems and mysticism; a concept retained in NexGen Systemology to indicate etheric concentrations of energy into wheel-mechanisms that process *ZU* energy at specific frequencies along the *ZU-line*, of which the *Human Condition* is reportedly attached *seven* at various degrees as connected to the Gate symbolism.

49 **realization** : the clear perception of an understanding; a consideration or understanding on what is "actual"; to make "real" or give "reality" to so as to grant a property of "beingness" or "being as it is"; the state or instance of coming to an *Awareness*; in *NexGen Systemology,* "gnosis" or true knowledge achieved during *systematic processing*; achievement of a new (or "higher") cognition, true knowledge or perception of Self; a consideration of reality or assignment of meaning.

50 **imprint** : to strongly impress, stamp, mark (or outline) onto a softer 'impressible' substance; to mark with pressure onto a surface; in *NexGen Systemology,* the term is used to indicate permanent Reality impressions marked by frequencies, energies or interactions experienced

lying excessive effort to make a journey toward accumulation of "things" rather than a reduction. Former methods have not proved effective in producing much more than an incredible collection of cliché axioms and fancy spiritual doctrines that yet continue to keep the Human Condition in a fragmented state.

Within our Systemology, at each gradient of *Awareness*, a Seeker is systematically processed to "lighten their load" of *stuff*, because quite frankly, it will not all fit through as one moves further and further. And it was not meant to. Even the astral "levels" and energetic "layers" envisioned around the Alpha-Spirit's[51] consideration of a "finite body" should be *lessening*, not *increasing*, as one reaches towards *Infinity* on the *Pathway*. For this reason, many who have attempted "astral work" and "Gatewalking" (*&tc.*) in the past, and based on the esoteric instruction and other paradigms predating Mardukite Zuism and Systemology, have not found true successes toward the ultimate goal that could have otherwise been reached.

Many underground esoteric and mystic practitioners, that have known no better, *have* actually traversed the sevenfold

---

during periods of emotional distress, pain, unconsciousness, loss, enforcement, or something antagonistic to physical (personal) survival, all of which are are stored with other reactive response-mechanisms at lower-levels of *Awareness* as opposed to the active memory database and proactive processing center of the Mind; an experiential "memory-set" that may later resurface—be triggered or stimulated artificially—as Reality, of which similar responses will be engaged automatically; holographic-like imagery "stamped" onto consciousness as composed of energetic *facets* tied to the "snap-shot" of an experience.

51 **alpha-spirit** : a "spiritual" *Life*-form; the "true" *Self* or I-AM; the *individual*; the spiritual (*alpha*) *Self* that is animating the (*beta*) physical body or "*genetic vehicle*" using a continuous *Lifeline* of spiritual ("*ZU*") energy; an individual spiritual (*alpha*) entity possessing no physical mass or measurable waveform (motion) in the Physical Universe as itself, so it animates the (*beta*) physical body or "*genetic vehicle*" as a catalyst to experience *Self*-determined causality in effect within the *Physical Universe*; a singular unit or point of *Spiritual Awareness* that is *Aware* that it is *Aware*.

system—but they have only done so from within the *first* sphere or "Gate," not realizing that the system repeats itself as a fractal-like[52] macrocosm[53] and microcosm in relative[54] "directions" of magnification; seven times in each of seven Gates. Most practitioners have either become lost in entanglement[55] of the "Gates" at a *first level* of understanding or end up abandoning their reach on the *Pathway* altogether.

Even many of the brightest and most aptly trained and skilled individuals in such practices have found themselves permanently encircling the first level of continuity with a genuine feeling that they have "arrived" and therefore tend to look no further, only fragmenting the continuity of what they have found into a greater amount of potential correspondences. This is because there *is* a continuity at each level of understanding whereby everything can be made to seem to fit within *that* potential level of knowledge accessible from *that* Point-of-View; just as much as we could restrict a total knowledge of purely physical phenomenon using a purely

---

52 **fractal** : a wave-curve, geometric figure, form or pattern, with each part representative of the same characteristics as the whole; any baseline, sequence or pattern where the 'whole' is found in the 'parts' and the 'parts' contain the 'whole'; a pattern that reoccurs similarly at various scales/levels on a continuous whole; a subset of a Euclidean space explored in higher-level academic mathematics, in which fractal dimensions are found to exceed topological ones; in NexGen Systemology, a "fractal-like" description is used specifically for a pattern or form that has a reoccurring nature without regard to what level or scale it is manifest upon. Examples include the formation of crystals, tree-like patterns, comparison of atoms to solar systems to galaxies, &tc.

53 **macrocosmic** : taking examples and system demonstrations at one level and applying them as a larger demonstration of a relatively higher level or unseen dimension.

54 **relative** : an apparent point, state or condition treated as distinct from others.

55 **entanglement** : tangled together; intertwined and enmeshed systems; in *NexGen Systemology*, a reference to the interrelation of all particles as waves at a higher point of connectivity than is apparent, since wave-functions only "collapse" when someone is *Observing*, or doing the measuring, evaluating, &tc.

physical understanding of chemicals and forces and still be made to seem "correct" for *that* level of understanding and knowledge base.

More important than determining or demonstrating if any of our knowledge is representative of some "Absolute Truth," the emphasis of Systemology is toward specific ancient lore which is found to be objectively[56] effective in predicting and workable in producing targeted results.

Our concern in presenting the "Standard Model"—and likewise why it is not introduced directly until *Grade-III*—pertains to previous associations an individual tends to attempt to apply to this material as just more "esoteric lore" to incorporate into an existing databank. Our model is specific but representative; fluid as opposed to rigidly fixed; interconnected systematically rather than a compilation of parts treated in exclusion. All of the parts and facets and elements it represents, maintain a complete energetic circulation of communication with one another as a dynamic system; a system that is always changing, shifting and altering its apparent[57] face; and hence why these systems continue to persist with solidity.

Therefore, we have found, as a basic barrier to increasing an individual's *Awareness*—and as a basis of the "problems" facing the Human Condition—inability to adjust significances and reassign "importances" for new evaluations, while simultaneously under the hold and command of reactive-response programming and other heavily imprinted (or energetically charged)[58] past experiences. As this personal inability contin-

---

56 **objectively** : concerning the "external world" and attempts to observe Reality independent of personal "subjective" factors.

57 **apparent** : visibly exposed to sight; evident rather than actual, as presumed by Observation; readily perceived, especially by the senses.

58 **charge** : to fill or furnish with a quality; to supply with energy; to lay a command upon; in *NexGen Systemology*—to imbue with intention; to overspread with emotion; application of *Self-directed (WILL)* "intention" toward an emotional manifestation in beta-existence; personal

ues to be validated,[59] presumably across multiple lifetimes, the Self finds itself becoming more and more the "effect" of fixed mental implants and finite considerations of reality—and thus we find ourselves now stuck here, as the ultimate result of trillions of Alpha Spirits all succumbing[60] to the same downward spiral of considerations and manifestation, imprisoned in a very solid Physical Universe.

An individual's apparent personal stability is often based on conditional "agreements"[61] they have made concerning Reality—which is to say a determination of considerations about what is *real.*

At its core, this is actually so important, that any useful meaning it might have carried was lost to the cliché sentiment that "everyone creates their own reality." But such statements have done nothing to effectively and successfully liberate considerations of the *Self* from its material entrapment. We tend to speak of "well-adjusted" individuals quite simply as those that seem to face new data and experiences *anew,* without overly fixating, comparing or automatically associating[62] all past data in judgment.

---

energy stores and significances entwined as fragmentation in mental images, reactive-response encoding and intellectual (and/or) programmed beliefs; in traditional mysticism, to intentionally fix an energetic resonance to meet some degree, or to bring a specific concentration of energy that is transferred to a focal point, such as an object or space.

59 **validation** : reinforcement of agreements or considerations as "real."

60 **succumb** : to give way / give in to, a relatively stronger superior force.

61 **agreement (reality)** : unanimity of opinion of what is "thought" to be known; an accepted arrangement of how things are; things we consider as "real" or as an "is" of "reality"; a consensus of what is real as made by standard-issue (common) participants; what an individual contributes to or accepts as "real"; in *NexGen Systemology,* a synonym for "*reality.*"

62 **associative knowledge** : significance or meaning of a facet or aspect assigned to (or considered to have) a direct relationship with another facet; to connect or relate ideas or facets of existence with one another; a reactive-response image, emotion or conception that is suggested by (or directly accompanies) something other than itself; in traditional

This, in itself, is milestones ahead of the standard issue[63] Human Condition—and a quite accessible first step in reaching toward our ultimate *metahuman destinations.*

---

systems logic, an equivalency of significance or meaning between facets or sets that are grouped together, such as in $(a + b) + c = a + (b + c)$; in NexGen Systemology, erroneous associative knowledge is assignment of the same value to all facets or parts considered as related (even when they are not actually so), such as in $a = a$, $b = a$, $c = a$ and so forth without distinction.

63 **standard issue** : equally dispensed to all without consideration.

:: ‖ ::

UNIVERSAL COMMUNICATION, CONTROL AND COMMAND
《 SYSTEMOLOGY GRADE-IV CRASH COURSE 》
WIZARD LEVEL-0 IMAGINOMICON EDIT

Systemology of "Communication, Control & Command" is an emphasis of material for *Grade-IV* Metahuman Systemology. At this Grade, we apply the same training and processing "routes" to individual "Seekers" working alone with books and resources *and* those practicing systematic processing as "Professional Pilots"[64] of Systemology and "Ministers" of Mardukite Zuism. A complete course on these subjects for *Grade-IV* is provided as the volume *"Metahuman Destinations."* For present purposes—to both newcomers and returning Mardukite Systemologists—a crash course[65] of fundamentals will suffice in carrying the total spirit of Grade-IV into this present manual.

The Standard Model of Systemology demonstrates a vast network of communication between our proposed points of "zero" and "Infinity"—most of which, as it relates to the individual themselves, is experienced along a personal energetic continuum of potential "beingness" that we call the ZU-line. Combined, the two "concepts" represent all possible interactive points between an individual and a universe—*any* universe.

The relay of energy, a message or signal—or even locating a personal POV (viewpoint) for the Self—along this

---

64 **pilot** : a professional steersman responsible for healthy functional operation of a ship toward a specific destination; in *NexGen Systemology*, an intensive trained individual qualified to specially apply *Systemology Processing* to assist other *Seekers* on the *Pathway*.

65 **crash-course** : a very intense or steep delivery of education over a very brief time period, usually applied to bring a student "up-to-speed" or "up-to-date" for receiving and understanding newer or cumulatively more advanced material.

continuum is referred to as *communication.*

Communication relayed from an operative center or organizational cluster, which incites[66] new activity elsewhere on the ZU-line, is considered *control.* Abilities of the Self (I-AM), from its ideal exterior[67] POV as Alpha Spirit, to direct a communication for control that is perfectly duplicated along the ZU-line without fragmentation is true *command.*

From a systematic approach, *communication* is the primary catalyst[68] by which all *Life* is learning and experiencing existence. We are directing and receiving communications from the external[69] environment while interacting with the Physical Universe (*beta-existence*). These are all processed by communications internal[70] and interior[71] to the Mind–Body connection, upon which experience and command of the Human Condition seems primarily anchored.[72]

---

66 **incite** : to urge on or cause; instigate; prove or stimulate into action.

67 **exterior** : outside of; on the outside; in *NexGen Systemology*, we mean specifically the POV of *Self* that is '*outside of*' the *Human Condition,* free of the physical and mental trappings of the Physical Universe; a metahuman range of consideration; see also '*Zu-Vision*'.

68 **catalyst** : something that causes action between two systems or aspects, but which itself is unaffected as a variable of this energy communication; a medium or intermediary channel.

69 **external** : a force coming from outside; information received from outside sources; in *NexGen Systemology*, the objective '*Physical Universe*' existence, or *beta-existence*, that the Physical Body or *genetic vehicle* is essentially *anchored* to for its considerations of locational space-time as a dimension or POV.

70 **internal** : a force coming from inside; information received from inside sources; in *NexGen Systemology*, the objective '*Physical Universe*' experience of *beta-existence* that is associated with the Physical Body or *genetic vehicle* and its POV regarding sensation and perception; from inside the body; within the body.

71 **interior** : inside of; on the inside; in *NexGen Systemology*, we mean specifically the POV of *Self* that is fixed to the '*internal*' *Human Condition,* including the *Reactive Control Center* (RCC) and Mind-System or *Master Control Center* (MCC); within *beta-existence*.

72 **anchor (conceptual)** : a stable point in space; a fixed point used to hold or stabilize a spatial existence of other points; a spatial point that

Humanity has run through many phases of intellectual reach to properly resume this control, ever since perfected knowledge of the Mind–Body connection became fragmented thousands of years ago. Yet, there is an inherent *knowing* that behind, back of, and beneath the "surface" of what we are consciously facing as reality in this Physical Universe, there is an entire existence that is blocked, occluded, occulted[73] or otherwise obscurely hidden from Human view, if following along to the beat of standard issue programming.

Physical sciences have offered little more than further "agreements" to confine our considerations of thought and spirit to this Physical Universe. Eventually an individual finds that all conceptions of potential beingness are either "reactive" or else tied strongly to "mental programming implants"[74] that selectively direct and fix our attentions on

fixes the parameters of dimensional orientation, such as the corner-points of a solid object in relation to other points in space; in *NexGen Systemology*, "beta-anchored" is an expression used to describe the fixed orientation of a viewpoint from Self in relation to all possible spatial points in *beta-existence* ("physical universe"), or else the existential points that fix the operation of the "body" within the space-time of *beta-existence.*

73 **occulted / to occult** : hidden by or secreted away; to hide something from view; otherwise *occlude*, to shut out, shut in, or block; to *eclipse*, or leave out of view.

74 **implant** : to graft or surgically insert; to establish firmly by setting into; to instill or install a direct command or consideration in consciousness (Mind-System, &tc.); a mechanical device inserted beneath the surface/skin; in *Metahuman Systemology*, an "energetic mechanism" (linked to an Alpha-Spirit) composing a circuit-network and systematic array of energetic receptors underlying and filter-screening communication channels between the Mind-System and *Self*; an energetic construct installed upon entry of a Universe; similar to a platen or matrix or circuit-board, where each part records a specific type or quality of *emotionally encoded imprints* and other "heavily charged" *Mental Images* that are "impressed" by future encounters; a basic platform on which certain *imprints* and *Mental Images* are encoded (keyed-in) and stored (often beneath the surface of "knowing" or *Awareness* for that individual, although an implanted "command" toward certain inclinations or behavioral tendencies may be visibly observable.

the lowest denominator of beta-existence; that which we refer to as the "RCC" or "Reactive Control Center," which generates bio-chemical and emotional experiences internally in a physical body ("genetic vehicle").[75]

The purpose of any esoteric initiatory or mystical gradient system that mirrors facets of the "Gates" or "Levels" (which we demonstrate as a "zero-to-eight scale" on the Standard Model) were originally intended to systematically and progressively remove the standard issue programming, emotional encoding[76] and other implants that had been taken on, reinforced and validated during the course of an exceptionally long spiritual existence.

By reducing the weight of these lower level energy masses from the "banks" of the "spirit," an initiate was treated to a progressive journey toward a greater metahuman POV that put them back in contact with the ZU-line from their true and ideal state.

While a methodology of using "Gates" proved successful in the beginning (many thousands of years ago), these organized efforts to spiritually liberate individuals from the material system trappings of this Physical Universe (Earth-Gate or Zero-Gate) did not continue undefiled[77] for very long. In no short time thereafter, we find the clear path obscured

---

75 **genetic-vehicle** : a physical *Life*-form; the physical (*beta*) body that is animated/controlled by the (*Alpha*) *Spirit* using a continuous *Lifeline* (ZU); a physical (*beta*) organic receptacle and catalyst for the (*Alpha*) *Self* to operate "causes" and experience "effects" within the *Physical Universe*.

76 **emotional encoding** : the substance of *imprints*; associations of sensory experience with an *imprint*; perceptions of our environment that receive an *emotional charge*, which form or reinforce facets of an *imprint*; perceptions recorded and stored as an *imprint* within the "emotional range" of energetic manifestation; the formation of an energetic store or charge on a channel that fixes emotional responses as a mechanistic automation, which is carried on in an individual's spiritual timeline or personal continuum of existence.

77 **undefiled** : to remain intact, untouched or unchanged; to be left in an original "virgin" state.

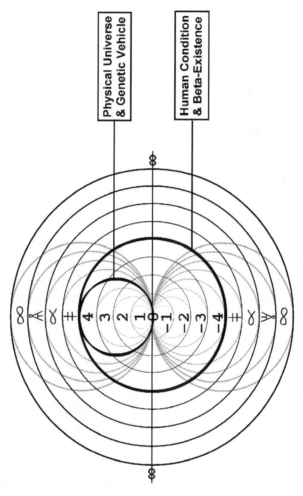

and confounded into "*Mystery Traditions*" with a now fragmented knowledge dispersed across varying cultures
throughout the globe. This is the true nature of the "Tower of
Babylon Incident" whereby complete, clear and present access to the "Gates of Understanding" was cut off from
humanity. This is explored more directly in "*Tablets of Destiny*" and gleaned from the Grade-II "Mardukite Core."

In Systemology we do more than just suppose there is more
than inert material continuity of this Physical Universe—we
go forth to codify and systematize the understanding avail-

able to us on the Standard Model. As such, we have noted the existence of the "RCC" and "MCC" in previous texts, plotted at "2.0" and "4.0" respectively on the ZU-line. In fact, our primary introduction of the Standard Model and its systematic structure is a primary emphasis of education and systematic processing demonstrations provided in *Grade-III*.

What we have done with the Standard Model is provided a "systemology" for the Mind–Body connection that, when operated by a Self-Honest individual, is under the command of Self as the Alpha Spirit, free of entrapment to low-level considerations and automated reactivity to the environment. Between "0.1" and "4.0" is the "internal" nature of the Mind–Body connection, as within the range of *Awareness* and experience of the Human Condition,separate from "external" qualities attributed to the continuity of the Physical Universe at *zero*.

It is at the zero-point of our model that the most "solid" aspects of the "genetic vehicle" meet or match frequencies of "solid matter" in this Physical Universe. We tend to treat the entire range of "0.0" to "4.0" as *beta-existence*, because it reflects the total scope of physical, emotional and mental parameters[78] as experienced "internally" from the POV of an Alpha Spirit operating its *beingness* "within" physical conditions of a "genetic vehicle"—and this is hardly an optimum[79] position of command for a god-like Spiritual Beingness.

(0.0) : "External" (continuity of objective beta-existence; Physical Universe)

(0.1) to (4.0) : "Internal" (*Self*, operating as POV in a "genetic vehicle")

---

78 **parameters** : a defined range of possible variables within a model, spectrum or continuum; the extent of communicable reach capable within a system or across a distance; the defined or imposed limitations placed on a system or the functions within a system; the extent to which a Life or "thing" can *be*, *do* or *know* along any channel within the confines of a specific system or spectrum of existence.

79 **optimum** : the most favorable or ideal conditions for the best result; the greatest degree of result under specific conditions.

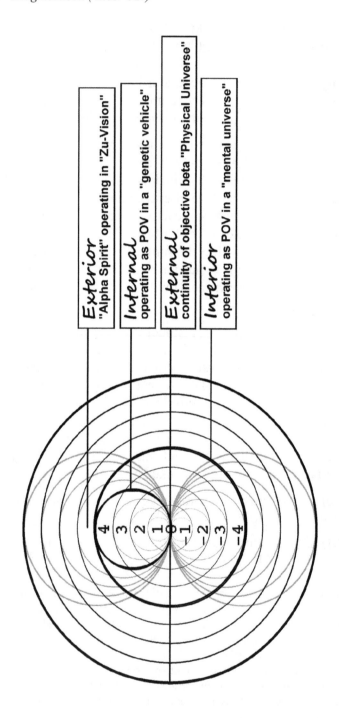

Exterior
"Alpha Spirit" operating in "Zu-Vision"

Internal
operating as POV in a "genetic vehicle"

External
continuity of objective beta "Physical Universe"

Interior
operating as POV in a "mental universe"

To accomplish goals of accessing these higher *realizations* to continue our graded *Pathway*, it became necessary to codify and systematize a wider-angle view of our model that would resolve the "problems" that we were left with in processing toward a *Homo Novus*[80] "metahuman" state.

What we are simply concerned with now is a further reach that extends our progression on this *Pathway*, beyond simply the "internal" workings of the genetic vehicle we are operating, but the communications throughout the "interior" of our personal "mental universe"—which includes the Mind–Body connection (between "0.1" and "4.0") *in addition to* the full "interior" of the personal Mind-System (even independent of a specific "physical body") carried on an individual's persona energetic continuum (or ZU-line) all the way down to the (sub?) range of "–4.0" on our Standard Model.

This means that using our systematic reasoning,[81] the full operating system of the "Mind" exists for each individual as a "mental universe system" that extends from "4.0" to "–4.0" on our Standard Model demonstration. That entire zone of existence is marked as "interior" (using our semantics), because the *beingness* of an individual is still operating from a POV "interior" to the mental systems—particularly "beta" mental systems—thus it's stated that the individual is *still* very much "in their head" (figuratively speaking). This, of course, adds another dynamic to our model.

---

80 **Homo Novus** : literally, the "new man"; the "newly elevated man" or "known man" in ancient Rome; the man who "knows (only) through himself"; in NexGen Systemology—the next spiritual and intellectual evolution of *homo sapiens* (the "modern Human Condition"), which is signified by a demonstration of higher faculties of *Self-Actualization* and clear *Awareness*.

81 **rationality / reasoning** : the extent to which a player seeks to play (make decisions, &tc.) in order to maximize the gains (or else survival) achievable within any given game conditions; the ability and willingness of an individual to reach toward conditions that promote the highest level of survival and existence and make the best choices and moves to see the desired goal manifest.

(4.0) to (0.1) : "Internal" (*Self*, operating as POV in a "genetic vehicle")

(4.0) to (-4.) : "Interior" (*Self*, operating as POV in a "mental universe")

It became evident, as we plotted out the work for the Wizard Grades, that we would have to make certain of our distinctions regarding these classifications on the Standard Model; particularly the differences between POV that are "internal," "interior" or "exterior"—because it becomes quite relevant when accessing the upper-routes.

This matter is not fancy word play and semantic tricks. Previous "traditional" attempts at our goals for Wizard Level-0 were ambiguous lower-Grade instructions regarding "astral vision" and "spirit bodies"—which *did not* provide actual effective tools for getting an individual *exterior* to even a "mental universe" fixed to an intermediate[82] "Mind-System." Greater clarity was needed to complete "*Imaginomicon*" (*Liber-3D*) and realize our most basic goals for the Wizard Grades, as we move upward through the *Gateways to Infinity*.

Δ Δ Δ Δ Δ Δ

The abilities of an Alpha Spirit throughout its own creative journey are linked precisely to the communication systems that are demonstrated on the *Zu-line* of the Standard Model. We see that when an individual is operating from their "MCC"—represented with the symbol of the upward pointing triangle—they are "facing up" or "confronting" the reality of their universe, reaching and extending across spheres of influence in the existential or objective universe, and is learning from the association and incorporation of its own experiential knowledge.

In our previous manuals for Systemology, a *Seeker* or *Pilot* is

---

82 **intermediate** : a distinct point between two points; actions between two points.

primarily dealing with "*products of*" the Mind-System when treating conditions found within the "internal" systems. It was not until we began to systematize knowledge of *how* emotional encoding, imprinting and other programming, actually takes place and the way in which it is even stored between lifetimes as part of a spiritual identity,[83] that we realized that there was a more deeply ingrained chain of potential "terminals"[84] or "nodes" by which all of these later programs, tendencies, fixations, compulsions,[85] avoidances (*&tc.*) could even attach to an individual in any way. Since a few of us began to call these types of interior facets[86] "implants" early on in our research, the name stuck.

On an energetic level—whether physical kinetics,[87] emotional charges and mental circuits—we find varying "lines" and

83 **identity-system** : the application of the *ZU-line* as "I"—the continuous expression of *Self* as *Awareness* across a "*Spiritual Timeline*"; see "*identity.*"

84 **terminal (node)** : a point, end or mass on a line; a point or connection for closing an electric circuit, such as a post on a battery terminating at each end of its own systematic function; any end point or 'termination' on a line; a point of connectivity with other points; in systems, any point which may be treated as a contact point of interaction; anything that may be distinguished as an 'is' and is therefore a 'termination point' of a system or along a flow-line which may interact with other related systems it shares a line with; a point of interaction with other points.

85 **compulsion** : a failure to be responsible for the dynamics of control—starting, stopping or altering—on a particular channel of communication and/or regarding a particular terminal in existence; an energetic flow with the appearance of being 'stuck' on the action it is already doing or by the control of some automatic mechanism.

86 **facets** : an aspect, an apparent phase; one of many faces of something; a cut surface on a gem or crystal; in *NexGen Systemology*—a single perception or aspect of a memory or "*Imprint*"; any one of many ways in which a memory is recorded; perceptions associated with a painful emotional (sensation) experience and "*imprinted*" onto a metaphoric lens through which to view future similar experiences; other secondary terminals that are associated with a particular terminal, painful event or experience of loss, and which may exhibit the same encoded significance as the activating event.

87 **kinetic** : pertaining to the energy of physical motion and movement.

"connections" formed with various "terminals" of existence that we may have a communication with. Many Seekers discover that they have a great many "ties" with various objects and people; but specifically as a representative symbol that is interacted with in *beta existence*. These same "terminals" may be contacted or envisioned internally using mental faculties[88] just as they are sprung up on automatic as "screens" to our view, whenever they are triggered or stimulated by the environment.

It has been realized that the average individual carries a great deal of energetic "charge" on their personal "mental images"[89] which are treated as a reality substitution for the objective universe. In brief, the individual is interacting and reacting based on the mental and emotional stores connected to a "terminal" rather than the objective nature of the "thing." An individual goes as far as to "create" their copy of the objective universe based on automatic mechanisms and even begins to take for granted the concept that walls and other solids are *more real* than anything that could be created by the Self. When the individual has ceased to consciously create, they have succumbed to considerations that they are simply an effect. Naturally, the more numerous the strong "ties" to terminals in the Physical Universe, the stronger the "pull" to remain at such a level in order to receive whatever the individual is now wired to experience as an effect.

"Systematic Operating Procedure 2-C" is a Professional Piloting methodology introduced in the text "*Metahuman Destinations*" (*Liber-Two*). There are other "Routes" explored in *Grade-IV* specifically for *Wizard Level-0* contained in "*Imaginomicon*" (*Liber-3D*) that pertain to handling "*mental images*"

---

88 **faculties** : abilities of the mind (individual) inherent or developed.

89 **mental image** : a subjectively experienced "picture" created and imagined into being by the Alpha-Spirit (or at lower levels, one of its automated mechanisms) that includes all perceptible *facets* of totally immersive scene, which may be forms originated by an individual, or a "facsimile-copy" ("snap-shot") of something seen or encountered; a duplication of wave-forms in one's Personal Universe as a "picture" that mirror an "external" Universe experience, such as an *Imprint*.

directly. Prior to approaching this final threshold[90] of the fourth *Gate* and *Grade*, *"Metahuman Destinations"* focused on clear communication relay between the most accessible considerations and terminals using these methods. Such techniques tend to be "generalized" in their approach so that a Seeker may insert their own applicable examples and yet still arrive at the ultimate conclusion or end-state *realization* that each systematic process is intended to achieve.

"Processing" or "systematic processing" that we "run" in our Systemology is composed of "Processing Command Lines" (PCLs) that function on the Mind-System very similarly to how you might operate a computer. These are essentially "command postulates" delivered by a *Pilot* that knows the way to where a *Seeker* wants to go, until the *Seeker* is certain in their ability to get there on their own. This, of course, actually requires properly directed attention and the Seeker's willingness[91] to provide their actual *presence*[92] to a "processing session."

The key is to always process with what *is* within the reach, accessibility and willingness of the Seeker as they are at present and then cumulatively extend that willingness to reach or *do*, building on the validation of what *is* within the known control of the individual. What we are then doing is reversing the programming and imprinting that has been stored, which has been found to limit the power of thought and consideration to smaller and more fixed parameters. This

---

90 **threshold** : a doorway, gate or entrance point; the degree to which something is to produce an effect within a certain state or condition; the point in which a condition changes from one to the next.

91 **willingness** : the state of conscious Self-determined ability and interest (directed attention) to *Be, Do* or *Have*; a Self-determined consideration to reach, face up to (*confront*) or manage some "mass" or energy; the extent to which an individual considers themselves able to participate, act or communicate along some line, to put attention or intention on the line, or to produce (create) an effect.

92 **presence** : the quality of some thing (energy/matter) being "present" in space-time; personal orientation of *Self* located in space and time and handling the energy-matter present.

degradation took place systematically throughout the course of the *Self's* own journey, projecting its POV through more and more rigid and condensed universes until finding all of the remaining "willingness" for consideration right now here in this beta-existence, tightly wound up as a box that we prize, guard and protect: the artificial personality.[93] It is *this* that entraps the Human Condition to beta-existence.

The basic premise that we began with is very simple to consider, perhaps just as simple to manifest in today's world. Systemologists learn to think systematically and holistically,[94] applying the fractal-like gradient scale of the Standard Model to daily life—and those training to be "Pilots" and "Ministers" within our tradition go on to expertly apply these same elements to processing procedures systematically designed to elevate *Actualized Awareness* from POV controlled by lower-level energy-driven mechanisms. Here we provide a *Seeker* with the tools to finally return effective command of their experience of *beta-existence* and the Human Condition to *Self* knowingly as Alpha-Spirit.

---

93 **personality (program)** : the total composite picture an individual "identifies" themselves with; the accumulated sum of material and mental mass by which an individual experiences as their timeline; a "beta-personality" is mainly attached to the identity of a particular physical body and the total sum of its own genetic memory in combination with the data stores and pictures maintained by the Alpha Spirit; a "true personality" is the Alpha Spirit as Self completely defragmented of all erroneous limitations and barriers to consideration, belief, manifestation and intention.

94 **holistic** : the examination of interconnected systems as encompassing something greater than the *sum* of their "parts."

:: III ::

.: Grade-IV Treatment of The Standard Model :.
CONDENSATION OF UNIVERSES AND
FRAGMENTATION OF THE HUMAN CONDITION

Most sources alluding to the true Cosmic History—one that predates this version of planet Earth and even *this* version of the Physical Universe—are based on the most ancient writings we have access to; carefully scribed at the inception[95] of writing systems during this current version of human civilization. These narratives relay mythographic symbolism and as a result we find development of specific portrayals of a literal "mythology" that now, thousands of years later, have all been blown down for the "straw men" that they are. But!—they were all inspired by something, some memory, and the oldest of these recollections may be found on the *Arcane Tablets* and records from ancient Mesopotamia.

Previous relays of "Cosmic History"—including the systemological interpretation of the *Enuma Eliš* that is provided in *"The Tablets of Destiny"* (*Liber-One*), which directly contributed to the formation of our Standard Model—describe a linear pattern that reflects the "condensation of universes" and degradation of the Alpha Spirit as it became imprisoned within the POV and considerations of *beta-existence* and entrapped to the low-level hard-wiring of the standard-issue Human Condition.

We know very succinctly *how* it happened; progressing from an Infinite Nothingness; to individuation of Alpha Spirits; and onward through more condensed Universes and increasingly fragmented reality associations with their existence. This is reflected strongest in the "Gate-System" paradigm of ancient Babylon; then afterward, remnants appear in various lore regarding systems like various forms of *kabbalah* and *chakras*, which attempted to achieve the same reach of actualization.

---

95 **inception** : the beginning, start, origin or outset.

But methods proposed over the past four millennium have done little for the Human Condition other than enforce[96] more stringent considerations toward more restrictive reality agreements; such that, by our measuring—using a greater understanding of the Standard Model than before—is going to send the entire Physical Universe "out the bottom" quite soon, relative to our Spiritual Timeline.[97] Direction of movement has been "downward" for too long, sending our Awareness to follow along, leading considerations to further "spiral inward"—validating and reinforcing the track direction we are unknowingly on, following standard issue programming. Without correction, this actually is quite a dangerous direction for an *eternal spirit* to be headed in for its existence. It undoubtedly echoes a truth that is otherwise buried in unnecessary religious dogmas and moral conventions.

As an individuation, *Spiritual Beingness* or *Self*—an establishment of the personal identity continuum or track on the "Spiritual Timeline" known as "I"—the Alpha Spirit first practices being selectively "out of communication" with what is "not-I" near the uppermost level of our Standard Model (*ZU-line*). Esoterically, it has been referred to as the "*I-not-I monad*," but really it is *Self*-"*Aware*" of its *Self* as *Self* at the highest point of *beingness* that is possible from this static[98] point (at "7.0" on the Standard Model).

In order to differentiate[99] "I" from the "not-I," the Alpha

---

96 **enforcement** : the act of compelling or putting (effort) into force; to compel or impose obedience by force; to impress strongly with applications of stress to demand agreement or validation; the lowest-level of direct control by physical effort or threat of punishment; a low-level method of control in the absence of true communication.

97 **spiritual timeline** : a continuous stream of *Mental Images* or record of experiences that defines the "past" of a spiritual being (or *Alpha-Spirit*) and which includes impressions form all life-incarnations and significant spiritual events the being has encountered; also "*backtrack.*"

98 **static** : characterized by a fixed or stationary condition; having no apparent change, movement or fluctuation.

99 **differentiation** : an apparent difference between aspects or concepts.

Spirit adopts a selective practice of imposing various barriers, communication lags and distances to perceive across, so as not to simply be the mirror of other "I's" (Alpha Spirits) also differentiating themselves as wave peaks, crests or uppermost tips of icebergs emerging from out of the Infinity of Nothingness ("8"). At the highest level of *knowingness* and *beingness*—prior to the fragmentation of "Alpha Thought"[100] in order to experience Shared-Games Universes ("6")—an Alpha Spirit maintained a perfect undefiled command of its own Personal-Home Universe.

An individual still very much occupies its own Personal Universe and is able to shift its considerations and creations freely by command postulates, generating the space and energy at will and without requiring any automated machinery. The whole of an individual's experience of existence is consciously created by *Self*, and in the beginning, the Alpha Spirit *knew* it was *creating* the conditions of its own *beingness* without inhibition[101] or restriction. We speak in relative linear terms here, because the static position of *Self* as Alpha Spirit continues to remain unchanged in the present—only its considerations of *Point-of-View* (*POV*) and Self-identification[102] given an experience of "time" as a successive degradation of personal willingness, reach and creative ability.

The only effective corrective measure inherent in the system

---

100 **alpha thought** : the highest spiritual *Self-determination* over creation and existence exercised by an Alpha-Spirit; the Alpha range of pure *Creative Ability* based on direct postulates and considerations of *Beingness*; spiritual qualities comparable to "thought" but originating in Alpha-existence (at "6.0") independently superior to a *beta-anchored* Mind-System, although an Alpha-Spirit may use Will ("5.0") to carry the intentions of a postulate or consideration ("6.0") to the Master Control Center ("4.0").

101 **inhibited** : withheld, discouraged or repressed from some state.

102 **identification** : the association of *identity* to a thing; a label or fixed data-set associated to what a thing is; association "equals" a thing, the "equals" being key; an equality of all things in a group, for example, an "apple" identified with all other "apples"; the reduction of "I-AM"-*Self* from a *Spiritual Beingness* to an "identity" of some form.

is to simply run this programming and its circuits *backwards.* The way through and out is actually a *backtrack*; not some newly fragmented direction of action. Behind the considerations assumed and energetically imprinted on a personal "Spiritual Timeline," the *Self*—Alpha Spirit—is still there, bright, beautiful and powerful; the "I" that *is* the *Actual Awareness* of the individual... if you can just remember what you chose to forget...

In a shared "Creative Universe," other Alpha Spirits can also create. The Alpha Spirit is aware of their own creations and how they are separate as barriers and energetic masses at a distance, freely shifted and arranged at will; but they *are still* barriers of a sort, even only to maintain ones own individuality. This is not a crime; it is completely natural. But, it also sets up the Self for a practice in being the effect of another being's creations—and a desire to create automated energetic machinery to resolve this for them. Since an Alpha Spirit can put up its own screens and images and walls, it can also shield or filter or create walls.

Of course, what this did at a higher level of Self-determinism and creation is *knowingly* put a condition in place by which a once "all-knowing" Spirit *could* now be "surprised" by unexpected creations found on the other side. Enter: the inception of "*Mystery*" and a clear way ahead by which additional fragmented conditions and agreements resulted in further condensation of "*Space*" and "*Energy*" to the point where such "things" were now considered of value; and the way ahead was clear for establishment of "Games Universes."

> To be a "player"[103] in a "Games Universe," the Alpha Spirit identifies *Self* with lower states and conditions of *beingness* to share a common reality agreement with other players. An Alpha-Spirit, which cannot be affected except by the consideration that it can, agrees to

---

103 **player** : an individual that is making decisions in a game and/or is affected by decisions others are making in the game, especially if those other-determined decisions now affect the possible choices.

be the consideration of effect just to be part of the Game.[104]

Δ Δ Δ Δ Δ Δ Δ

Willingness of reach and extent of withdrawal is learned and "tracked" along the *Spiritual Timeline* of an individual, carried from "lifetime" to "lifetime"—or "incarnation"[105] to "incarnation" since it is actually one continuous lifetime for the Alpha Spirit—for personal consideration. Unless otherwise directed, it apparently is only added to, never discharged, thus subjecting the Alpha Spirit to accumulate more and more solid energetic masses and more stringent considerations for existence as they descend into more and more solid, rigid and fixed POV from which to grant *beingness* even to themselves.

When the Alpha Spirit first occupied only POV in what is now an "exterior" existence or Alpha Universe, acceptance and rejection of energy communications was originally based on personal inclination and determination; but slowly these tendencies formed into patterns that we assigned as "aesthetics"—a *sense* of "beauty" or "ugliness" that transcends standard-issue beta-concepts of analytical thought or even emotional imprinting. "Aesthetic Consideration" is not really a quality that inherent to beta-existence. It is applied from a higher position than can be measured as *beta-Awareness*— meaning, markedly higher than "4.0" on our Standard Model.

Personal tendencies toward "aesthetics" laid further groundwork for potential miscommunication and automation even above the level of "thought" connected to the Mind-System. Of course, a highly actualized being would be able to fully change their considerations and willingness to reach by a

---

104 **game** : a strategic situation where a "player's" power of choice is employed or affected; a parameter or condition defined by purposes, freedoms and barriers (rules).

105 **incarnation** : a present, living or concrete form of some thing or idea; an individual lifetime or life-cycle from birth/creation to death/destruction independent of other lifetimes or cycles.

matter of personal choice. That which inhibits executing this directive fully is not a fault with the *Self* or Alpha Spirit maintain its true existence at "7.0," but from accumulation of energetic fragmentation along the "lines" between the "I" and command of its own POV *beingness.*

What we find to be the case early in our spiritual existence is not much different than what we discover to be true about the systems we find our POV now occupying: the entire matter is related to a communication of energy along specific channels[106] and circuits.[107] The only thing that has changed is the rigid automation of these channels and the fixed solidity found in physical mediums of communication exercised in *beta-existence.* This is why an understanding of the systemology of communication, control and command is functionally useful and effective "across the boards" and not simply in one or a few specific instances.

Even in the earliest "Creative Universes" we can see seeds of fragmentation stirring. Just as we might withdraw our reach, close off communication and reject creations of others, so too can others demonstrate a rejection of admiration toward our own creations. All various channels of energetic exchange[108] are created and then treated with some consideration that could be very well reduced to whether or not we "*like*" such-and-such. As *Self* moves its POV to more strict and narrow

---

106 **channel** : a specific stream, course, current, direction or route; to form or cut a groove or ridge or otherwise guide along a specific course; a direct path; an artificial aqueduct created to connect two water bodies or water or make travel possible.

107 **circuit** : a circular path or loop; a closed-path within a system that allows a flow; a pattern or action or wave movement that follows a specific route or potential path only; in *NexGen Systemology*, "*communication processing*" pertaining to a specific flow of energy or information along a *channel*; *see* also "*feedback loop.*"

108 **energetic exchange** : communicated transmission of energetically encoded "information" between fields, forces or source-points that share some degree of interconnectivity; the event of "waves" acting upon each other like a force, flowing in regard to their proximity, range, frequency and amplitude.

parameters of reality agreements, the automatic nature of these inclinations and tendencies is not only a personal hindrance to Self-determinism, but it could also be manipulated and programmed, then passed off and accepted as a "personality" that is quite artificial in nature when compared to the truest ideal state of the Self as Alpha Spirit.

Once a *Seeker* is able to understand the base structure of their own programming here in *this beta-existence* that the POV is presently confined to with *Systemology Wizard Level-0*, then we can press further onward into treating *Higher Universes* that we have "fallen" through to eventually arrive here. Such work continues throughout the "Wizard Grades." We are now charting our *backtrack* through minefields and trappings that we have picked up along the way. No steps are to be skipped along this course if we are to progress surefooted[109] on the *Pathway* ascending toward a true metahuman evolution for the Human Condition.

Δ Δ Δ Δ Δ Δ

Simultaneous with the condensation of universes and the agreement to confine the POV of *Self* to such universes, the *Self* became fragmented as a result of its own consideration that it could be. This started with the basic acceptance and rejection of energy very early on the timeline and later developed into various automatic mechanisms that we might consider "solids" from a purely physical perspective and semantic. As most of us know, "solid matter"—any solid form—in some way obscures the view of what is behind or in back of it. This is no less the case when we consider the creative forms and vices that were composed even in higher reaching Spiritual Universes.

Once we find *Self* in a position of operating a Mind-Body connection from a Mind-System ("4.0"), the implanted programming for a standard-issue Human Condition is simply a matter of logic—and entirely and systematically

---

109 **surefooted** : proceeding surely; not likely to stumble or fall.

demonstrable with the Standard Model. The sequence of diminished ability and rigidity of fixed agreements and considerations becomes quite apparent when we take a step back and look at mechanisms inherent in beta-Awareness; but let us examine them one by one, from the inside out—keeping in mind that *Self* is somehow convinced to agree to each one of these conditions along the way as part and parcel for the course down the spiral. But hope is not lost. We are able to clearly see these systems for what they are now, and the way out is very much in reach.

Let us consider that at the root behind all systems in existence, the most fundamental "Prime Directive" is simply *to exist*, which is a consideration of "*to be.*" But, this is obviously not the only driving factor; it is simply the most basic one applying, by definition, to *all* "existences." What we are interested in now are the *implanted* directives that may be introduced to the programming of the Mind-System; which is essentially everything between "0.1" and "4.0" on our Standard Model—and which we have quite adequately divided into two "control centers" that relay communications toward the command of the Human Condition; one which is primarily "reactive" and one which is primarily "analytical"—referred to as the "Reactive Control Center" (RCC) and "Master Control Center" (MCC) at "2.0" and "4.0" respectively on our Standard Model.

Naturally, in our truest, highest, most ideal state, the Alpha Spirit cannot be affected; but *what if* the *Self* made a sequence of agreements that led to an unknowing automated assumption that the "spirit" *is* the "body"? By forming this connection of pre-programmed considerations for a POV, we discover the "Mind-System" as it pertains to a "Mind-Body" connection. The POV of this Mind-System is not the actual *Self* either, but it *is* what many philosophers and mystics have treated as a "higher self" (from their perspective), although it is still very much tied to whatever implants and programs it is operating on, even in the upper-levels of *beta-thought* near "4.0" on our model.

Using the expanded version of the Standard Model (that includes sub-zero classifications), it is easy to demonstrate basic "fragmentation" inherent to the assumption of a "physical body" by simply threatening the *survival* or *existence* of that "body." It's literally that simple. Just get an eternal *Spiritual Being* to believe and postulate its own existence *as* a mortal body and suddenly it can be conditioned with "pain" (from the body) and also additional programming through various states of "unconsciousness"[110] or reduced beta-Awareness.

Sub-levels of the Mind-System, beginning with identification and registry of "pain" and "unconsciousness" for a genetic vehicle, are deeply embedded and encoded *implants*—or rather, specific *imprints* encoded on specific *implants*. In the past, the primary issue with referring to any of this as "un–" or "sub–" anything, is a presumption that these inner workings are fundamentally inactive, except during perhaps sleep or physical unconsciousness (such as coma states); but this is not the truth at all. If anything, it is the clear view and upper command from the Alpha Spirit ("7.0") and control of the Mind-System ("4.0") that periodically drops out. But so long as POV is restricted to standard fragmentation of the Human Condition, these other sub-systems are *always on* and can be incited later to trigger direct reactive-response mechanisms outside the command and control of Self-determinism.

Now, it might seem that we have gone as far as we can possibly go down the "Ladder" upon reaching the Earth Plane. Assuming the cosmic pattern continues, for those who have not achieved Ascension toward Higher Universes, when this Physical Universe collapses, the only POV left lower will leave *Self* "hanging on" as a mere perpetually enduring existence, functionally as static as a rock at a "zero-point" continuity in juxaposition to the true stasis of the Alpha Spirit.

---

110 **biological unconsciousness** : the organism independent of the sentient *Awareness* of the *Self* to direct it; states induced by severe injury and anesthesia.

Before Self is "aware" of controlling a "body" it must *know* that it can *have* "things." And whatever it must *know* at this level of programming must be equal across all living systems that maintain even a cellular-organic[111] "reactive-response" nature. But again—the problem and solution were the same and it was not hard to realize that emotional encoding is linked to *having* and thereby could be affected by the opposite qualities of "loss."

As a POV connected to sensory functions of an organic "genetic vehicle," the *Self* takes on the hard-wired programming that enables sensory reception of data, using a "physical body" to perceive material qualities of the physical environment. Programming and encoding at "2.0" on the Standard Model would thus be connected to a POV that is "aware" of the physical nature of creation (*beta-existence*) and that its composition of condensed solidified energy points creates matter, mass... "things."

Creative Ability of the Alpha Spirit while operating within a Home Universe, or even a shared Creative Universe, allows anything to be created and dispersed an infinite number of times without even a consideration of requiring energy. On the other hand, considerations for creations and position of energy-matter in *this* Physical Universe is concentrated and identified in such a way where a "thing" is uniquely rare from any other "thing" and cannot be truly duplicated even if resembling the same form.

By treating "things" with finite consideration in exclusion to all other "things," we generate an agreement with the concept of "possession"—or else a concept of *owning* or *having* "things" that are unique in finite creation to any other "thing" that is, was or could be. Fluid instantaneous and unlimited creation of "things" becomes something of a scarcity as one progresses down the condensation of Universes. As a

---

111 **organic** : as related to a physically living organism or carbon-based life form; energy-matter condensed into form as a focus or POV of Spiritual Life Energy (*ZU*) as it pertains to beta-existence of *this* Physical Universe (*KI*).

result, at each level, there is a heavier tendency or desire to "hold on" to things more strongly or tightly. This only occurs when the Alpha Spirit becomes convinced it cannot easily create them again.

Therefore, as soon as Self enters the POV of any Games Universe where material things are scarce and therefore should be *had, protected* and treated with high regard, emotional imprinting enters the picture—because now the Self can "lose" things; and this sense of "loss" (at "2.0") is treated as the same nature of threat to survival and existence as we might treat the care, protection and stewardship of a "physical body" (at "1.0"). Therefore, the most basic implant at this level is the command: *"knowing* and *being* is precise identification with the *having* of things and the avoidance of *pain."*

ΔΔΔΔΔΔΔ

When treating the interior of the Mind-System, the "RCC" (at "2.0") constitutes only one part of the range that maintains the Mind-Body connection To the upper part of mental command (of beta-thought), we give the name "Master Control Center" (or MCC), plotted at "4.0" on the Standard Model. Within this upper band[112] of "beta-thought"—between "2.1" and "4.0"—Self may occupy all manner of POV within the Mind-System.

At the level of "1.0" we can say that the observable programming of the Human Condition from the POV of the genetic organism is "fight-versus-flight"—and this is compounded by the other half of the RCC system at "2.0" with a primary "stimulus-response" automation system installed. That about wraps it up for the "genetic vehicle" as a bio-chemical emotional entity. Just above this level, we discover the larger framework of the Mind-System; and its manner of computation is wholly different from the "identity-based" imprints of

112 **band** : a division or group; in *NexGen Systemology*, a division or set of frequencies on the ZU-line that are tuned closely together and referred to as a group.

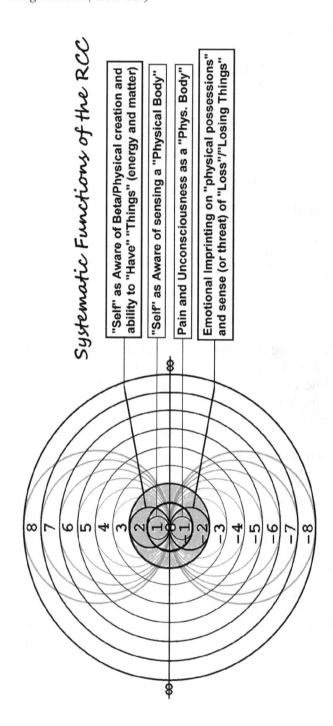

Systematic Functions of the RCC

"Self" as Aware of Beta/Physical creation and ability to "Have" "Things" (energy and matter)

"Self" as Aware of sensing a "Physical Body"

Pain and Unconsciousness as a "Phys. Body"

Emotional Imprinting on "physical possessions" and sense (or threat) of "Loss"/"Losing Things"

Systematic Functions of the MCC

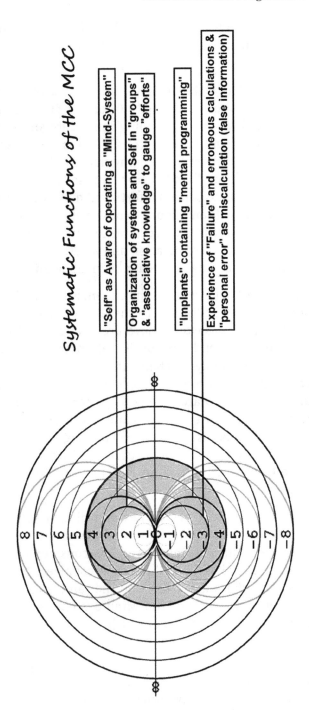

"Self" as Aware of operating a "Mind-System"

Organization of systems and Self in "groups" & "associative knowledge" to gauge "efforts"

"Implants" containing "mental programming"

Experience of "Failure" and erroneous calculations & "personal error" as miscalculation (false information) the RCC, which tends to generalize "knowledge" as emotional encoding and includes all *facets* found within an experience indiscriminately.

Within the band of beta-thought, or else the Mind-System that operates between "2.1" and "4.0" on our Standard Model (under the MCC), we find "grouping" and "categorization" of associated knowledge. Although analytical and not reactionary, the MCC can still be fragmented by individual experiences of "failure" and "error." It uses its stores of information to calculate certain efforts and make evaluations[113] about the Universe, then it looks to observable cues in the environment to see if this is correct. Misleading or erroneous[114] knowledge leads to miscalculation and a deteriorated mental state when personal data is repeatedly invalidated.[115]

It is a Self-Honest "clearing" of the channels that restores full command of the Mind-System to the Alpha Spirit. Too many of the functions and systems have been set on "automatic." The lower one descends in consideration on the Standard Model, the more solidly mechanistic and automatic the programs and circuitry become. These lower mechanisms tend to push an individual toward having a "pattern" or "tendency" outside of full *Actualized Awareness* and *Self-Determinism*. Eventually an individual is no longer knowingly at *Cause* for anything; and when one finally succumbs to being the total effect of a Universe, there is no direction left to go but out the bottom.

The latest 21st century researches and discoveries of Mardukite Zuism and its Systemology have supported the fact that *there are solutions* to all of what is considered "human problems" and it has been further recognized that these problems and solutions are one and the same and given any consideration only because the Mind-System is running in such a way as to perceive them as such.

---

113 **evaluate** : to determine, assign or fix a set value, amount or meaning.
114 **erroneous** : inaccurate; incorrect; containing error.
115 **invalidate** : decrease the level or degree or *agreement* as Reality.

The Mind-System is primarily occupied with computations of knowledge and effort in order to solve problems; and its computations are perfect to the degree of the programming that it is given and the state of fragmentation that it is operating at. [To gauge this in any relative workable form, we developed the *"Beta-Awareness Scale"*—as described fully in the text *"Crystal Clear"* (*Liber-2B*).]

In summary: personal fragmentation and Universe implants, in relation to the systematic structure of our Standard Model, logically follows an orderly sequence.

4.0 Mind-System (Human Condition)
–4.0 ... able to experience "programming"

3.0 Associated Knowledge (Calculations)
–3.0 ... able to experience "failure"

2.0 "Having" (Emotional Association)
–2.0 ... able to experience "loss"

1.0 Physical Body (Genetic Vehicle)
–1.0 ... able to experience "pain"

IMAGINOMICON

— LIBER 3D —

UNLOCKING HIGHER UNIVERSES AND TRUE SPIRITUAL FREEDOM

:: 0 ::

THE "CREATIVE ABILITY TEST" {"CAT"} WIZARD LEVEL - TRAINING REGIMEN

PURPOSE:

The *"Creative Ability Test"* *(CAT)* was developed for *Mardukite Systemology* to assist Seekers in not only gauging personal progress during their "Wizard Level" and *"Pre-A.T."* grades of work, but also to directly accelerate *"Creative Ability Training"* based on methods described throughout materials of "Metahuman Systemology"—specifically:

> *Creative Ability* maintained by an individual *Alpha-Spirit*, in its management of a *genetic vehicle* (to experience *beta-existence*), and also while operating independently *exterior* to reality agreements with the *Human Condition* and *Physical Universe.*

Unlike the *"Beta-Awareness Test"* *(BAT)*—first introduced in *"Crystal Clear,"* then reprinted in the *"Systemology Handbook"* and *"Way Into The Future"*—where a numeric assessment is applied on a gradient scale of fixed values for an observable evaluation on the Standard Model for *Beta-Existence*, the *"Creative Ability Test"* *(CAT)* is relatively subjective and virtually "unlimited" in its application.

BACKGROUND:

The author accumulated a large collection of esoteric exercises and New Thought techniques over a 25-year period. These were then tested by members of the Systemology Society and evaluated for relevance to the "end-goals" of Mardukite *Grade-IV* "Metahuman Systemology" and "Wizard Level" work. A precise intensive study of "background theory" for the exercises is *not* necessary for them to be effective —however, supportive technical knowledge is found throughout our related publications: *"The Complete Mardukite Master Course,"* materials from *"The Systemology Handbook"* (primarily

"*Tablets of Destiny*" and "*Crystal Clear*") and "*Metahuman Destinations*"—in addition to information in this present volume and its appendix.

After two years of intensive experimentation with innumerable "basic techniques" by many *Seekers* around the world reporting their results to the Systemology Society, surprisingly few exercises survived our rigorous testing and scrutiny for inclusion as both a Wizard-Grade "primer" and "*Creative Ability Test*" (*CAT*). Some versions of these exercises have appeared in previous Mardukite and Systemology publications; others may bare striking resemblance to "mystical" and/or "occult" techniques found elsewhere in esoteric lore—as recorded during the past 6,000 years, since the inception of cuneiform writing.

APPLICATION:

A Seeker will notice that as they develop greater degrees of *Creative Ability*, these "exercises" may be repeated with cumulatively better results. The "*CAT*" is not a traditional gradable "test." These "exercises" are approached on a gradient scale of "success" that relatively extends to *Infinity*. An individual will get a "sense" of their own present *ability*, which admittedly, can always be expressed "stronger," "longer" or "clearer" with additional practice.

"*Time*" is a common measure used by Seekers to chart their personal development; the *duration* period an individual can maintain duplication of an exercise with perfect clarity. Another measure is the actual degree of "*clarity*"—which is to say, a subjective certainty of completion or perfection successfully realized—that is maintained while carrying out exercises. This will all undoubtedly *increase* with each effective pass through "creativeness training sessions."

Data that *may* be recorded (for training purposes) is virtually identical to traditional "systematic processing sessions," including: the session environment (*location, weather, day of the week, &tc.*); your apparent condition (*a personal Beta-Awareness* or *Emotimeter evaluation*) at the start and end; the specific exercises or techniques applied; the duration of time spent on each exercise and the entire testing session; energy handling (*clarity of the operation, certainty of success, new realizations*); the material objects encountered and other "body phenomenon" (*solid forms, imagery, physical/emotional reactions, discomfort or pings sensed from the genetic vehicle*).

INSTRUCTIONS:

Even if an exercise seems "familiar," pay particular attention to specific wording of directions for each application, treating each step in its own unit of time (separate from previous exercises). The "*CAT*" may be *Self-Administered* or *Piloted*. In either case, to provide lasting "gains," it is necessary to focus validation on what an individual *is able* to do, rather than "exercising" in the direction of failure and shortcomings. We have found it more effective for beginners to cycle through as many of the basic steps of each exercise as possible during a single "creative training session"—because, when starting out, Seekers are likely to "try" too intensely on the extended particulars of a particular exercise, in exclusion to others, straining for a specific result or effect to occur. No effort should be applied; a *Seeker* should emphasize validating what they *can* do with each pass.

:: NOTICE :: Exercise cycles applicable for this "test" and "training regimen" follow an intensive systematic methodology resulting from twenty-five years of esoteric research and experimentation with numerous applied philosophies of spiritual technology. Although we are quite casual in their relay here (emphasizing light practice to encourage accumulating greater certainty), actual realizations and stable gains develop only by pushing through whatever fragmentation appears during practice—discomfort, somatic[116] pings,[117] in-

---

116 **somatic** : specifically pertaining to the physical body, its sensations and response actions or behaviors; also "*pings.*"

117 **ping** : a short, high pitched ring, chime or noise that alerts to the presence of something; in computer systems, a query sent on a network or line to another terminal in order to determine if there is a con-

trusive thoughts, reactive images, various emotional responses. Only by working through these to the height of personal certainty and clarity are they useful tools for defragmenting such automatic phenomenon.

At first, a Seeker may only be able to focus for a few minutes on the more basic steps of each exercise cycle, *realizing* it to the extent that present *Actualized Awareness* and attention allows—even if the extent of "success" is a vague *sense* of certainty. As the individual continues their studies and practice—increasing their understanding, willingness and ability —the "test" results become more vivid, certainty is stronger, greater realizations provide for higher "ledges" of Actualization, and personal development relevant to approaching *Gateways to Infinity* is demonstrably more apparent.

As an individual works toward *Spiritual* (or *"Alpha"*) *Actualization*—emphasized for the "Wizard" (or *"A.T."*) work of our Systemology—any one of these exercises produces increasingly better results the longer its clarity is able to be held. It is not unreasonable, as an individual advances, to eventually apply 30, 60 or even 120 continuous minutes—and entire *two-hour creative session*—toward a single exercise with increasing results.

Each section represents a specialized cycle, building upon previous cycles. Even after greater certainty is established on a particular cycle: for each new creativeness session, an individual should start at the beginning ("#1") and move through each, however briefly, before going to the next. There are no other "short cuts" to getting *through* and *out* from the trappings of this *Beta-Existence*—our Systemology *is* the most direct path we can access and best chance humanity has had toward its own Ascension, for at least 6,000 years.

---

nection to it; in *NexGen Systemology*, the sudden somatic twinge or pain or discomfort that is felt as a sensation in the body when a particular terminal (lifeform, object, concept) is 'brought to mind' or contacted on a personal communication channel-circuit; the accompanying sensations and mental images that are experienced as an automatic-response to the presence of some channel or terminal.

Due to debut appearance of the "CAT" in a rather introductory position for *Liber-3D*, an individual is likely to overlook true significance behind the following cycles of exercises in lieu of researching "deeper meaning" or "studies" behind this methodology. But, those who have walked this part of the *Pathway* ahead of you can attest that, indeed, *the whole meal is tasted within the first bite*. In the beginning, a *Seeker's* sense of reality on many of these experiences will be mostly "imaginary" in nature—but as real practice continues, actual perception will increase, permitting certainty and ability to *create* a higher ledge of *Beingness* to reach from, as we continue our journey upward the *Pathway* approaching the *Gateways to Infinity*.

:: NOTICE :: Before proceeding take factual note that the directives for this training regimen *do not* include personal intention or commands for a creation or image to persist. Any "masses" *Imagined* or *Copied* and any *Mental Images* "manufactured" in our Systemology exercises and systematic processing should be handled by consideration or command postulate, either: discarded, reduced down to a ball to toss away, dissolved to nothing, treated as being given away—or even pushed into the body from time to time to satisfy the illusion of replenishing energy (though all energy is actually manufactured by the Unlimited Self when necessary). The Alpha-Spirit is a god-like artist with unlimited *Creative Ability*, access to limitless ink and pad of unending paper at their disposal. But over time, it became increasingly fixed on its one track of compulsive creation. Once we can rehabilitate *Self* with certainty of its own *Creative Ability* again—only then might an individual be convinced enough to finally tear off that top of sheet of paper and regain the freedom of its true *Spiritual Beingness*.

Δ Δ Δ Δ Δ Δ Δ

CREATIVE ABILITY TRAINING
GRADE IV - WIZARD LEVEL-0

—#1— "PRESENCE: ENVIRONMENTAL SECURITY"

• *Look around your environment and spot objects that are acceptable—that you don't mind being present.*

• *Look around your environment and find objects that you wouldn't mind having.*

• *Look around your environment and spot locations where you are not.*

• *Look around your environment and notice persons that are not present; objects that are not present;*
animals that are not present; locations that are not present; times and incidents that are not happening.

—#2— "MENTAL IMAGERY: TURNING ON PICTURES"

• *Recall an actual event that has happened. When was it? Where was it? Who was there? What is its duration? Imagine the scenery. Notice as many facets of perception as you can—time of day, sensations, touch, weather, humidity, objects, brightness, smells, tastes, sounds, communications, dialogue, emotions of others, personal emotions, gestures, body positions, external motion, personal movement, &tc.*

• *Repeat the above step several times (with eyes closed if it is easier); recalling, imagining and looking at times/events which are acceptable to view, noticing all the details and facets—for example: when you saw something beautiful; when you heard something you enjoyed; when you smelled something pleasant, &tc.*

• *Continue until a clearer perception of Mental Imagery is realized.*

:: *Persistent Blackness/No Images—Imagine a duplicate of the blackness in the same space as the one you're looking at. Make a copy of it beside it. Make another copy. And another. Several more. Push the copies together and compress into nothing. Make eight more copies; then push them together and throw it away. Make eight more copies; push them together and then push them into the body. Continue this step until the compulsively generated blackness is under your control and you can perceive imagined or recalled images.*

—#3A— "PRESENCE: BETA-EXISTENCE SPACE-TIME"

• *Select two walls in a room with a clear path to walk between them. Start in the center facing one wall and get the sense that you are making the body perform these actions: Look at that wall; Walk over to that wall; Touch that wall; Turn around. Repeat the actions numerous times between both walls, each time giving the same attention to each action as if it's the first time.*

• *To advance this further, perform the previous step as directed, then from the center of the room with eyes closed, perform it again using only directed attention to alternate your Awareness between the walls and touch them. Then, repeat the actions, focusing on getting an actual sense of the perception of touching the wall. If this doesn't happen right away, just imagine the feel of the wall.*

—#3B— "PRESENCE: SPATIAL CORNER-POINTS"

• *Eyes closed, sitting near the center of a room—Reach up with Awareness and locate an upper corner-point in back of the room. Then find the second upper-corner. Focus all Awareness on these back two corner-points without thinking anything else. Keep all attention on these corner-points.*

• *To take a step further as an advanced practice, during a separate creative session, perform the same procedure treating all four back corner-points.*

• *This exercise can be extended to include all eight corner-points defining a room. This demonstrates basic principles behind the "imagined" or "spiritual" version of this exercise called "Creation-of-Space."*

—#4A— "FACSIMILE-COPIES: WHAT ARE YOU LOOKING AT?"

• *Eyes closed. What are you looking at? Imagine another copy just like it. Make another copy next to it. And several more. Then compress them all together into a ball and discard or toss away.*

• *Eyes open. Spot an object in the environment. Imagine a duplicate or copy of it right beside it. Spot another object and repeat.*

Continue to do this with various objects.

• *With eyes closed, get a sense of looking at the objects in the environment. Imagine a duplicate or copy beside each, one by one.*

• *With eyes closed, while indoors, get a sense of looking at objects outside the environment/room/building; and imagine a duplicate or copy beside each.*

• *Practice each of the above—but imagining a perfect duplicate of the object, making it in the same space, using the same energy-mass; then consider that the object is there again; then make a perfect duplicate; then consider the object is there again. Alternate repeatedly.*

:: *Persistent Images/Imprints—Imagine a duplicate of the image in the same space as the one you're looking at. Make a copy of it beside it. Make another copy. And another. Several more. Jam the copies together into a ball and compress into nothing. Make eight more copies; then jam them together into a ball and toss it away. Make eight more copies; jam them together into a ball and push them into the body. Continue this step until the compulsively generated image is under your control.*

—#4B— "FACSIMILE-COPIES: IDENTIFICATION AND BODIES"

• *Eyes closed. Imagine a duplicate (identical copy) of your presently owned human body out in front of you. Make a copy next to it. And another. And several more. When you have eight or so, push them together into a ball and collapse it into nothing. Imagine another duplicate. Make a copy next to it. And many more copies; then push them together into a ball and toss it away. Continue this step until you feel comfortable in creating bodies.*

–*Imagine a duplicate of your present body as ideal and healthy; then unmake it. Make it again; then unmake it. Alternate repeatedly.*

–*Looking into a mirror. Get the sense that there is "something there"; then get the sense there is "nothing there." Alternate these considerations repeatedly.*

• *Eyes closed. Imagine a busy or crowded place, mall, depot or street corner. Place your point-of-view in a fixed location; then look around and spot objects, motions and people in this scenery.*

Practice this for multiple locations (preferably until an increase in actual perception).

–*Choose the location you like best from the previous stop to use for the remaining cycle of exercises; Imagine making a facsimile-copy of your present human body to use as a point-of-view; then unmake the body and remain looking as an Awareness. Alternate repeatedly.*

• *Perform the previous step, but this time: Imagine an identical copy of the body out in front of you, using a point-of-view outside the body to look around the location; then use a point-of-view from inside the body to look around the location. Alternate viewpoints repeatedly.*

–*Perform the previous step, but this time adding: Get the sense of other persons acknowledging your presence when they are near or walking by (even if they don't look at the body).*

• *Select a basic solid object (pyramid, cone, cube, sphere, &tc.); Imagine using the "object" as your body to practice each previous step of this locational-cycle of exercises; making and unmaking, alternating viewpoints, spotting other objects, noticing motions and persons, and receiving acknowledgment ("hellos") for your presence. Now add to this cycle: unmaking the body and point-of-view in one spot, then making it again at other spots in the location. Get a sense of moving that body like a "playing piece."*

–*As before; Imagine using a duplicate copy of your present body.*

–*As before; Imagine use of an elderly body.*

–*As before; Imagine use of a child body.*

–*As before; Imagine using a body of a different gender.*

–*As before; Imagine using a body that appears strong.*

–*As before; Imagine using a body that appears wise.*

–*As before; Imagine using a sparkly cloud of silvery-white energy for a body with small golden balls for eyes.*

–*As before; using only the point-of-view as an Awareness with nothing added as a body.*

—#4C— "FACSIMILE-COPIES: MACHINERY AND BODIES"
• *Select an object that has a basic mechanical function "to produce a flow." (This may be best practiced with a "sink" or "water-spigot"*

until there is an independent reality on electricity and basic motions.)

–*With eyes open. Look at the mechanical-object in its "off" condition and imagine an identical duplicate beside it. Look between the two and spot any differences, adjusting your created duplicate to match the original. Continue until satisfied with the certainty of duplication.*

–*Turn the mechanic-object "on" and look at it in this condition, noting the motion and getting a sense of the energy-flow driving it. Adjust your imagined duplicate to match this in every way, noting the motion and getting a sense of the energy-flow involved.*

• *For advancing these steps, with eyes closed; use an object not present.*

• *Select a mechanic object that has a basic "motor" function. (This may be best practiced with an "electric fan" until there is an independent reality on generators and engines.)*

–*Apply the previous basic steps for imagining duplicate machinery; this time giving particular attention to its internal mechanics: at basic, a circuit or energy flow that drives or propels spinning motion of the blades and is started and stopped by a switch. As it runs (is "on") get a sense of the internal mechanics and match this energy and motion in your duplicate.*

• *For additional practice: use more complex machines; use machinery not present; use electronic devices. A basic study in physical mechanics on "how things work" is of benefit.*

• *Eyes closed. Imagine being a "motor-vehicle"; create the machine, the internal mechanics, and get the sense of identifying with it as a body. Establish a point-of-view from the car, while maintaining a sense of the energy and motion mechanically operating inside of it.*

• *For advancing this step further, move your point-of-view through each mechanical system of the vehicle as you imagine it running: steering, brakes, the engine, transmission, &tc. (to the best of your reality on these systems). Get a sense for how it operates from the inside.*

• *Apply basic directions for using a solid object in locational-cycle exercises (#4B), this time using a vehicle (such as a car) for a body. Run the whole cycle using the vehicle: everything from "making*

and unmaking" to considerations as a "playing piece."
• *Imagine the creation and unmaking of various machinery, devices, motors, vehicles, engines, generators, and power plants. Imagine as much detail in your creations as you can.*
–*Additionally; Imagine being various machinery. Alternate your point-of-view between inside and outside various vehicles and machines.*

• *Imagine the creation and unmaking of various personal "mental machinery": devices that inform you of things, so you don't have to know; devices that react for you, so you don't have to remember; devices that show impressions of what things are, so you don't have to look; devices that make your creations invisible as soon as you imagine them; devices that turn mental images into dark screens and black clouds when you try to remember them; devices that make mental images for you, so you don't have to create. Consider other mental mechanism that could be created.*
–*Additionally; Imagine being various mental machinery. Alternate your point-of-view between inside and outside various mental machinery.*

• *Eyes open, outdoors, public area. Spot a person that is standing or sitting for a while (like at a bus-stop). Imagine the creation of an identical duplicate copy beside them. As in previous steps; look between the two and spot any differences, adjusting your duplicate to match.*
–*Additionally; if the person leaves your view during practice, simply select another. If they change positions or spots in the area, adjust your duplicate copy to match the motion. Practice this step with several persons.*

• *Eyes open, outdoors, public area. Spot a person that is standing or sitting for a while (like at a bus-stop). Imagine the creation of an identical duplicate copy beside them. As in previous steps; look between the two and spot any differences, adjusting your duplicate to match.*
–*Additionally; if the person leaves your view during practice, simply select another. If they change positions or spots in the area, adjust your duplicate copy to match the motion. Practice this step repeatedly.*

• *Once certainty is established with the previous step: use the step to duplicate a person; this time giving particular attention to copying the internal parts of that body (bones, organs, muscle, &tc.) and get a sense of the organic systems functioning inside (as with the previous exercise on machines).*

-*Additionally; apply this step to duplicate a moving person, copying the motion in your duplicate. Get a sense of how the internal organic machinery drive various motors and systems during the motion. Practice this step with several persons. Practice this step repeatedly.*

—#5A— "CONTROL: WHAT IS THAT BODY DOING?"

• *Get the sense of you making the body do "what it's doing." Get the sense of making the body sit in a chair. Get the sense that you're making that body hold a book, &tc.*

• *Get the sense that you are behind the body, controlling its movement by strings or beams. Decide when to lift a finger of the body and then do so, imagining its control by a string. Decide when to lower it and then do so. Practice this on other movable parts of the body.*

• *Decide to conduct some activity (walk outdoors, &tc.) and focus Awareness behind the body's head. Expand your POV to encompass the entire space around the body. Move the body around, still using its eyes, but imagine controlling the body from behind it.*

• *Perform the previous step, emphasizing attention on the presser (push) and tractor (pull) energy beams directed to control movement of the body.*

:: *Compulsions/Ticks and Twitches—Consider a behavior that the body does compulsively on its own. Now decide to do this on your own determinism and you do so. Decide to stop and you do so. Start it again and decide to increase/exaggerate the action; then you do so. Decide to decrease the action and you do it. Decide to stop again an do it. Repeated this cycle until the behavior is under better control.*

—#5B— "CONTROL (PRESENCE): DISTANCE & CONNECTEDNESS"

• *Eyes open. Spot two objects and notice the differences between* them; then note the distance between them. Then get a sense of the space between them.

• With eyes closed, repeat the above step.

• Eyes open. Look around and spot an object that you wouldn't mind connected to you. Get the sense of making that object connect to you. Then get the sense that it is separate from you. Alternate. Determine how you could make it connect. Then consider in what ways it is different from you.

• With eyes closed, repeat the above step.

• Eyes open. Spot an object. Decide that you will walk over to the object and do so. Decide that you will reach out and touch the object and do so. Decide that you will let go of the object and do so.

• With eyes closed, repeat the above step by extending your Awareness.

• Walking outdoors; get the sense of being stationary and moving space around you, then get the sense of moving through space.

• Eyes open, then eyes closed. Indoors and outdoors; spot two objects and notice the distances between the objects and you. Then get a sense of the space between them and you.

• Perform the above step using three objects.

• Look around and spot something that is still; then spot something that is in motion. Alternate repeatedly.

• Eyes closed, repeat the above step, using a point-of-view from spaces or locations where you are not.

—#6— "ALTERNATION: BELL, BOOK & CANDLE"

• Select a small simple object (such as a "bell, book or candle") that is easily moved. Locate two spots. Move the object uniformly back and forth between these exact two spots at a consistent speed. Reach and let go for every spot change, leaving the object in precisely the same position at each spot for a moment.

• Select two small dissimilar objects (such as a "bell, book or candle") that are easily moved. Locate two spots (on a table). Place an object in each spot. Pick up "Object-1" and look at it. Notice its weight, its feel and its appearance. Get the sense of you making it more solid. Put it back in the same exact spot and position. Pick up

"Object-2" and look at it. Notice its weight, its feel and its appearance. Get the sense of you making it more solid. Put it back in the same exact spot and position. Alternate this step between the two objects, each time treated as the first time.

• *Continue the previous step until there is no compulsion toward automatic actions or responses, no fluctuation in attention and no desire to "leave" the exercise.*

• *For advanced practice, perform the physical version of the previous step, then close your eyes and imagine six walls forming a room that is not located in the Physical Universe. Imagine two tables or pedestals in the room. Imagine "Object-1" is on one table; hold it still and make it more solid. Imagine "Object-2" is on the other table; hold it still and make it more solid. Imagine "Object-1" floating up in the air; get a sense of its weight, its feel and its appearance; then have it float back down. Imagine "Object-2" floating up in the air; get a sense of its weight, its feel and its appearance; then have it float back down. Alternate as described above.*

• *Continue the previous step until there is increased perception of actual solidity and weight (in addition to imagined).*

—#7— "ALTERNATION (POV): AWARENESS OF SPOTS"

• *Eyes open. Locate a spot on the body, decide to reach out and touch it, then do so. Decide when to let go and do so. Find another spot on the body, and repeat the step. And again.*

• *With eyes closed, repeat the above step.*

• *Locate a spot in space, decide to move the body and touch it, then do so. Decide when to let go and do so. Find another spot in space, and repeat the step. And again.*

• *With eyes closed, repeat the above step.*

• *Locate a spot on the floor, decide to move the body over it, then do so. Find another spot on the floor, and repeat the step. And again.*

• *With eyes closed, repeat the above step.*

• *Locate two spots on the floor, decide to move the body over one, then walk toward it. Before reaching the spot, decide to change your mind and move the body over the other one instead. Find another two spots on the floor, and repeat the step. And again.*

• *With eyes closed, repeat the above step.*

• *Locate three points in the body; direct all attention on these three points in the body. Locate three points in space; direct all attention on these three points in space. Alternate these repeatedly—three points in the body; three points in space.*

• *With eyes closed, perform the above step; rapidly and repeatedly.*

• *Continue until there is perception separate from a body.*

—#8— "PROCEDURE 1-8-0, ROUTE-8: NOTHINGNESS"

• *Eyes closed. Imagine you are extending your Awareness, reaching through the entire Physical Universe, as far as you can imagine. Now reach a little further beyond and outside of all dimensional space and find the Nothingness. Hold your point-of-view on the Nothingness, without thinking or imagining anything else.*

–*Extend your reach out on the right side, getting a certainty of the Nothingness.*

–*Extend your reach out on the left side, getting a certainty of the Nothingness.*

–*Repeat the previous step for each other direction; reaching in front, reaching behind, reaching above, reaching below.*

–*Extend your reach out to the right and left simultaneously, holding the perception of Nothingness in both directions.*

–*Repeat the previous step for each direction-pair: in front of and behind you; then above and below you.*

–*Extend your reach out on all six sides of you at once, maintaining a certainty of Nothingness in all directions.*

• *To take practice a step further, alternate between this point-of-view with eyes closed and the point-of-view of the Physical Universe with eyes open. Look around each time and orient Self to the environment.*

• *Alternate getting full perception of Nothingness and full perception of the Physical Universe.*

:: 1 ::

IMAGINATION—HANDLING MENTAL IMAGES AND CREATIVE ABILITY

IMAGINATION is the vehicle or catalyst for an individual's *Creative Ability*. Such abilities originate at the level of the "Spirit" or "*Alpha Spirit*"; they are "*Alpha*" qualities originating within one's own "Personal Universe" apart from any programmed or encoded "reality agreements" concerning *Beta-Existence*, which is to say, the "Physical Universe." The two "Universes" are separate—and it is only when an individual confuses the Reality of *one* with the *other* that they tend to find the experience of Life and Existence especially difficult... and *fragmented*.

Being an Alpha quality, Imagination is above or *senior* to "Associative Thought" of the Mind-System as it applies to an individual's experience of *Beta-Existence*. Where the common denominator of personal thought and effort in *Beta-Existence* is toward the Existential Prime Directive: "*To Survive*"—the "name of the game" in all upper-level Universes and truer Alpha echelons[118] of spiritual existence is always: "*To Create*."

The Spirit is able to create, essentially, from *Nothingness*—and does not require fragmentation or condensation of *other* "energy-matter" *parts* in which *to be* creative. In this wise, an Alpha Spirit exists and operates in an unlimited Home Universe that defies some of the hardest-held beliefs about the Physical Universe. For example, fixed "conservation of energy," which is an untruth given the fact that *Life*—or the Spirit—is able to employ *Imagination* and literally imbue *Beta-Existence* with energies from a point *exterior* to it. Perhaps this is what accounts for an "expanding" Physical Universe, something we wouldn't expect to see *if* all energy-matter really *was* rigidly "conserved" as a fixed constant.

Although present-day "adult" society may pay a lip-service in

---

118**echelon** : a level or rung on a ladder; a rank or level of command.

support of "imaginative ability"—and what is laughingly called "creative thinking"—all typical demonstrations of social education and "enforced reality" suggest that the value of Imagination has been ranked quite low, put somewhere on a back-shelf beside "childish" things and "play." For the average individual, ability and willingness to "play" or "pretend"—just as "To Create"—diminishes over time as more and more fixed "thought-forms"[119] or "beliefs" (and other "imprinting" and "programming") are accumulated.

Most individuals are taught to put personal value in "experience" and in order to get a sense of that worth—to feel as if they can show something for it; or *have* something as the ultimate goal—the information is stored for "future" use—the only valid use being evaluation of "effort" necessary to "act" in the Physical Universe (*Beta-Existence*) using a "body" that exists to communicate at that material continuity level. But unfortunately, as an individual puts more and more energy into storing data and other "*Mental Images*" that mirror *Beta-Existence*, their considerations and willingness become increasingly rigid and fixed—essentially forming "energy ridges" and "mental machinery" that an Alpha-Spirit uses to manage and control experience with a physical body-form (*Genetic Vehicle*). This is also one aspect of how an *exterior* Alpha-Spirit became entrapped *interior* to the Human Condition of the Physical Universe.

Some schools of philosophy and spirituality have sought a resolution to this entrapment by treating the entire subject of the Physical Universe—and its facets of *space-time energy-matter*—as "unreal" or a "delusion." Such modes of operation contradict earlier agreements and postulates the Alpha-Spirit is already "carrying" concerning the Human

---

119 **thought-form** : apparent *manifestation* or existential *realization* of *Thought-waves* as "solids" even when only apparent in Reality-agreements of the Observer; the treatment of *Thought-waves* as permanent *imprints* obscuring *Self-Honest Clarity* of *Awareness* when reinforced by emotional experience as actualized "thought-formed solids" ("*beliefs*") in the Mind; energetic patterns that "surround" the individual.

Condition, so the individual gets "hung up" or "stuck" in a "Mystery" concerning their certainty on Reality. These other methods have already been attempted by our organization and were found unworkable and unproductive to our reaching the ultimate goal of returning to the Spirit its own (true and original) Actualized Awareness and ability of operating as Self, independent and *exterior* to *Beta-Existence.*

In spite of the numerous times an Alpha-Spirit has connected with a *Lifeform* in a *Beta-Existence,* the fact remains that we continue to consistently apply spiritual energy to create our "Personal Universe" in *Alpha-Existence.* Of course, the Self-Determined knowledge of this gradually fades to black as an individual enshrouds their considerations of Self and Reality with further "agreements" concerning the nature of the Physical Universe in exclusion to all others. For this reason, most other traditional "sciences" and "applied philosophies" have failed to do anything other than keep our considerations and attentions entrapped *interior* to *Beta-Existence*—providing no regard for the Spirit, its nature and abilities.

On a practical level—and in regards to "systematic processing"—before a *Seeker,* or *Pre-A.T. Wizard-In-Training,* focuses attentions too heavily on Higher Universes—their creation and management—the individual must arrive at full realization and *Awareness* that the Alpha Spirit *is* at *Cause* in *creating* them; that Self *is* at *Cause* in *determining* its own true spiritual existence and that the mechanics of *Beta-Existence* are wholly separate, but mirrored in an individuals consideration of a Personal Universe.

The nature and existence of this Physical Universe, however, is simply the result of all the lowest common denominator agreements made by countless Alpha Spirits participating[120] in this *reality* as a Point-of-View (POV) remote from, and simultaneous with, their own true continuing position as a *Spiritual Being* inhabiting a Personal Universe within

---

120 **participation** : being part of the action; affecting the result.

Alpha-Existence—with is marked at "7.0" on our Standard Model. It is at this "point" that the Alpha-Spirit may turn "180 degrees" to *confront*[121] the *Infinity of Nothingness*, but the fact that we are here now suggests that we became far more interested in potential *Somethingness*—and the whole nature of the "game" or "action" as we moved through a progressive condensation of Universes is fundamentally *"Communication,"* meaning the creation and origination of all types of directed *Energy-Matter* through *Space* across *Time*.

It is apparent within our Standard Model, our Systemology— and even allegories from the "Arcane Tablets"—that as an Alpha-Spirit was increasingly unwilling to confront communications of a "game" within a particular Universe, their considerations for existence as Self "fell down" or "degraded" to increasingly "lower" condensations of former Universes. Descriptions of the pathway back "up" and *out* are often relayed to "esoteric initiates" using symbolism of ascending "Gates"—although this application is frequently misunderstood when treated exclusively within paradigms of former mystical religions and occult practices. In any case, an individual essentially has gone "out of" *Communication* with "higher" spiritual levels on their descent *interior* to the present Human Condition. The "Wizard Grades" of our Systemology *systematically* pursue a repair of this.

"Imagination" is the most appropriate semantics we can apply to the Alpha-Spirit's *Creative Abilities* as experienced in the Human Condition. It is a crude word to use, at best, given that most individuals associate it with "unreal," "artificial" or "mental fluff." Although an Alpha-Spirit may direct imagery (energetically down the ZU-line) to the "Mind-System" for *Beta-Existence:*

---

121 **confront** : to come around in front of; to be in the presence of; to stand in front of, or in the face of; to meet "face-to-face" or "face-up-to"; additionally, in *NexGen Systemology*, to fully tolerate or acceptably withstand an encounter with a particular manifestation or encounter.

> Imagination is a *creation* originating directly from
> the "Spirit"—not a *product* of the "Mind."

However, as a *Being* descends in their considerations, *Point-of-View* (POV) and lower "seats" of *Beingness*—particularly below "4.0" on the Standard Model—cumulative programming and implanting of the "surrounding" Mind-System *caves in* on the individual. This promotes the type of automated reactive tendencies and preset patterns of thought and stimulus-response behavior that is treated in our *previous* Systemology materials concerning systematic "Beta-Defragmentation."[122] Once a Seeker has effectively *cleared the slate*[123] using Grade-III "Tech" from *"Crystal Clear"* combined with our initial Grade-IV advancements in *"Metahuman Destinations,"* then they are better prepared to realize for themselves—as an *Actualized Awareness*—the targeted goals of "Wizard Level-0" relayed throughout this *present* book.

Δ Δ Δ Δ Δ Δ

Each and every one of us has the ability to *incite* or *dissolve* "creation" with our *Attention*—our focused application of *Self-Directed Awareness*. We tend to do this several times a day: forming an intention[124] in the "Mind," *creating* an entire *"Mental Image"* within our "Personal Universe" of Reality and

---

122 **beta-defragmentation** : toward a state of *Self-Honesty* in regards to handling experience of the "Physical Universe" (*beta-existence*); an applied spiritual philosophy (or technology) of Self-Actualization originally described in the text *"Crystal Clear"* (*Liber-2B*), building upon theories from *"Systemology: The Original Thesis."*

123 **slate** : a hard thin flat surface material used for writing on; a chalkboard, which is a large version of the original wood-framed writing slate, named for the rock-type it was made from.

124 **intention** : the directed application of Will; to intend (have "in Mind") or signify (give "significance" to) for or toward a particular purpose; in *NexGen Systemology* (from the *Standard Model*)—the spiritual activity at WILL (5.0) directed by an *Alpha Spirit* (7.0); the application of WILL as "Cause" from a higher order of Alpha Thought and consideration (6.0), which then may continue to relay communications as an "effect" in the universe.

then often *erasing* it. Ability to *"Imagine"* is an innate faculty of Self as Alpha-Spirit, while still maintaining a communication with this shared "Physical Universe" separately. Within the higher levels of an Alpha Spirit's "Home Universe" and other shared "Creative Universes" within Alpha-Existence, the same faculty we describe as "imagination" in *Beta* is actually pure *"Creation"*—perhaps the highest ability and directive purpose *of* the Alpha-Spirit.

Of course, an individual is no *more* "free" to *Self-Determine* the nature of their own *"Creations"* or *"Creative Ability"* than they are in confronting and handling other elements of the *"Reactive Control Center"* and Mind-System *if* their considerations are still fixed locally and exclusively to the Point-of-View (POV) of the *Human Condition*, particularly the specific *Genetic Vehicle* to which it is operating. Such considerations inherent to the *Human Condition*, such as "I" or "Self" being "held in," "snapped in" or "keyed-in" *to* the "body" are direct "pass-not" barriers to achieving any higher states of graduated development within the "Wizard Levels" of our Metahuman Systemology.

Imagination is a *"Creative Ability"* of an Alpha-Spirit that is *superior* to "Thought"—originating from above "4.0" on the ZU-line and *exterior* to the Mind-System attached to POV exclusive to the *Human Condition*. This is not to say that, in some relative respects, the Alpha-Spirit does not carry its own "spiritual" equivalent of a "Mind" (in *Alpha*) that is then attached to considerations of the *Human Condition* with each *incarnation* using a *genetic vehicle*. Without such, there would be no carry-over record of a "spiritual continuum" or "spiritual lifeline" that marks the "Eternal Journey" that an individual experiences—but this is not the same, *one-to-one*,[125]

---

125 **one-to-one ('a'-for-'a')** : an expression meaning that what we say, write, represent, think or symbolize is a direct and perfect reflection or duplication of the actual aspect or thing—that "A" is for, means and is equivalent to "A" and not "a" or "q" or "!"; in the relay of communication, the message or particle is sent and perfectly duplicate in form and meaning when received.

with the Mind-System referred to at "4.0" on the Standard Model.

The Alpha-Spirit is the "I"—the *Self* or individual as they actually are. At its highest point of *Being* or *Beingness* ("7.0" on the Standard Model), the Alpha-Spirit is a *unit* or *point* of Awareness, which is *Aware* of its *Awareness*. At its most basic state, *this* is all that an Alpha-Spirit really is, free of all other considerations, creations and even postulates of knowingness. All the rest is *secondary* and first *realized* into being in order for it to be actual; and all as the *product of* the Spirit. Unlike former philosophies—and even early schools of epistemology[126]—we have discovered that the *Self* or "I" or Alpha-Spirit *is* the "I-AM"; not the Mind. "Self" is not *a* "Thought."

Descartes broadcast his error widely, when he famously wrote "I think; therefore, I am" (in his logical proof called the "*cogito*"). But he wrongly identified the "thinkingness" with the "beingness" of *Self.* Although it received far less attention, eventually this error philosophically earned a correction in Jean-Paul Satre's insight: "The consciousness that says 'I-Am' is not the same consciousness which 'thinks'."

> The *Being* is *Aware* that *it is* "thinking"
> —that *Awareness* is not a *part of* the "thinking."
> The *Being* is independent of the "thought."

What we have here, is a consideration of various potential POV or "viewpoints"—that we might otherwise consider "seats" of *Beingness*—whereby an individual is operating their *Awareness* from. It is bad enough to be "stuck" in a Mind-System POV, but when operating solely on considerations that *Self* is *a* "physical body," an individual has dropped extraordinarily low in *Beta-Awareness* (as demonstrable on the Standard Model).

---

126 **epistemology** : a school of philosophy focused on the truth of knowledge *and* knowledge of truth; theories regarding validity and truth inherent in any structure of knowledge and reason.

Systemology Wizard Levels emphasize techniques that go *beyond* the scale of *Beta-Awareness* (the range of "0" and "4" on our Model). Materials directed to specifically target "personal defragmentation" of lower *Beta* levels is available within the texts: "*Tablets of Destiny,*" "*Crystal Clear,*" "*Power of Zu*"‡ and "*Metahuman Destinations.*" This earlier work is quite necessary for most Seekers to establish successful certainty and effective reach and reality on the higher goals in place for Grade-IV (*Wizard Level-0*), which includes not only full Awareness and responsibility[127] for the creation and personal experience of "Mental Imagery," but also the operation of imagination and "Creative Ability" *independent* and *exterior* to the "Human" Mind-System. These are the keys to unlock *Gateways to Higher Universes.*

To adequately complete Grade-IV Wizard Level-0, an individual should *know* to the fullest extent of their *Beingness* that they are *not* the "physical body" (*genetic vehicle*)—to the same extent that they had once fixed or trapped their *knowing* in a consideration that they *were* identified as some other "body" or such. This is not an intellectual trick of semantic philosophy or something learned from books; an individual *must* knowingly maintain a full *Actualized Awareness* "outside of" the *Beta* range and limitations of the *Human Condition* in order to move forward and "upward." Establishment of *Self* as Alpha Spirit is not some arbitrary "rule" that our organization on Earth is imposing for social purposes. The gradient structure of the "Gateways" we illuminate[128] in our Systemology is already established as it is: the same "route" by which an individual once "descended" to reach their present conditions.

Previous attempts at reaching the same goals as our Systemo-

---

‡ Materials from "*Tablets of Destiny,*" "*Crystal Clear*" and "*Power of Zu*" may also be found in the Grade-III Master Edition anthology "*The Systemology Handbook.*"

127 **responsibility** : the *ability* to *respond*; the extent of mobilizing *power* and *understanding* an individual maintains as *Awareness* to enact *change*; the proactive ability to *Self-direct* and make decisions independent of an outside authority.

128 **illuminated** : to supply with light as to make visible/comprehensible.

logy often resulted in failure because of an overemphasis on handling "energy" directly. It is now concluded that an individual's inability to directly handle "energy" is supported by the amount of "relays" and "screens" and "filters" and "catalysts" that have been fixed in place to prevent them from doing so—barriers to direct communication and knowingness. Thus, if an individual *were* practiced in handling energy directly, there would be no dependency on using the sensory-organs and perceptions of a *genetic vehicle*. One could still do so by choice; but there would be no compulsive necessity behind such intentions.

Systemology Wizard Level-0 redirects emphasis on precise control, and responsibility for, the "Mental Images" and "Masses"—*forms, objects, manifestations* and *"terminals"*—that an individual maintains an energetic circuit-flow[129] with. It was discovered during the "2019 Crystal Clear Convocation" that when an individual properly *Self-Directed* handling of their *realizations* of consideration connected to *imagery* and *symbols* representing the "terminals" themselves, the energy-flows simply followed in suit; the circuitry connected to them "defragmented" as if the operator handled the energy. Elements of this are previously described in *"Metahuman Destinations."*

Imprinted and encoded information and memory develops into the basis of an artificial personality, one which the individual *identifies* with and operates a POV from. Of course, the Alpha-Spirit also possesses its own "personality" of sorts—a basic *Individual Identity* or *Beingness*. However, in regards to the *Human Condition*, additional considerations are then attached to this *Beingness* as one makes increasingly more agreements entrapping the individual within an artificial personality POV. For most individuals, there is no POV *outside of*—or *exterior* to—*Beta-Existence* and what it "means" to be "Human."

---

129 **flow** : movement across (or through) a channel (or conduit); a direction of active energetic motion typically distinguished as either an *in-flow, out-flow* or *cross-flow.*

Information imprinted and encoded on the Mind-System shares characteristics specific to a library or databank of specific details. These details are stored based on classifications: assigned significances for consideration in association (or comparison) with other previously established details. This forms a "set" or "data set"—contributing to the common phraseology: "Mind-Set." Of course, total capability (or creative range) for the Alpha-Spirit (or *Self*) is not restricted to any particular Mind-Set, unless it considers or "postulates" that it does, as an Alpha-Thought—in which case:

In its misguided *Self-Direction*, the Spirit *is* powerful enough to *forget* its own nature, if it *commands* it to be so, even if pressured or coaxed into agreeing to the same.

Δ Δ Δ Δ Δ Δ

Using previous material provided in Grade-III, Grade-IV and this present volume, a Seeker, Master—or *Pre-A.T.* Wizard-in-Training—increases Self-Determinism and understanding, and thereby their certainty to "face up to" or *confront* "Reality," which is to say: the agreements and significances made regarding not only *Beta-Existence*, but the subject of *all* "Universes." In *this* book, we tend to emphasize control and responsibility for "Mental Imagery"—control of the "associative knowledge response" to our experience of the "world-at-large." To be fully *Actualized*, an Alpha-Spirit must be free, once again, to fluidly consider potentiality of the ALL—AN.KI —or else the total potential sum and differentiation of considerations for all existences, *Alpha* and *Beta*.

Highest potential creativity of the Spirit and its upper-level *Point-of-View* (POV) is brought down to lower points of *Beta-Awareness* and fixed within the parameters of *that* existence, becoming obsessively attached to a *genetic vehicle* (or "physical body") POV for its sense of *Beingness*. Through a long sequence of programmed imprinting on implants reinforced with excessive emotional encoding:

> an individual comes to believe certain factors
> are true of *Self* and their Personal Home Universe,
> when they actually only pertain to considerations
> of the *genetic vehicle and* the Physical Universe.

Fragmentation of Beta-thought reduces an Alpha-Spirit's true spiritual individuality as it begins to "identify" itself with other "things." When it has too solidly identified with agreements of low-level *Awareness*, it falls in the domain of being an "effect" of *Beta-Existence*, succumbing to the "Physical Universe" or otherwise "mundane forces." Having forgotten the nature of its own creations, it is convinced on the dependency of a *Beta-Existence* to provide the force, energy, space, matter and so forth—providing the individual with an entirely *other-determined* "reality" in which to exist. This fact is the real delusion of the Physical Universe; not the solidity of its material substance. It continues to persist in existence, as a sort of "prison for Alpha-Spirits," because no one takes responsibility for its original creation and every Observer consistently alters what it *is*.

Inability to control or manage *Self-Determined* flows of energy (communication, reactivity, mental images, &tc.) is remedied by practice of consciously, intentionally and knowingly *Self-Directing* these flows in the same way that their handling has come to be "automated" as "push-button responses" managed by the *Beta*-environment or Physical Universe. The key component to this type of practice or "creativeness processing" is *Imagination*—literally the personal control of "Mental Imagery" and recording of experience.

> Mechanism in the Mind-System store data for "Mental Imagery" which entangles the same energy and *Awareness* that is *imprinted* during an experience or *Imprinting Incident*.[130] Not only does this reduce an individual's *Act-*

---

130 **imprinting incident** : the first or original event instance communicated and *emotionally encoded* onto an individual's "*Spiritual Timeline*" (recorded memory from all lifetimes), which formed a permanent impression that is later used to mechanically treat future contact on that

ualized Awareness, but also leads to giving the responsibility of creating and handling *Mental Images* over the automated mental machinery. This same *imprinted* data creates energetic turbulence[131] later when reactively incited as an individual's "Reality" by perception of the external environment during encounters with a similar *Activating Event*[132] that stimulates circuitry for a programmed response with a certain *facet*.

As explained in former Systemology texts, *Imprints* are essentially "stamped" holographic-type imagery—a snap-shot of energetic *facets* associated with an experience. When an individual is not maintaining high levels of *Actualized Awareness*, energetic-flows result in emotional encoding or programming stored on existing implants. Insufficient *"Presence"* and *Self-Determinism* is being applied to its handling. Automated response-mechanisms are "unconsciously" generated in place of it; they generate a "Mental Image"—and an Alpha-Spirit *"looks"* at *that* in place of the actual energy.

When *Self* is not knowingly at *Cause* in the experience of *Life*, no responsibility is taken for the creation of that experience —or one's own Personal Universe. The individual, as an *effect*,

---

channel; the first or original occurrence of some particular *facet* or mental image related to a certain type of *encoded response*, such as pain and discomfort, losses and victimization, and even the acts that we have taken against others along the Spiritual Timeline of our existence that caused them to also be *Imprinted*.

131 **turbulence** : a quality or state of distortion or disturbance that creates irregularity of a flow or pattern; the quality or state of aberration on a line (such as ragged edges) or the emotional "turbulent feelings" attached to a particular flow or terminal node; a violent, haphazard or disharmonious commotion (such as in the ebb of gusts and lulls of wind action).

132 **activating event** : an incident or occurrence that automatically stimulates a conscious or unrecognized reminder or 'ping' from an earlier *imprinting incident* recorded on one's own personal timeline as an emotionally charged and encoded memory; an incident or instance when thought systems are activated to determine the consequence or significance of an activity, motion or event—often demonstrated as *Activating Event → Belief Systems → Consideration*.

tends to put up more "resistance" to the Physical Universe as *Cause*—therefore making the considerations and agreements to *Beta-existence* more solid and apparently less controllable (one thinks) by *Self.*

In *Metahuman Destinations*, the subject of energy-flows is treated as "circuits" on "channels of communication"; the nature of "terminal nodes" is also defined. By understanding Systemology, we can see that the flows on these circuits are fixed by our "resistance" *against* some rejection, barrier or communication break with Universes and Spheres of Existence all the way down to present time *Beta*-experience. Over the course of our very long spiritual existence, this has created more solid barriers and added greater solidity to our fixed considerations of what something *is.* And this has come to happen "on automatic"—using automated response-mechanisms to handle the "circuitry"—*we* have created—for us.

> If we consider the nature of
> emotionally encoded *Imprinting*,
> we often find "snap-shots" of
> what we are resisting against.

For example, in a resonating "Image" remaining from a physical accident, it is a "snap-shot" of what we are attempting to *stop*, and thereby *control*. Failing this, the "Image" remains—it becomes a barrier-wall or backdrop on our Reality (for that "channel"). Of course, in essence, because we don't want to *see* or *communicate* with it, we tend to "flip" the "Image" around and only see the "backside," which is apparently some kind of "blackness" representing "Mystery."

But *facets* of the *Imprint* (and it's mechanisms) are all still in existence "running in the background," yet now even less under control of *Self*, which no longer *sees* it for what it *is*. This energetic solidity and fragmentation hinders a *Self-Honest* state of true Spiritual Freedom and *Creative Ability*. A remedy for this is found with one of the primary theories behind the application of "systematic processing":—

> to get an individual to consciously, willingly and
> knowingly practice actions that are otherwise
> taking place unknowingly on automatic
> or using response-mechanisms and other filters.

Such mechanisms and filters were once our own creations, but *control* of them became more automatic the longer they were used and the greater they were relied upon as "sensors" for information and experience. Keep in mind, that this same quality of energetic communication is taking place all up and down the Standard Model (ZU-line), including throughout the Mind-System.

We are now treating what *Self* experiences as obstructing "screens" or "fields" *and* the automatic-response "*Imagery*" (along with its associations of identity). Without this component, the "Route-1" methods described in "*Tablets of Destiny*" concerning the "Reactive Control Center" (the "RCC" at "2.0" on the Standard Model) have a "*limited*" application. They benefit a Seeker up to the point of overemphasizing validation of preexisting "RCC" patterns—as do "behavioral modification" exercises, or "cognitive therapies."

Thus, we systematically practice knowingly "duplicating" or "copying" *Mental Images* that are otherwise considered an imposition or barrier. When an individual recognizes that they "own" it, then the responsibility and command-power of creating all *Mental Imagery* experienced, increases.

:: 2 ::
ROUTE-ZERO—USING "CRYSTAL CLEAR" AND OTHER PROCEDURES FOR GRADE-IV "PRE-A.T." WIZARD TRAINING

An individual fragments—and defragments—*their own "Mental Image"* stores, considerations (programming; postulates), thoughts (reasoning; association) and emotional encoding (as a personal imprint) *all* regarding "some thing" (a form or mass; "terminal"). The "things" *remain* "things"—there is no delusion in this respect; it is the *significances* "imagined" *about* "things" that compose our own "image" of Reality. For this reason, "systematic processing" tends to practice a fluidity of energy-communication (as an alternation) along each channel to each "terminal" as way of freeing up the unlimited consideration an Alpha-Spirit naturally maintains at its highest state.

There is often too close a "reality association" with our imprinted responses and implanted circuitry to the automated *Mental Imagery* experienced as *Beta-Existence* from a POV of the *Human Condition*. An individual loses control of their own "Personal Universe"—which they are continuing to create and experience—as more of their attention is fixed on mirroring "identity associations" and "reality agreements" with the "Physical Universe."

Therefore, materials for Grade-IV (*Wizard Level-0*) place greater emphasis on applications that promote responsibility and certainty to control *Mental Imagery*—the ability to *know YOU* are creating the *Imagery*; that you can *choose* to make it more 'solid' and 'real' or simply 'dissolve' it; and a realization that no thing is permanent or can affect the Spirit, except as a consideration that it can.

"Routes" of systematic processing given in previous materials have one thing in common: they are treating the *past* in *this* lifetime—"scanning" this lifetime or "resurfacing" a specific event, or an even that is linked to communications from an earlier event and its *facets*. Such methodology is not only effective for *this* lifetime, but to have any greater applications, the Seeker would require an increased Reality on *former* lifetimes—and quite often, the "screens" and "filters" maintained in the operation of *this* lifetime are acting as "blinders" to any higher spiritual realizations.

"Route-1"—as demonstrated in theory for *"Tablets of Destiny"*—assists an individual in reclaiming some of their former energies "entwined" or "entangled" with holding on to emotional intensity of former experiences. It was intended to *assist* an individual in reaching enough *Actualized Awareness* to apply other forms of systematic processing. The method by itself is somewhat limited due to its exclusive treatment of instances where the Seeker is at "effect" of something other-determined—"what others have done to you"—and therefore can potentially reinforce "victimization" if used intensely for all purposes, in addition to over-validating functions of reactive mechanism.

"Crystal Clear" introduced "Route-2"—or else, "Analytical Recall"—which had far greater application in addressing personal significances, reasoning and *facets* of "associated knowledge" tied to an event, *any* event or consideration. "Route-3" from *"Metahuman Destinations"* worked along a similar philosophy; though it went beyond only events, treating "terminals" that our communication lines of energetic channels are tied to, and *three* specific circuits of *facet imprinting*:

Circuit-1: what *Self* has done (outflows);
Circuit-2: what *Self* has received (inflows); and
Circuit-3: what *Self* has observed of others (crossflows).

Of course, all of these former "Routes" are still primarily treating actual incidents from *this* lifetime—and their "Recall." There is no question that they are all effective methods for the goals in place at each step of the way; and it is highly recommend that a reader of this book actually work through previous materials. But—you are *here* now—and if these other

"Routes" should have demonstrated anything to you as a *Systemologist*, it is that you are *here* in the present where "past events" are *not*.

Too much time is spent trapped in "old" viewpoints (POV) where an Alpha-Spirit was so overloaded with energy that they have, in essence, "stuck" themselves—or rather, part of their Awareness—there on a "*Spiritual Timeline*" to *figure it out* for eternity. But there is really nothing to figure upon when the truth of the matter is: those events and conditions are *not* here and now—regardless of what "similar" *facets* of existence we may be confronted with that seem to "snap us" *unwillingly* "back in time" to relive an experience or *filter* and *process* present experiences from that POV.

Wherever an "energy-flow" has been fixed in place, or control of a "channel" has been abandoned, or considerations concerning a given "terminal" have been calcified[133] or fragmented with debris, an individual can be said to be "out of communication" with that aspect or part of existence. And since all parts work *systematically*, there is an ensuing *systematic* break-down of the remaining systems—at least as it concerns *Self-Determinism*, control and command, of and by *Self*— as Alpha-Spirit. To be effective at all:

the "Routes" of "systematic processing" rely on
a Spirit's ability to *control* and *dissolve* its own *creations*,
even when not explained as such in the directions.

When we consider the Grade-III anthology, "*The Systemology Handbook*"—containing "*Tablets of Destiny,*" "*Crystal Clear,*" "*Power of Zu*" and "*Systemology: The Original Thesis*"—in addition to the Grade-III "*The Complete Mardukite Master Course*" Academy Lectures *and* the first half of the Grade-IV material published as "*Metahuman Destinations,*" the present author

---

133 **calcified** : in nature, to calcify is to harden like stone from calcium and lime deposits; in philosophic applications, refers to a state of hardened fixed bone-like inflexibility; a condition change to rigidly solid.

has already dedicated *over half-a-million words* to establishing of a complete basic theory and applied philosophy for development of this "New Thought" science of "Mardukite Systemology"—of which we will not take up space to rehash in the present volume, while our goal remains to reach *higher* still.

Methodology for an additional "Route" for Grade-IV has not been previously provided. It is, however, unofficially listed as "Route-0" for "Unit Three" of "*Metahuman Destinations*"—and its steps are oversimplified for the outline (in that book) of "Systemology Operating Procedure 2-C." No other information is given for it, other than it would be covered in "*Liber-3D, a forthcoming Grade-IV textbook*"—the present volume you now hold in your hands.

Δ Δ Δ Δ Δ Δ

The two-step process given for "Route-0" in Pilot Procedure SOP-2C[134] is: *Imagine* and *Create It*—which sufficed to give an idea of the direction that "*Pre-A.T.*" work was headed. This might even be better stated as: *Imagine/Create* and *Make it More Solid*; or even *Realize It* and *Make it More Actual.* Additionally, SOP-2C "Route-3" lists a further "*A.T.*" application as "Circuit-0," which is what *Self* has created (or is creating) for *Self*—"What *Self* has done to *Self*"—as a method for emphasizing responsibility for creating all *Mental Images* and "identity associations" of what things *are*. This is incredibly "covert" goals for the processing, but more or less direct to the point.

Any point where the Alpha-Spirit is using a Mind-System to experience *Beta-Existence* from a POV *interior* to the *Human Condition*, a significant amount of its own spiritual energy is

---

134 **SOP-2C** : *Standard Operating Procedure #2C* or *Systemology Operating Procedure #2C*; a standardized procedural formula introduced in materials for "*Metahuman Destinations*" (*Liber-Two*); a regimen or outline for standard delivery of systematic processing used by *Systemology Pilots* and *Mardukite Ministers*; a procedure outline of systematic processing, which includes applications of "*Route-1*," "*Route-2*," "*Route-3*" and "*Route-0*" as taught for *Grade-IV Professional Piloting*.

taken up in the "unknown" validation and solidification of various "*wall-like screens*" and "*filter-mechanisms*" that inhibits free circulation of energetic-flow between an Alpha-Spirit's true Beingness and any of its potential creations or POVs.

Fragmentation of any kind "blocks" the clear communication that is maintained between *Self* and anything which it is still creating or in "possession" of. We carry a lot of energetic "ties" with us to the things in our past that we have had a significant amount of attention fixed upon—and other times when our attention was too dispersed to properly focus on the information that was being processed at the time. The former "Routes" have been quite successful in allowing a Seeker to resume communication with that which they have "*screened*" or "*filtered*" in the past and reclaim the control and command of those channels.

In many ways, basic goals of our applied spiritual philosophy —Mardukite Systemology—have not changed in the slightest. What we have found, however, working through the appropriate gradients of understanding—and the "Gateways" they correlate to—is that as an individual's *Actualized Awareness* increased up the tiers[135] of the *Pathway*, a wider-encompassing "arsenal" of tools is suddenly accessible and effectively workable. Such options must first be within the realm or Reality of the operator, who must also be fully able to understand and employ them properly.

In essence, all of our "Routes" have approached the same goal on a gradient scale: the *conversion* of old fixed *Mental Images* and the channels of energy-flow that *Self* maintains with these creations. In "Route-1" we called it *Resurfacing* (or *Cathartic Processing*);[136] "Route-2" is obviously *Analytical* or *Recall*

---

135 **tier** : a series of rows or levels, one stacked immediately before or atop another.

136 **catharsis / cathartic processing** : from the Greek root meaning "pure" or "perfect"; Gnostic practices of "consolamentum" where an individual removes distorting/fragmented emotional charges and encoding from a personal energy flow/circuit connected or associated with some terminal, mass, thing, &tc.; in *NexGen Systemology*, the

Processing; and "Route-3" is commonly referred to as *Communication Processing.*[137] This leaves us with with the obvious classification of this present "Route-0" methodology as *Creativeness Processing*—as applied to our *Grade-IV Pre-A.T. Wizard Level-0*. We have then, now, a very concise schedule of procedure.

"Route-1" Resurfacing/Cathartic Proc. (*Tablets of Destiny*)
"Route-2" Analytical/Recall Processing (*Crystal Clear*)
"Route-3" Communication Proc. (*Metahuman Destinations*)
"Route-0" Creativeness Processing (*Imaginomicon*)

In view of the fact that each "Route" added was able to accomplish goals of former "Routes" at a higher-level of operation, it is no surprise that systematic use of *Creativeness Processing* has characteristics of not only achieving goals of all other "Routes"—if properly applied—but simultaneously bringing an operator to an even higher gradient, tier or ledge of stable reach in their progression of *Actualized Awareness* as an Alpha-Spirit.

The "keyword" used for most basic "*Processing Command Lines*" (PCLs) of "Route-0" is: "Imagine." It was originally introduced to our spiritual technology during the "2019 Crystal Clear Convocation," but held back for "higher-level" examination after we realized many *Seekers* required working through "*Crystal Clear*" material several times in order to have a strong Reality on it. We developed "*Metahuman Destinations*" and "Route-3" not only to introduce "Professional Piloting Procedures" to Systemology, but also to make certain a *Seeker* had cleared *enough* channels—had enough "reactivity"

---

emptying out or discharge of emotional stores.

137 **communication processing** : a methodology of Grade-IV Metahuman Systemology that emphasizes analysis of all Mind-System energy flows (information) transmitted and stored along circuits of a channel toward some terminal, thing or concept, particularly: what Self has out-flowed, what Self has in-flowed, and the cross-flows that Self has observed; also "*Route-3*."

under their control—before making their Mental Imagery and other creations any "stronger."

"Route-0" methodology may be applied directly to the same type of "terminals" and "events" targeted by all other "Routes," but only if "IMAGINE" is applied properly in the *Processing Command Line* (PCL) and then also executed properly in practice. For example, one can easily replace "RECALL" with "IMAGINE" in all formerly suggested PCLs. The action of "*Imagining*" or "*Creating*" also frees up a wider range of potential applications for *Systematic Processing*—including those that increase an individual's ability to "*confront*" (and what they formerly were unable to adequately "*recall*" or have "*screened*"/"*filtered*") or points of *Recall* that prove too turbulent for a *Seeker* to "*confront*" when approached by other "Routes."

Any "thing" or "scenario" that might be treated by another method of systematic processing can be treated in *Creativeness Processing* (Route-0) *if* the "terminal" or "subject" is within the reach of the practitioner. If not, then the same methodology can be employed on a gradient scale—getting an individual to simply *Imagine* some small part of the whole, each time gradually increasing the amount of scope or magnitude that they *are* willing and able to "*confront.*" This is especially applicable to *any* "thing" or "terminal" associated with reactive *Mental Images*; or to the "mass" or "situation" in one's environment, producing or associated with a particular *facet*, that automatically stimulates generation of a particular *Image*. When phenomenon occurs as reactive-responses, they are said to be "out of the communication"—and thereby "control"—of the operator.

Δ Δ Δ Δ Δ Δ

Effectiveness of "Route-0" is dependent on an individual *creating* and *imagining*—independent of memory, Beta-thought or "associative reason." In no way should an *Imaginary Scene* or *Mental Image* be a duplicate or "*facsimile*" of something that has actually happened unless the technique specifically calls for it. The purpose of this is to resume control of the very mechanisms and functions that have already caused "associations of identity" to be fixed automatically in "*facsimile imprints*" of experience on a "reaction-response" basis.

The term "*Mental Image*" is not restricted only to "visual scenes" or literal "pictures" held in the Mind—or within one's Personal Universe. As a Seeker learns in their former study of Mardukite Systemology, the *facets* of an *Imprint* include perceptions of other "senses" and the information they can provide. In addition to scenes depicting places and things, "*Crystal Clear*" suggests several other significant *facets* including: brightness/dimness, time of day, time of year, sounds, noises, vocal tones, spoken language, hardness/softness to touch, weights, physical efforts, tastes, smells, temperature, humidity, motion/movement, body actions, body position... the potential list is nearly endless.

Imagination originates from a "higher" point on the Standard Model than Beta-Thought. It occurs outside of or *exterior to* this *Beta-Existence* and the *Human Condition* POV, from a point of "Alpha-Thought." This is referred to as "postulates" in past literature: the decision for something *to be* or *not to be*—a much higher level or faculty of the Alpha-Spirit than considerations and associations taking place in "thinking." In fact, it is these higher faculties that were once used to *create* the *circuitry* of the Mind-System for the "thinking," as the willingness and ability of the Spirit began to slump into states of *Beta-Awareness*. It is therefore the rehabilitation of *Creative Ability* that allows an Alpha-Spirit the understanding and certainty to regain the freedoms it holds in its truest state.

Perhaps one of the benefits to having a *Professional Pilot* administer "Route-0" early on is: an individual new to this systematic approach may repeatedly succumb to drowning in *real* scenes from their past—which is not the purpose of this technique. Benefit gained from *Creativeness Processing* is not as a result of a *Seeker* "facing up to" the Reality of *this* Physical Universe; instead, their ability to *confront* this *Beta-Existence* is increased by first practicing within their own Personal Universe—which is a truer spiritual existence that they have since abandoned communication with by unknowingly superimposing their experience and POV of *Beta-Existence* from the *Human Condition.*

We are therefore dealing with a higher-level of processing and skill when dealing with *Creativeness Processing.* The range of "Creative Alpha-Thought" occurs in the domain of approximately "6.0" on the Standard Model—exceeding even the level of "Will-Intention" at "5." We are then, of course, treating the POV of *Self* from a higher echelon than "Beta-Thought" or the "surface thought" between "2.1" and "4.0" in the Mind-System; and naturally well beyond the "below-surface thought" of "reactive-response" mechanisms from "2.0" on downward. Thus, *Creativeness Processing* logically follows the original systematic progression of work along the *Pathway.*

Although "Route-0" is intended to steer away from *real* "scenes" from *this* lifetime, this Physical Universe is not the only *Beta-Existence* that an individual has occupied—nor is *this* lifetime the only incarnation-cycle that has been experienced in *this* Physical Universe. Unfortunately, the more times that an individual's POV is entrapped in *Beta-Existence*, the more their considerations begin to fall "in line" or "in step" *with* the Physical Universe more solidly.

When occupying low-levels of *Beta-Awareness* for too long, an individual often "mechanizes" their considerations—rather than willingly controlling their "postulates" and knowingly setting forth "actions" to *create* effects. An individual may also come to believe that the Physical Universe is all there is —that they have been given use of all the materials and energies within it and must use the efforts of this *Beta-Existence* in order to *Be* or *Have* anything in a Spiritual Universe. Yet, we discover that the Alpha-Existence—and one's own Personal Universe—does not actually require any physical effort in order to *Create*, which only requires the "postulate" or "consideration" that things *are* in order *to be.*

Defragmenting and controlling the "stores" of *Mental Imagery* seems particularly important for our *Spiritual Actualization.* The Alpha-Spirit "records" personal experience as *Mental Imagery* on a "*Spiritual Timeline*" and this is carried between lifetimes. Some "genetic memory"[138] is taken on from the continuing legacy of the *genetic vehicle* itself, but for the most part, it is our own *created* and *carried* "storage" of "things" that seems to affect our "mode of operation" the greatest—particularly when one is under the impression that *Self* and the *genetic vehicle* are the same POV; at which point it is very hard to distinguish whether the Spirit *or* the "Body" is in control of the experience, or even differentiate their identification.

An individual is often occupying a POV surrounded by "*screens*" and "*Imprints*" that are based on fixed locations in "space-time" that they refer to as "experience." But these experiences tend to "change" the perception of what and who the Alpha-Spirit *thinks* they are; which is a big step down from *knowing.*

Communication of energy is retained as a continuous flow (or "wave") on a particular "channel" up to *now* in present time. In truth, an individual isn't really *stuck* anywhere themselves, so much as they have *stuck* "pictures." But the individual is no longer carrying *Actualized Awareness* on that "channel" in the *now*, which is why it is not "actual" *Awareness*, but instead, a "Reality" or agreement that has kept a "presence" of *Awareness* fixed on some point in the past.

---

138 **genetic memory** : the evolutionary, cellular and genetic (DNA) "memory" encoded into a *genetic vehicle* or *living organism* during its progression and duplication (reproduction) over millions (or billions) of years on Earth; in *NexGen Systemology*—the past-life Earth-memory carried in the genetic makeup of an organism (*genetic vehicle*) that is *independent of any* actual "spiritual memory" maintained by the *Alpha Spirit* themselves, from its own previous lifetimes on Earth and elsewhere using other *genetic vehicles* with no direct evolutionary connection to the current physical form in use.

The subject of *"Point-of-Views"* (POV) and *"Identity Phases"*[139] is treated in previous materials, but much like what is formerly described as *"Imprints," "facsimiles"* and *"snap-shots,"* an application of these semantics seems more "correct" or understandable to a *Seeker* when approaching our Systemology on the basis of *"Mental Images."*

A *Point-of-View* (POV) *is* a "point" in which to view out from. These *"screens"* and *"filters"*—and circuits of *Mental Images*— are *"Identity-Phases"* an individual takes possession of; a pattern of "thinkingness" to substitute true "Knowingness."

In other words, an individual gets to "play a game" by assuming a "role"—and there is, of course, nothing wrong with the ability of the Alpha-Spirit *to Be* anything it chooses, so long as it *is* knowingly and willingly *choosing* to do so on its own Determinism; and also freely able to "get up" from the *Game.*

It is also important to realize *when* we *are* "playing a game"; and that the experience of moving little pieces around a board is not the same as the Identity of the *Self*—as Alpha-Spirit—that *is* the one playing the *Game* from a truer POV that is outside of—or *exterior* to—the Reality of the "game-board" dimension.

---

139 **phase (identification)** : in *NexGen Systemology,* a pattern of personality or identity that is assumed as the POV from *Self*; personal identification with artificial "personality packages"; an individual assuming or taking characteristics of another individual (often unknowingly as a response-mechanism); also *"phase alignment."*

:: 3 ::

ESTABLISHING THE ALPHA-SPIRIT

The applied spiritual philosophy of Mardukite Systemology is rooted on one primary axiom: that the *Self* is a point or unit of *Spiritual Awareness* that we refer to as the *Alpha-Spirit*—the first-form or primary principle of "I-AM" that exists as a center of an Alpha-Existence. The *Alpha-Spirit* has *one* true lifetime or continuous eternal Alpha *Beingness*, which is only separated by consideration of individual life-cycles (*incarnations*) that it has located its POV and identified as a *Beingness* to some level or plane of communication: in order to *do* something, in order to *have* something.

Self-Actualization, as it applies to our *Metahuman* and *Spiritual* "Systemology," is a higher state of *Beingness, exterior* to the *Human Condition*, that includes a true *Self-Honest* perception and realization of the "I-AM." Although the concept has appeared in the semantics of many spiritual philosophies and mystical religions in the past, the *map* is not the *territory*—and in the past 6,000 years we have found few demonstrations of these higher ideals experienced by individuals still entrapped within the POV of the *Human Condition*. In short: former attempts have not delivered satisfactory results.

It is true that many who remain suspended within "parameters" of the *Human Condition* cannot *actually* conceive of *Self* as a "Spirit" operating *exterior* to states of "feeling" (sensation) and "thinking" (associative reason), which have far too long substituted actual states of "*Knowingness.*" Even magicians, mystics and priests—with their "astral bodies" and "mental bodies" and "etheric bodies"—are still yet unable to *realize* a *Self* that is not tied to forms and bodies. We have experienced phenomenon of *Seekers* in processing: some of which are stuck in a body POV; some of which are stuck in a head POV; some of which are stuck apart from wanting anything to do with control of "bodies," leaving the one they identify with to run completely on its own stimulus-response impulses.

As techniques within this book demonstrate, *Self-Actualization* of *Self-Awareness*—which we refer to as gradients of *Actualized Awareness*—is not being *Aware* of the "outside world" in *Beta-Existence*, or even of one's own *genetic vehicle* as separate from other "bodies" and forms—such as impressed by the mystic's "I–Not-I monad." Upper-level states of *Spiritual Awareness* (and "Zu-Vision")[140] that often accompany the completed experience of "Beta-Defragmentation" (*Self-Honesty*) surpass even an *Awareness* of operating one's own Mind-System, as we have realized that Descartes was only part of the way "there" when he stopped with "thinkingness."

"Individuality"—as the true nature of *Self*—is plotted high, one-to-one with the Alpha-Spirit, at "7.0" on the (*Zu-line*) Standard Model; higher than the range of even Alpha-Thought, which is the product of the Alpha-Spirit—and well beyond the level of "association" and, of course, "identity." The I-AM—*Self* as Alpha-Spirit—*is* an Individual. It is above any of the personality-persona-packages and *genetic vehicles* and *forms* that it may later attach to its own consideration of *Beingness.*

The basic methodology and "esoteric exercises" suggested are meant to assist a Seeker in more fully *realizing* the *Awareness* of "Spiritual Individuality" as opposed to the "*beta-personality.*" The total *realization* of "I" as *Self* as Alpha-Spirit *is* a prerequisite to the attainment or *Actualization* of that high-level Awareness. This is not "word-play"; the fundamentals of this principle are outlined more clearly in the text "*Crystal Clear*" and many other collected works within the "*Systemology Handbook*" anthology. An actualization of these same fundamentals is also necessary for a *Seeker* or "*Master*" to achieve the highest goals for "*Wizard Level-0.*"

---

140 **Zu-Vision** : the true and basic (*Alpha*) Point-of-View (perspective, POV) maintained by *Self* as *Alpha-Spirit* outside boundaries or considerations of the *Human Condition* "Mind-Systems" and *exterior* to beta-existence reality agreements with the Physical Universe; a POV of Self *as* "a unit of Spiritual Awareness" that exists independent of a "body" and entrapment in a *Human Condition*; "spirit vision" in its truest sense.

Practice of *Self-Awareness* falls within a subset of the domain of *"Imagination,"* which we might refer to as *"POV Processing"* when administered systematically. Mystics and adepts would practice such exercises until they became as habitual to consider as the former considerations once were of being fixed within the *Human Condition*. Once the stable gains for Grade-IV have been achieved—as an individual reaches closer to total *Beta-Defragmentation*—the basic methodology of the present volume provides for more certain and lasting results.

The most critical component to operating "out" and *exterior* to this *Beta-Existence* is to attain a "crystal clear" certainty and realization—complete reality agreement—that the I-AM, *Self*, is: not the Mind, not the Body (or any *genetic vehicle*), but is commander and operator of these instruments in *Beta-Existence* from a point of true *Spiritual Awareness* that is not directly identifiable within the boundaries or parameters of the Physical Universe; it simply operates the machinery there. As an individual Alpha-Spirit becomes fragmented by "associative thought," the circuitry of the Mind-System offers POV that make it seem as though the individual *is* confined to within those Systems as a point of *Beingness*. But these "implants" are not truth—the total remedy for which falls within an even higher pursuit that we might refer to as *"Alpha-Defragmentation."*

In order to get a *realization* that *Self* is apart from—and the superior master to—the *genetic vehicle* as a "body," the Seeker should take time to focus *Awareness* through each part of the body: beginning with the feet and moving up into the head (and including the brain). In the past, mystics referred to these techniques as *"Activating the Light-Body"*—but, what we have found in our Systemology is that the *Awareness* itself act as "Light," not any "body." The Alpha-Spirit operates as an *Awareness* independent of *any* "body"—even a "spiritual" one. Of course, it has had many layers or levels or dimensions of "energetic body" assumed during its experiences through various "Universes"; and the more rigid, solid and condensed the energy-matter of a Universe, the more rigid and solid the *genetic vehicles* are for Life to communicate at that level of *Beta-Existence.*

When *Self* is operating as an *Awareness* "outside" sensory perceptions and energetic rigidity of a "material body," it may, in effect, *look into* the *genetic organism* and view its workings—practice in which will demonstrate that the "I" or *Self* is not identical or identified *as* the "body." For some it is easier to consider that they are operating *exterior* to this Physical Universe, but are "projecting" their *Awareness* to a POV that *is within* another form or "body" to experience a *Beingness.*

"*Creativeness Processing*" tends to operate best on a gradient scale of reality—the Seeker achieves the best results by systematically treating a whole in parts until they are prepared to maintain a full realization on the whole. For example, in the treatment of the "body" with these methods:

> Begin with full directed attention—as *Awareness*—on just the feet (even prior to treating the entire limb), or if that proves challenging at first, just one toe of one foot. Then concentrate that *Awareness* in that location; and using *Creative Ability*, imagine that: if the feet were nonexistent, then *Self* would still continue to exist unchanged as the Alpha-Spirit. Next, consider that they are useful tools for communicating activity when operating a *genetic vehicle* in the Physical Universe, but they are not the "feet" *of* the Spirit; and *Self* is not dependent on the feet of a "body" to act.

It is important to clarify that the *genetic vehicle* is not to be disowned or rejected at this juncture—for that is not the intention of the exercises. An individual who is not getting along well in this lifetime, or is experiencing a great deal of pain, is already excessively and compulsively "out of communication" with the "body." The *genetic vehicle* is exactly that—a vehicle or instrument or tool that should be cared for like we might any other "possession," but it should not be obsessed over or confused as an "identity" for *Self.*

The same exercise may be continued with the remainder of the body—the pelvic region (sexual organs), digestive tract, chest, arms, neck, head, &tc.—treating each with the same considerations, and moving off from each with the same realizations, as with the feet. When this is accomplished throughout the whole body, then the *Seeker* may look to consider the "body" as the whole of the *genetic vehicle*, an instrument useful for communication in the Physical Universe, biologically adapted to this *Beta-Existence*; but that *Self*—I-AM; Alpha-Spirit—*is* above and superior, independent and apart, from the *genetic vehicle*, and exists *exterior* to it in a "Spiritual Universe."

Δ Δ Δ Δ Δ Δ

Practice of *exterior* "Zu-Vision"—the *Awareness POV* from *Self* independent of a "body" and *Beta-Existence*—ensues until a *Seeker* has an increased *realization* on the matter; and this practice requires "Imagination" and *Creative Ability* for that *realization* to become *actual*. It is here that an individual must be careful not to invalidate their own experience—or for a *Pilot* to invalidate a *Seeker*—concerning exactly what is taking place within the realm of "Imagination" and one's Personal Universe. An individual *"imagines"* the potentiality of something until it is *realized*, from which it may then be *actual*.

It is interesting to discover a few workable premises for our Systemology scattered throughout human history—pieces waiting to be picked up and assembled into foundations for a new level of "*Metahuman*" understanding. For example: although we have since developed more precise and systematic applications of our philosophy and spiritual techniques, we read similar suggestions for practical exercises voiced by *William Walker Atkinson* (1862-1932)—one of the founding pioneers of American "New Thought" over a century ago. We find written in his esoteric library of arcane teachings:—

"Let the Neophyte,[141] in imagination, leave the physical body and gaze upon the latter. A little mental practice will enable one to do this in imagination, thus bringing fully to mind the realization that it is possible for the *Self* to leave the body and dwell apart from it. When the mind has once grasped this possibility, the body will ever after be recognized as merely a physical machine, sheath or covering, of the *Self*—and one will never again commit the folly of identifying the 'I' with the physical body.

"Then let the Neophyte imagine themselves leaving behind their physical body, until, as Holmes says: '...thou at length are free, leaving thine outgrown shell by life's unresting sea.' Let them then consider themselves as occupying other and different bodies, one at a time, in different phases of life and condition, in different ages, &tc. This will bring about the realization that *Self* is something higher and independent of the particular physical shell or machine that it is now using, and which it may have at one time considered identical with itself. Then will the particular body occupied seem, in reality, to be '*my body*' instead of '*I*' or *Me*."

Of course, where one does find persistent difficulties in managing the *genetic vehicle*—or some reoccurring psycho-somatic condition—it is found that the Mind-System "short-circuits" energetic communication flows to locations of the "body" that are injured. Being a composite system, that "part" of the *genetic vehicle* is treated unaffectionately by the "automated" network—and this causes the *pings* and *pains* of life to continue being *created* as they are until *Self* resumes control and responsibility for total command of the "body."

As an experimental example, when a particular part of the *genetic vehicle* has been injured or pains us, we "prefer" to *not*

---

141 **neophyte** : a beginning initiate or novice to a particular sect or methodology; novitiate or entry-level grade of training, study and practice of an esoteric order or mystical lodge (fellowship).

"think" about it—or put any *Awareness* onto that region of the "body" because it "hurts." An individual can go as far as to start "damning" and "cursing" that part of their "body" and even succumb to lower levels of physical mutilation—all simply to avoid actually *confronting* that part of a "body" any longer. A better approach is to "imagine" *Mental Image* copies or create Self-Determined *facsimiles* of that "part" within the vicinity of the "part." This reestablishes that the "part" exists and that there is no "mental shortage" of energy passed to the "terminal." As a "Route-0" application of *Communication Processing*: an individual might even *imagine* literal spoken communications between *Self* and the "part," complete with *Hello's* and acknowledgments.[142]

By working with *Imagination* and *Creative Ability* in one's Personal Universe, a *Seeker* is able to focus more of its attentions on the incidents and experiences *exterior* to this *Beta-Existence* that are recorded on one's *"Spiritual Timeline."* Although the recovery of "Past-Life" memory is set for a higher gradient in our Systemology—such as in Grade-V (*Wizard Level-1*)—we are a building up a greater certainty of *realization* toward our Alpha-Existence, which of course, must be attained and actualized as a Reality for us to reach any further.

For now, the *Seeker* may contemplate—or *Imagine*—the etheric and incorporeal nature of the Alpha-Spirit that exists independent to *this* Universe. That they may experience the *Mental Imagery* that is conjured in the old Mystic Initiations drawn from the *Chaldean Oracles*, wherein a "Neophyte"— while mentally separated from the "body"—is brought to confront *Mental Images* of the "rushing fires" or "swirling waters" and physical elements that would otherwise consume and waste the flesh, but to which has no hold or influence on the eternal qualities and individual existence of *Self* as a "unit" of *Spiritual Awareness*.

---

142 **acknowledgment** : a response-communication establishing that an immediately former communication was properly received, duplicated and understood; the formal acceptance and/or recognition of a communication or presence.

Theories of Alpha-Defragmentation *could* be derived from a variety of mystical teachings and esoteric exercises—however the longevity and certainty of their stable results has always been in question, even among most "New Age" practitioners, which still seem to operate more on the basis of "thought" and "Mind" than the "Spirit." Consequently, many are on a "route" that does little more than validate the traditions they participate in. There is no sense of *Knowingness* attained; only that there *must* be some *thing* to *know*. Therefore, these organizations and groups continue to swell in numbers composed of members that simply have not *realized* anything "greater than" whatever their new presentation of old beaten ideas has to offer.

Many ongoing "Alpha-Defragmentation" experiments at the Systemology Society are born from archaic "New Thought" formulas found in old forgotten corners of dusty esoteric libraries—many of which bare similarity to various methods of "Eastern Tradition," although we emphasize *Self-Actualization* as an Alpha-Spirit—a point of pure *Spiritual Awareness*—that is not the same as an "Astral Body" or even a "thought," although it is capable of *creating* both "thoughts" and "bodies." The very fact that *Self* is able to *observe* all these faculties should suffice for one to *realize* that they—the actual I-AM—is above, superior to, and fully able to control and command its own *creations.* Even when we are presented with something *externally*—creations of others—the actual *facsimile* "copy" we store in our databanks and all associations we identify with it are completely our own *creations* to manage.

Δ Δ Δ Δ Δ Δ

At the end of Grade-III work, during the "2019 Crystal Clear Convocation" a special process was given to attendees—and later published in *"Crystal Clear"*—originally referred to as "SP-2B-8A," but when combining full knowledge of the "Standard Model" with the "Spheres of Existence," it was designated "Systemology Procedure 1-8-0." It became apparent after *"Tablets of Destiny"* that, even for basic "Beta-Defragmentation," a *Seeker* would have to *realize* well "beyond" the point they sought to effectively *actualize* as a stable gain.

"*Systemology Procedure 1-8-0*" remains the primary experimental *route out,* if actualized, even should we later discover more direct or effective means of achieving similar *realizations.* Although the concept seems basic, the present author can attest to the fact that over two decades of experimental practice with variations of the same, used by different operators, continues to yield great results. For us, it first began in the late-1990's, when reading from *Atkinson's* esoteric library of arcane teachings:—

> "Let the Neophyte meditate upon the great Ocean of Life in which the individual entities are but focal Centers of Consciousness and Force. Let them picture themselves, in imagination, as being an actual Center, with all the Universe revolving around them; see themselves as the pivot around which the Universe moves— the Central Sun around which the infinite world and planets circle in their cosmic flight. Let them feel themselves to be the focal Center of the Cosmos.

> "And this is indeed, in accordance with the centuries of old occult axiom, which informs us that 'the Cosmos is infinite—its circumference is nowhere—its center is everywhere.' Let the Neophyte lose all thought of the outside world in this meditation—let them regard it as totally unmanifest if they like—but see *Self* in Actual Existence and in Full Power. Let them realize 'I-AM' to the fullest extent of their power of imagination and conception."

Our development of "Systemology Procedure 1-8-0" began with the various routes for which it was named for—though it is also named for the compass-direction of our *Pathway,* which is 180-degrees *back the way we came.* All of its "routes" were particularly advanced by Grade-III standards, but allow for a gradual progression of increased *realization* (personal reality) with practice.

The text for "*Crystal Clear*" only included directions for one of them: "Proc. 180, Route-1" (*SP-2B-8A*) exactly as given below. This was originally intended to move *Awareness* "out" from the *genetic vehicle* and personally experiencing one's impressions of *each* "Sphere of Existence"—along the "Zu-line"—on their approach to *Infinity*; but it was never written as such in the instructions and previously has only described that way at the Academy for *Professional Piloting Flight School.*

"Systemology Procedure 180, Route 8" is given in the "*Creative Ability Test*" (CAT), emphasizing its ultimate destination: the "Infinity of Nothingness"—directly experiencing the "Infinity of Nothingness" in all directions. The third and final tested demonstration is "Proc. 180, Route 0," whereby an individual directs their *Beingness* as an Alpha-Command to any point in space-time for any Universe—though it is generally practiced with the local planet and local solar system first. This would include *Processing Command Lines* (PCLs) such as "*Be* outside the body" or "*Be* above the Earth" and other similar practices that effectively prepare an individual to operate independent of the *genetic vehicle* (in "*Zu-Vision*").

To sum up very concisely—we have an advanced methodology called "Systemology Procedure 180" that includes practice of the following formula:

(1) Self-Awareness;
(8) Nothingness; and
(0) Beingness.

In essence, it is this basic applied philosophy that actually provides us with all other high-level defragmentation. However, other practices, procedures and methods of systematic processing are also employed in order to increase the ability and certainty of reach that an individual actually has to attain these higher-levels. This would be no great task *if* it were just a matter of subtly reminding everyone of their *true Spiritual nature*; but most individuals have been systematically plunged into *Beta-Existence* (and the *Human Condtion*) pretty deeply—so, it requires a greater systematic approach to allow someone stable lasting results along the way *through and out* of the dross.[143]

Δ Δ Δ Δ Δ Δ

For reference purposes, the procedural instructions for "*Systemology 1-8-0, Route-1*" are given below exactly as they first appear in the text "*Crystal Clear.*" This same formula can be applied for each of the "Spheres of Existence."

"SYSTEMOLOGY 1-8-0, ROUTE-1"

—IMAGINE your Awareness as outside and *exterior* to the body.

—FOCUS your *Awareness* on the *Eighth Sphere* of *Infinity*.

—IMAGINE the *Infinity* of *Nothingness* extending out "infinitely" on all sides as a great Ocean of Cosmic Consciousness.

—FOCUS your *Awareness* from *Self* as a singular focal point of individuated consciousness in the center of the *Infinite Ocean*.

—SENSE that the *Nothingness-Space* all around you is rising up as tides and wave-actions of invisible motion; its abyssal stillness broken by the singular point that is *You*.

—SENSE that as you press your *Awareness* against the *Nothingness*, there is no resistance, there is no sensation—no feeling of any kind.

—IMAGINE your totality of *Awareness* as the singular focal point of *Infinity*—then REALIZE that the waves you see crashing up against you and rippling into *Infinity* are an extension of your every thought, will and action.

—REALIZE that you are the *Alpha Spirit*; that "wave peak" in an otherwise *Infinity of Nothingness* stretching out within and back off all that was, is and ever will.

—REALIZE that your conscious *Awareness* as "I", your direction of WILL as *Alpha Spirit*, and the "central wave peak" born out of *Infinity* are all the same pure individuated ZU—are all *One; Infinity; None*.

---

143 **dross** : prime material; specifically waste-matter or refuse; the discarded remains collected together.

—WILL yourself to project *Awareness* ahead of you and see an extension of this ZU as your projection of Identity extending infinitely in front of you—all the way to the *zero-point-continuity* of existence—and back to *Infinity*.

—REPEAT this several times, IMAGINING this ZU as a *Clear Light* radiant extension from *Self*, directed across *Infinity* to *Zero-point* and back to *Infinity*; then REALIZE that you are dissolving and wiping out all *fragmentation* from the channel as you direct the *Clear Light*.

—REPEAT this several times, until you feel confidant in your current results for this cycle of work.

—RECALL the instance you decided to start this present *session*—get a sense of the Intention you *Willed* to begin the session.

—REALIZE that your *beta-Awareness* and the true WILL of the Alpha Spirit are One continuous stream and that the *Self* is superior to, and master of, the *genetic vehicle*; End the session.

:: 4 ::
THE CONQUEST OF BETA-EXISTENCE, MENTAL IMAGERY AND IMPRINTING

"A faithful reproduction of the world around us collapses, and
our world image, far from being identically duplicate with the
'real world', becomes but our specific interpretation of that
world; our world is but *our* version of *the* world."

—*J.J. Van der Leeuw*

Imagination takes place "above" *Beta-Awareness* and is even superior to the WILL of an individual, for it effectively initiates
the impulse for what a *Being* is "willing"—and how that will
later correspond to reasoning, efforts and action that take
place in *Beta-Existence*. *Imagination* most closely resembles the
Creative Ability of the *Alpha-Spirit* in its natural basic state, existing in a personal Spiritual Universe that is receptive to
spontaneous creation. Such instantaneous "manifestation" does
not appear to take place in *Beta-Existence*, where an individual
is using a *genetic vehicle* to apply limited physical effort toward changing *energy-matter* of the Physical Universe and
create effects in *Beta-Existence*.

Existence of "I-AM" *Self* as Alpha-Spirit is not dependent on
any *survival* in *Beta-Existence*, except as the consideration of
playing a "game" *here* and being able to continue the "role"
and "personality" of a *genetic vehicle* that is equipped for communicating efforts of "change" in *Beta-Existence*. This is, of
course, not the only Universe we could be operating in—but
so long as we are fixed to the low-level considerations of the
Human Condition in its present state, it *appears* as if it is the
"only game in town."

With *Imagination*, an individual is employing high-levels of
Creative Ability as an Alpha-Spirit independent of considerations tied to the *Human Condition*. The highest function of the
Alpha-Spirit is *Creation*; and this ability is reduced to functions of a Mind-System and associative reasoning when fixed
to a *Human Condition* POV. *Life*, as operating in *Beta-Existence*,

is simply playing a "game" of *survival*—trying to "get along" as best as possible, using associative reasoning of the Mind-System (rather than *Imagination*) to "solve problems" of *survival*; all the while waiting for something or someone *else* to open the prison-gates. Yet, it is only by our own consideration and realizations (or lack thereof) that keep us *creating* the "Gates" as intact and guarded.

Practice and certainty of *Creative Ability* is paramount[144] to a *Seeker* being able to "release the hold" on *Beta-Existence* and its *Imprints*, knowing they are completely capable of *creating* any of these *Mental Images* again—and therefore not restricted only to those which have been *impressed* strongly upon them by other "forces" as *Cause*. The Alpha-Spirit has become more comfortable with *somethings*—where something is better than nothing—in preference to *confronting* the Infinity of Nothingness. This is resolved by providing an individual with the certainty that they can *have* anything they can *create* at any moment; thus, they need not compulsively cling to what is keeping them "down."

An individual believes—or *feels*—as though they "*have*" something by retaining significances of past *Imprinted Imagery*, which they tend to maintain as a valid "present-time" POV. The logic behind this, of course, being that the experience must have some "value" or "*be something*" (solid) of which can be used at a later time—otherwise why would we keep it in storage. The individual starts wanting to keep it all—after having been implanted with the concept of "*loss*"—and starts energetically *pulling* these "solids" in on the "body" from the perspective of *Self* being *interior* to the *genetic vehicle.* This validates and strengthens entrapment of *Self* "inside" the *Human Condition.* Even the idea of "pushing" things *away* from interior to the *Human Condition* creates a "resistance" or "energetic turbulence" *against* some *thing*, adding further "solidity" to it as a *thing.* It is no wonder that the Alpha-Spirit has found itself in quite a "spiritual trap" by entering into this Physical Universe.

---

144 **paramount** : most important; of utmost importance; "above all else."

While confined to the *Human Condition* or any *Beta-Existence*, a *Seeker* is using automated mechanisms to consistently "pull in" *Mental Images, Encoded Events, Thoughtform Beliefs*—all of which are the very *Imprinting* that is keeping them "trapped" in their present "mode" or Reality (level of realization). The mechanistic defense given to their compulsive creation, when *confronted* directly in systematic processing, is: *"but, they did happen..."*—and it is true: these are *Images* imprinted from *real* events that are located to some specific space and time; but that space and time is not *here* and *now*. Thereafter, these *Images* are simply maintained as "coiled energy" stores that fix (what would otherwise be unlimited) *Awareness* to "compulsive creation" outside total *Self-Determinism*.

Imprinted "snap-shots" are often the result of repeated "stops"—injury, punishment, going out of communication— all of which cause an individual to retreat (or retract or withdraw) from "control" on a particular communication line or "channel." Or, they might become "obsessive" about it. But neither extreme (tendency) provides for proper energy flow. The unwillingness to handle it proper forms energetic barriers—false *Mental Imagery* as a "screen," "filter" or "wall" in place of the *Self-determined* flow connected with some "terminal" or "stimulus."

> Systematic processing has revealed that much of what we consider "personal fragmentation" is a result of our inherent nature to *create* and *collect*—in this case: "pictures" of experience—and to be able to carry evidence of this experience in the form of "energetically charged mementos"—and *Imprints* of the "moment"—that are kept in place as signals or flags intended to prevent an individual from having to experience such *again*. This also breaks down an individual's *Self-Determinism* and ability to "duplicate" with full *Awareness*.

While it may seem fine to remember an incident as a warning to keep from "making the same mistakes," those conditions of the past are no longer present as "the same" ever again— and many other *facets* of experience are also tied to an *Im-*

print, meaning that its inhibiting factors extend to domains aside from just that one exact scenario.

Experience with "spiritual advisement" and "systematic processing" within our tradition also revealed that an individual is likely to reflect their "mode" of handling *Imprints* and *Mental Imagery* in the same manner they treat physical "objects"; since both are "masses." Many individuals have a tendency to be irresponsible about "masses"—whether they are compulsively "collective" or "destructive" in that regard. A "psychotic" may be hell-bent only on destruction of things in absence of any realized ability to *create*. But in most cases, it will be found that a *Seeker* is as well off as they are able to freely "rid themselves" of "masses" and have more "space"; and as bad off as they are surrounded by physical objects and "mental masses" with no "space" for *Beingness*. A *Being* that *Knows* they can *Create* at any instant will find little value in storing and carrying *mass*.

When we consider what the Standard Model (*Zu-line*) of Systemology represents—in terms of *Space-Time Energy-Matter*—the point of *Beingness* for an individuated Alpha-Spirit ("7.0") is all *Space* with nothing really happening within it. The spiritual unit of *Awareness* that is "I-AM"-*Self* certainly is not a "mass" in itself, which is why it is relatively "Eternal." As we move (down the "Model") into the Personal Universe and Alpha-Thought ("6.0") generated by an Alpha-Spirit, we begin to observe "action" or else "space with motion" in it—or else "energy."

As best we can understand, the energy potential at this level of operation by the Spirit is essentially unlimited. However, as more and more energy is created finitely, we get a condensation of space and thus, by a direction and concentration of the spiritual (Alpha) equivalent of "effort"—which is Will ("5.0")—we arrive at an "object" or "*mental mass*." In theory: *space* condenses as *energy*, which condenses into *matter*; and the closer and more "solid" the *matter*, the more finite the appearance of *time* as "action across/over distance." This would explain the changing conditions as we move into "lower"

Universes and "shorter" cycles of action (sometimes depicted in "wave-form").

It is difficult to introduce the Systemology of *Imagination* and its *Mental Image Pictures* (thought-images) without also differentiating these "knowingly" *Self-created Images* from other thought-waves,[145] which is to say "thought-forms" or "*thoughtforms*"—the energetic patterns that surround an individual, which they are creating on automatic or else "unknowingly." Some philosophies in the past have treated these thought-forms as everything from "auras" to "light shields" to "entities"—because there *is* a resulting phenomenon that mystics and spiritualists have long sought to classify, but never as the thing actually *is*, and always in combination with some other semantics.

Δ Δ Δ Δ Δ Δ

When we treat the Systemology of *Creative Ability*, a *Seeker* increases in their ability to knowingly manage the "*mental picture*," but it is not the "thought-image" alone that is being handled so much as the energetic "thought-forms" attached to it. Frequencies of various energies impress against the fields of *Beta-Existence* and *Self* must then process this information into what it considers "recognizable."

> This means external energy is received by a sensor,
> relayed on a communication line,
> hits against a "screen" of sorts
> and then the Alpha-Spirit *looks* at *that* "image"
> rather than *confronting* the actual energy-flow itself.

From this the concept of the "*Mental Image*" is created—and

---

145 **thought-wave** or **wave-form** : a proactive *Self-directed action* or reactive-response *action* of *consciousness*; the *process* of *thinking* as demonstrated in *wave-form*; the *activity* of *Awareness* within the range of *thought vibrations/frequencies* on the existential *Life-continuum* or *ZU-line*.

we say "mental" because it is using the "field" of the Mind as a backdrop to do this; and we are not restricting this idea to only a "Human Mind," but the actual "field" of mental energy that does enshroud the *Human Condition* when operating such a *genetic vehicle.* It is also why someone operating *interior* to a fragmented Mind-System has difficulty *realizing* the goals of the Systemology Wizard Grades—and why we first begin a Seeker with former "Routes" supplied in our materials.

The value of our applied spiritual philosophy—as an effective technology—is proved to an individual only by application: to the acid-test[146] of everyday life. A *"Systemologist"* has entire Universes for a laboratory. As we are concerned with *Creative Ability*, this "spiritual technology" is a living truth only when it is applied—it provides a *Seeker* with little more than mental occupation as "knowledge" when treated solely as an intellectual pursuit. *Creativity* comes not from having and accumulating a collection of dry postulates, but in the act of *creating energy.*

Goals of our work are meant to be treated in the "objective" world that a *Seeker* experiences everyday. Although we may establish objective truths, the "knowledge" earned from book-learning alone becomes a very "subjective" ordeal. A Systemologist is not deluded into thinking that there is not an "objective" Physical Universe "out there" as a shared meeting ground of communications at this level of *Beta-Existence.*

Issues only emerge when this Physical Universe—and its reality agreements—are confused with the true nature of *Self* and its own truer "Alpha" existence, operating from within a Spiritual Universe. The *Human Condition* is often implanted to *forget* this key point; and it seems that it cannot simply be subtly reminded—thus, we have

---

146 **acid-test** : a metaphor refers to a chemical process of applying harsh nitric acid to a golden substance (sample) to determine its genuineness; in *NexGen Systemology*, an extreme conclusive process to determine the reality, genuineness or truth of a substance, material, particle or piece of information.

our systematic methods for a *Seeker* to gradually work this out for themselves.

Systematic processing employed at the former "Master Level" (*Grade-III*) of Systemology—and "Route-3" from (*Grade-IV*) "*Metahuman Destinations*"—should have at least increased a *Seeker's* reality on the fact that:

a) the "Alpha-Spirit" operates as an individual "I-AM"-*Self*,

b) in command of a *genetic vehicle*

c) by using a "Mind-System."

This much should at least be demonstrable before moving forward. At the "Wizard Levels," we are concerned with establishing the Alpha-Spirit as a *creative* force capable of generating space-time energy-matter; at the very least, from within their own Personal Universe. Furthermore, the "Wizard Levels" must establish to a *Seeker* that:

a) there *is* a "Personal Universe" or "Home-World Universe" that the Alpha-Spirit is native to in its original basic state of existence;

b) that the I-AM-*Self* (as this Spirit or point of *Awareness*) exists independent of a *genetic vehicle*—just as much as we are not our "cars"; and

c) that an individual can operate from a truer POV remote from the body, *exterior* to the body and *beta-fragmented* "Mind-System."

Although *death* is also a direct transition point of *Awareness* "exterior" to the command of a specific *genetic vehicle*, thousands of years of practices by various monks and shamans has demonstrated that "alternative states" have been hit upon many times by the *living*. But in the case of death, the *genetic vehicle* and considerations of its operator have become the overwhelming effect of *external* forces—and the Alpha Spirit abandons control of the organism. Of course, when not freed from the implanted Mind-System that is encoded by *beta-existence*, the individual typically remains fixed to this Physical Universe in their next "incarnation."

Contrary to the "thought-formed beliefs" established by various religions in the past 6,000 years, it is far more logical and demonstrable—not to mention more certain in regards to one's own *Self-knowledge*—that we have experienced "past-lives" and continue our "spiritual existence" beyond this one. The idea of an "eternal stopping point" seems to defy the truth that one has already had a reality on in their spiritual past. Of course, these "Implanted Mind-Systems" do not allow proper memory of past-lives on an individual's "*Spiritual Timeline*" very easily. The matter is not particularly dealt with in the "basic" Systemology work due to the likelihood of it distracting a *Seeker* from responsibilities of *this* life, while they are still increasing their horsepower of *Actualized Awareness* enough to properly *confront* the reality of higher "levels."

There is a vague concept relayed in the semantics available in *beta-existence* regarding what is most primitively understood as a contrast between an "external world" environment or "objective" physical universe and the "internal" subjective "consciousness" of the "I" or "Eye of the Observer." Our Systemology breaks down the concepts more *systematically*—as External, Internal, Interior and Exterior.

The basic issue of being *fixed* or *stuck* "*interior*" to the *Human Condition* is just *that*: it *is* a condition—a conditional parameter or limitation of standard-issue "*internal*" sensory perception of an "*external*" environment. Yet, different *Awareness* levels, which incidentally have nothing to do with a "body," can allow a wider "reality" or "scope" of consideration—and potential *realization*—by which to evaluate energy-flows or more directly establish a *Knowingness*.

Although there are many levels of condensation—each essentially a Universe unto itself—the basic systemology behind space, time, energy and matter, seem to be mostly in common across all levels as we understand them. In the Physical Universe, we are dealing a *beta-existence* that still operates on the same principles as "higher ones," but the manifestations present—and the standard-issue faculties to perceive them—fall in a very low-level range of existence for experience.

> An individual while maintaining considerations for a POV rigidly fixed *interior* to the standard-issue *Human Condition* is unable to *confront* the "actuality" of energy-matter directly and must therefore rely on "organs" and "sensory screens" of a *genetic vehicle* to give them "cues" of an *external* world.

That alone should trigger some signals that a true existence of *Self* could not actually be confined to this *beta-existence* when all indicators seem to illuminate the now apparent fact that it remote-operates the experience "from outside."

This was one of the frustrating issues the present author has found with the semantics of "remote viewing"—because the true position of *Self* is always "remote" from a *body*, it just seems to be particularly attached to one as an exclusive POV. That *Self* can also direct its viewpoints *elsewhere*—or into other objects—is no more or less "remote" than its fixing or localizing a POV to a *genetic vehicle*.

Δ Δ Δ Δ Δ Δ

Apart from the *Infinity of Nothingness*, the *Self* exists as a point or unit of *Spiritual Awareness* as the "I-AM" amidst that *Sea of Infinity*. All else is Universes—or what some have called "dimensions"—and we typically *know* them by their "space" and "forms" existing against a background matrix, which is itself backed by *Nothingness*. So, the Alpha-Spirit *creates* and *experiences* in a "World of Lights" no matter what level of condensation those *spots* and *points* may manifest as.

Even in the Physical Universe, the green trees and blue skies and yellow suns and white clouds are all simple demonstrations of color and form, which is information transferred onto a screen and then given some sense of conceptual "reality" meaning. Otherwise, all we really have is *forms* and *colors* —the same as what we are likely to perceive as the *thought-formed* "ridges" enshrouding the *Beingness* of *Self* and what mystics and esoteric practitioners have termed "auric bodies" or "astral shields" and the like. Condensation of universal energy-matter can obviously get as solid as a *genetic vehicle*—or a "rock."

Mental Imagery is always *generated* with energy created by *Self*, even when it is a "response" to some external stimulus and/or created using automatic-mechanisms and "filter-screens"—such as information received through the "eyes" of the *genetic vehicle* and then broadcast as an "image" in the *"Mind's Eye"* (as it used to be called; and as people generally are likely to understand it at first), which is then viewed by *Self*. But all that is actually taking place is an encounter with the *forms* and *colors* of an "impression."

These "impressions" give our directed *Awareness* "cues" of an objective Physical Universe (*beta-existence*)—qualities of light, color and form, which make up the visual *facets* of the images we register as our "view" of an "external" environment. These varying "qualities" are treated as *facets* of the experience in "systematic processing"—each *facet* representing some type of recognizable energy or potential perception that can be recorded. All of the significance and meaning—all of the data for reasoning and future evaluation—is entirely *Self*-generated and maintained as an experience. But the truth is that the considerations of the *imagery* are completely up to an individual to determine; as theosophical philosopher, *J.J. Van der Leeuw*, even suggests:—

> "We, as it were, clothe the nakedness of the unknown reality with the image produced in our consciousness. The same facts, which are true for the sense of vision, hold good for our perception through any of the senses; thus there is no question of 'should' but in our consciousness, no question of 'taste' or 'smell' but in our consciousness, no question of 'hardness' or 'softness', of 'heaviness' or 'lightness' but in our consciousness; our entire world-image is an image arising on our consciousness because of the action on that consciousness by some 'unknown reality'."

We address this directly in with the systematic procedure *'Bell, Book and Candle'*[147] treated at great length in the text *"Metahuman Destinations"* and also included in the "Creative Ability Test" (CAT) for the Wizard Grades. The "objective" Physical Universe is the external other-determined force generates actions that *Van der Leeuw* refers to as the "mysterious unknown reality"—because to an individual operating at low-levels of *Beta-Awareness* or even fixed within the *Human Condition* at all, it is that "outside world" that continuously is hungry for our *attentions.* It prompts compulsive *looking* and *validation* by maintaining itself as a Mystery. It literally gets the participants to do all the work in continuing the perception of its existence—even though an individual is really only interacting with a "world-image" that they themselves have created and then later refer to as an experience happening *to* them.

The form and fodder[148] of the Physical Body (*genetic vehicle*) is also a part of *Beta-Existence*—it is a part of the projected "world image" of a personal reality experience in a projected "world image" of a Physical Universe. Due to the hard-wiring of the Mind-System with the *Human Condition* and the amount of time the POV has been validated or "snapped-in" tighter through pains and pleasures and other contact with the Phys-

---

147 **"bell, book & candle"** : three dissimilar objects that are kept accessible during a processing session (the book is often a copy of *The Systemology Handbook* or a hardcover copy of *The Tablets of Destiny* with the dust-jacket removed if it is less distracting that way); a term meant to indicate a Pilot's "objective processing kit" of objects generally present in the session room (accessible on a shelf, table or pedestal stands); in *NexGen Systemology,* the name of an objective processing philosophy pertaining to command of personal reality; historically, a formal ritual used by the Roman Catholic church to ceremonially declare an individual "guilty of the most heinous sins" as "excommunicated (to hold no further communications with) by anathema"—whereby a *bell* is rung, a *holy book* is closed and all *candles* are snuffed out—thus we therapeutically use the same symbolism historically representing religious fragmentation for modern systematic defragmentation purposes.

148 **fodder** : food, esp. for cattle; the raw material used to create.

ical Universe—its energetic frequency vibrations and particles—the physiology[149] and sensory perception of the *genetic vehicle* incites "internal" stimulation of a type that registers "familiar" enough to seem as though *it* is actually happening *to* the Alpha-Spirit, when it is only happening in *beta-existence*. *Van der Leeuw* goes on from earlier:—

"It is the peculiar relation in which we stand to our own body, the intimate link we have with it and which we do not have with regard to any other object in the outer world, which makes us feel that we know all about its reality. We have an *inside* feeling of our body which we do not have in regard to a stone or a tree, our body appears to us as part of ourselves and we forget that it is as much part of that *outer* world as the tree or the stone, and that our perception of it as a visible and tangible object takes place in just the same way as our perception of the tree or of the stone. Even the *inner* feeling we have of our body is but a variety of sense-perception which exists for our body alone..."

We come to the conclusion that: all perceptions of an objective reality are *Self-created* or generated based on impressions or suggestions from participation (reality agreement) with a Universe—regardless of what the considerations may be in assigning value to those perceptions. It is quite clear that the standard-issue Human operator is not aware of any higher *Creative Ability* to change the nature of objective reality at will —or we would expect that they would not be manifest the experience and "world image" (reality) that they "knowingly" perceive.

Some individuals find it incredibly difficult to have any "reality" on what is *Imagined* and *Created* as *Mental Imagery* within one's own "Personal Universe"—or the "illusive" energetic qualities described of these "higher metaphysical" dimens-

---

149 **physiology** : a material science of observable biological functions and mechanics of living organisms, including codification and study of identifiable parts and apparent systematic processes (specific to agreed upon makeup of the *genetic vehicle* for this *beta-existence*).

ions. But!—even when dealing with the more condensed "concrete solidity" of the Physical Universe, *Self* as the Alpha-Spirit is still interacting with *fields* and *screens* and treating the "reality" communicated as *Mental Imagery*. In either case, whether experiencing a "Personal Universe" or a "Physical Universe"—an individual, as a *Spiritual Awareness*, is interacting from a point *exterior* to the projected images of a holographic-reality that appear viewable on the "*screen*" of perception and are treated as "experience."

This would all just be simple intellectual curiosities to ponder in our "free time" were it not for how detrimental these truths are to the *Human Experience* and the liberation of the *Human Spirit* to its higher states.

All of this information would be lost in large pools of untested philosophy if it were not the case that the Mind-System is implanted to accumulate programming and collect encoding to validate fixed "associations of identity" and rigid considerations for what things *are*. *Van der Leeuw* reminds us with a clear message:—

"When an event takes place in this world of reality, there is produced, in the consciousness of each creature concerned, an *Awareness*, or *mental image*, which is the event as we see it. Unreality or illusion never resides in the event, or the thing in itself, nor even in my interpretation of it, which is true enough *for me*, but in the fact that I take my interpretation to be the thing in itself—exacting[150] to it the stature of an absolute and independent reality.

"The illusion or unreality is neither in the thing itself, nor in the image produced in my consciousness by that thing—but in my conception of the image in my consciousness as the thing in itself; as an object existing independent of my consciousness. We can see the way we have to go: we must withdraw ourselves from the enticing images of our own production and turn to-

---

150 **exacting** : a demanding rigid effort to draw forth from.

wards that center through which the production of our world image takes place—*Self* as a unit of *Awareness.*"

We are quite close to completing a final leg on the current cycle of the spiral-like *Spiritual Timeline*; and generally by the end of such cycles of action, everything equals everything else and a Universe collapses into yet one more level of condensation—and if we allow identification of *Beingness* to get much lower, there is less likelihood for an individual to get themselves *through and out* again. Effective systematic processing should include an increased *Awareness* along with the ability to clearly differentiate—rather than associate and categorize—the qualities of *energies* and *forms* and Universes encountered.

First we *clear* the *slate*; then we can truly *create.*

:: 5 ::
PERSONALITY PACKAGES, IDENTITY PHASES AND VIEWPOINTS OF REALITY

"As this processing continues, the Neophyte will find, much to their surprise, that nertheless their most cherished and firmly rooted characteristics are sheared away from them, *Self* remains. They will find that when all their mental feelings, as well as the objects thereof, are removed from their mental vision, they, themselves, remain. They will find a *Something* remaining, that is back of, underneath and at the center of all these feelings and characteristics, and which persists in full vigor when the rest has been stripped away."

—*William Walker Atkinson*

"Personality-Persona-Programs" and "identity-phases" are taken up in our previous publications—though, even at Grade-IV, one is not yet likely to be totally free of such considerations. Until then, we continue to treat this cycle of systematic components at each gradient step—simply at a higher level of *realization*. Note that:

> of everything that is *identifiable* and *apparent*
> in the course of one's *Ascension* up the *Pathway*,
> it is perhaps the sense of *Self*, *Awareness* or
> knowledge of *Self* and image of *Self*
> that is most noticeably refined as a *Seeker* progresses
> with their work from our Systemology.

Just as Universes condense as we perceive lower and lower levels of existence, working our way back up through the *Gates* requires increasingly greater degrees of personal refinement. Metaphorically speaking, an individual is essentially purging additional levels of low-level artificiality with each *Grade* and *Gate*. Only energy-matter of a specific type or frequency is manifest at each tier of the *Pathway*—and behind each *Gateway to Infinity*.

An individual is allowed to carry less and less "mass"—
even "mental mass"—along with them at each level of
ascent. It is the "mass"—the rigidly fixed "resistance"
on the *Zu-line*—that keeps an individual's POV or sense
of *Beingness* suspended by the low-level "gravity" and
tethered to a locatable mass that "forces" can act upon.

When we've applied "game theory"[151] to our Systemology—
regarding Universes of *action* and "game-play"—we often
refer to the individual as a "player." This immediately de-
notes that we are assuming a "role" in which to "play" a
"game." One often forgets that this is what we are doing in
beta-existence. In a previous lesson, we discussed placing an
Awareness "on" and then "dismissing" the characteristic components of the *genetic vehicle* as a "body"—the same
methodology can be applied to scanning and locating the
characteristics inherent in the "personality package" or
"identity phase" that a *Seeker* is "wearing" as a "player" in
this "game."

Of course, it requires a bit of systematic processing and *Self-
analysis* to properly identify the "phase" an individual is operating from. This is something that is given attention right
from the beginning with the texts *"Tablets of Destiny"* and
"Crystal Clear." An individual must also first understand what
an "identity-phase" is, along with its components. Most often
they come under the heading of "tendencies" and "inclinations" that are over-identified with *Self* or "I-AM"—when
really they belong to the "personality package" one is wearing as the "Me" or "My" in order to "play a game."

An individual is already a *Being*, maintaining a *Beingness* that

---

151 **game theory** : a mathematical theory of logic pertaining to strategies
of maximizing gains and minimizing loses within prescribed boundaries and freedoms; a field of knowledge widely applied to human problem solving and decision-making; the application of true knowledge
and logic to deduce the correct course of action given all variables and
interplay of dynamic systems; logical study of decision making where
"players" make choices that affect (the interests) of other "players"; an
intellectual study of conflict and cooperation.

is the I-AM-*Self* or Alpha-Spirit (at "7.0" on our Standard Model) and which, in its own "Personal Universe" can *Create* anything and *Know* anything by *Being* it (and then not) without a concern of fragmentation. And that *is* our most basic state—but that isn't a *game*.

As the Alpha-Spirit seeks to *do* something apart from *Beingness* as *Self* in this basic state, we enter a realm of "Universes" and "Games" (at "6.0") just subordinate to former superior "Creative Universes." Below or after the "Game Universes" an Alpha-Spirit began emphasizing use of "Will" (at "5.0") during their "past-lives" in a "Magical Universe" (sometimes referred to as the "Magic Kingdom" in our *Systemology Wizard Levels*), which immediately preceded the type of effort-based "mechanistic" "electrons-on-a-wire" *beta-existence* that we identify as this "Physical Universe."

Thus:

BASIC PROCESSION OF UNIVERSE CONDENSATION

Home —> Creative —> Games —> Magic —> Physical

The key to understanding "phases"—particularly the unknowing ("unconscious") assumption of various roles, personalities and attributes—as with other elements of our Systemology, is through personal practice. If an individual is able to knowingly ("consciously") *create*, greater control may be attained over the "automatic-mechanism" that *Self* has continuously and obsessively *creating* on its own behalf. In this instance, *Imagination* again plays a key role in the resolution.

"*Systemology Procedure 1-8-0, Route-1*" is written out with a series of progressive steps that essentially just shoot the individual off toward "*Infinity*" as a preparation for "Proc. 180, Route-8," which is the instantaneous experience of the "*Infinity of Nothingness*" *on command*. But, the full intention behind this procedure as an exercise is not so clearly given in the original relay of the steps and so it is worth us reiterating the correction: an individual is meant to practice ("Imagine") *Beingness* of as many different "types" as possible within *each* "Sphere of Existence" *progressively* up to the "*Infinity of Nothingness.*" This full version described here is what effectively prepares a *Seeker* for applying "Proc. 180, Route-0," which is the practice of instantaneous experience of *any* "*Beingness*" or "*POV*" *on command.*

At first, *facets* of a "personality package" (a "role") or "Identity-Phase" (representative of a "specific person") may be more difficult to identify and analyze. It is often easier to first locate facets of a "role" because they are more widely understood "archetypes"[152] with socially educated definitions. For example: a mother, a father, a teacher, a priest, a lawyer, a politician—these are all "roles" that have certain attributes, characteristics or *facets* "associated" with them as a consideration. When we speak of "Identity-Phases," we mean more specifically the attributes, characteristics or *facets* "associated" with a *specific* individual: their beliefs, the way they talk, certain phrases they say, the mannerisms and behaviors —even physical ailments can be assimilated from persons we know and have assumed the "phase" of.

After working through a list of all roles and persons, the *Seeker* is likely to identify certain ones that correlate with significant "terminals" and "implants" in their own lifetime—or lifetimes. Some of this processing can be assisted greatly by mechanical "biofeedback"[153] aids (discussed in future materials) to pinpoint "terminals" and "points" on the *Spiritual Timeline* where a *Seeker* is carrying "emotional encoding." It is found that heavy charges of energetic "programming" can actually raise detectable levels of "mass/resistance" in the

---

152 **apparent** : visibly exposed to sight; evident rather than actual, as presumed by Observation; readily perceived, especially by the senses.

153 **biofeedback** : a measurable effect, such as a change in electrical resistance, that is produced by thoughts, emotions and physical behaviors which generate specific 'neurotransmitters' and biochemical reactions in the brain, body and across the skin surface.

fields surrounding the *genetic vehicle*. In the past, such observations were treated with exclusively mystical or esoteric semantics, which simply are not as workable at our current gradient on the *Pathway*.

Regardless of any aids to the technique, the basic systematic methodology for uncovering this information follows rules of *Analytical Processing, Route-2*—particularly when applying "alternating" PCLs. This continues until a *Seeker* comes to the *realization* that the role is simply a reality agreement; the specific identity/person (from their past) is not actually present; and none of these have anything to do with the true individual *Self*, which lies at the center, which has been *looking* out through a lens or POV that is artificial to the Alpha-Spirit.

PHASES: IDENTIFIER-SEPARATION (ALTERNATING, BASIC 3D)

—How are you similar to ___ ?

—How are you different from ___ ?

Δ Δ Δ Δ Δ Δ Δ

Self-Directing POV is simply a matter of *attention* as *Awareness*. Systematic processing is designed to uncover "where" (or on "what") *attention* is compulsively fixed; and in the case of confusions and energetic dispersals, "where" (or on "what") is unable to be concentrated or fixed on command of *Self*. Rather than treating "energies" directly, a *Seeker* is introduced to the mechanics of directing attention with "command of the Mind–Body connection" as explored in "*Metahuman Destinations*."

Furthermore, the ability to manage responsibility for thought activity, communications, ability to change or remain the same, attitudes of protest,[154] abilities to assist and help *Life*

---

154 **protest** : a response-communication objecting an enforcement or a rejection of a prior communication; an effort to cancel, rewrite or destroy the existence or "is-ness" (what something "is") of a previous creation or communication; unwillingness to be the Point-of-View of

achieve higher states of *Being,* and the circuitry carrying betrayal on all "Spheres of Existence," is also described (primarily in Unit-Three, *Liber-3C*) of *"Metahuman Destinations"*—and such is the immediate precursor of systematic processing to our present work for *"Wizard Level-0."*

The collected work from our previous materials should not be overlooked if a *Seeker* is expecting to achieve the highest level of *Self-Actualization* with this present volume. Previous work moved forward along an effective gradient scale. Comprehension and use of former material allows us to introduce POV or *"location-based processing"* in Grade-IV, which directly moves us outside the confines of emphasizing only *Beta-Awareness* and the Mind-System, and concentrating more of our attention on *Creative Abilities* and mastery of *"Zu-Vision."*

In its original state—and occupation of a "Home Universe" —the Alpha-Spirit, quite god-like, able to *Create* and *Be* any thing, uninhibited and devoid of external forces, other-determined creations, and enforced considerations.

Some mystics and spiritualists in the past have referred to this state as *Spiritual Innocence,* we have referred to various parts of it as *Self-Honesty,* but in whatever way the "clearing of the slate" is to be understood, this critical step is missing from past attempts to accomplish *Metahuman* or *Spiritual Ascension* "out of" this "Physical Universe." Yet, there are a few teachers that have discovered elements of the *Pathway* we travel, such as reflected in the words of mystic philosopher, *Deepak Chopra,* in his training of Wizards:—

"The wizard sees themselves everywhere they look, because their sight is innocent; unclouded by judgments, labels and definitions.

A wizard still knows they have a self-image, but is not distracted by such either. All these things are seen against the backdrop of the totality, the whole context

---

effect or (receipt-point) for a communication.

of life—where our worldview is also a looking glass.

"The 'I' is your singular point-of-view. In innocence, this point-of-view is pure, like a clear lens; but without innocence, the focus is extremely distorting. If you think you know something—including yourself—you are actually seeing your own judgments and labels.

The simplest words we use to describe each other—such as *friend, family, stranger*—are loaded with judgments. The enormous gulf between *friend* and *stranger*, for example, is filled with interpretations. A friend is treated one way; an enemy, another. Even if we do not bring these judgments to the surface, they cloud our vision like dust obscuring a lens."

When we are dealing with POV, we are treating the same fundamentals as *Creation*, which is *Being—Beingness*, "to be." This contrasts greatly with conditions of *beta-existence*, wherein an individual is forced "to move" or "use effort" in order to accomplish similar results in the Physical Universe. When a *Seeker* is operating "*Proc. 180, Route-8*" and "*Proc. 180, Route-0*" there is no sense of movement; and no effort is necessary. The Alpha-Spirit says "*Be*" and it *is so*. Of course, at *Systemology Wizard Level-0*, this may still seem somewhat out of *reach* to *actualize*—but it can be practiced and *realized* and then gradually *actualized* further until there is a better handling of what is behind all of this. A *Seeker* should also not underestimate the value of using the *Creative Ability Test* (CAT) exercises consistently while pursuing the other parts of the material.

An individual has spent most of their spiritual existence *operating* or *occupying* various POV, none of which are the actual perspective of the "undefiled Self" as Alpha-Spirit. Now, it is true that any POV can be assumed by *Self* as directed attention allows—but we have found the standard-issue *Human Condition* is quite "fixed" (or entrapped) in POV exclusively *interior* to "beta-existence" (and confined to a *genetic vehicle*), consistently reinforced and validated by experience of "internal sensation" prompted by an "external" Physical Universe. Management and responsibility of a POV extends to "*Zu-Vision*" and "Actualized Technologies" of the "Wizard Grades."

At the true Alpha-Spiritual state, the I-AM-*Self* (Alpha-Spirit) is not actually located in space—*any* space; but, down the course on the *Spiritual Timeline*, by the point of it when they are occupying the *Human Condition*, an individual considers (thinks) themselves locatable in *beta-existence* "space-time" and therefore forms reality agreements that fix or restrict their *Awareness* to beliefs that they must operate exclusively from the POV they consider themselves located, as a POV, in "space-time." This is what leads to the erroneous belief of: "Okay, I'm a spirit, but only after I die."

When assuming a POV in a *beta-existence*, the Alpha-Spirit fixes its attention on a *living system* that is anchored in that space-time—the "physical body" itself is a composite organic mass of energetic concentration made solid. The Alpha-Spirit establishes a locational POV and begins to "identify" with a *form* that *can be* contacted or reached. Dependency on energetic *mass* permit a *Spiritual Being* to carry a platform or field of implants and records along from one *incarnation* to the next.

If a POV is too badly fractured or damaged, the individual generally abandons control and responsibility of it. Thus, we also tend to emphasize systematic processing that manages implants that signal "ability to hurt" and "ability to experience loss" in Grade-IV. As more and more POV are considered "unsafe," the Self-determination of *reach* gradually diminishes; hence the condensation and collapse of Universes that the Alpha-Spirit formerly maintained communication with.

> Personal experience of a Higher Universe "collapses" when all "points" in "space" are treated as "unsafe."

Even in *beta-existence*, an individual *withdraws* from increasingly more "space-time energy-matter" as they *associate* more "terminals" and "things" with pain and loss—including ability to manage *Mental Imagery* that represents the same *facets.* An individual eventually succumbs and "quits" as a result of over-associating *Self* with the "external world" and internal mechanisms of a "body"—both of which are objectively temporary in comparison to Alpha-Existence.

Δ Δ Δ Δ Δ Δ

Our standardized methodology of "Route-0" is traditionally classified as "*creativeness processing,*" but we have found that this also includes processing "acceptance of viewpoints" or increasing the "ability to confront POV"—which all seem to go hand-in-hand. This is applicable to "Wizard Levels" because rather than *reducing* every energetically turbulent "charge" on the "line"—such as is emphasized in our introductory work, "Route-1" in "*Tablets of Destiny*"—a "Wizard" must effectively demonstrate abilities to manage and handle "POV" at face value. This is a bit of an extreme gradient for some, but its benefits are necessary for securing stable gains, increasing *Actualized Awareness* and progressing further upon the *Pathway.*

Abilities to directly *confront,* manage, handle, ...*create* "energy" is increased as one cumulatively works with methods of each higher "route" within our applied philosophy—*Route-1, Route-2, Route-3* and our anomaly in numeric sequence, *Route-0.* Each has developed out of the former; each has its own specialized uses—and all are effective in what they are.

It may also be said that each "Route" can be used for getting "quicker" results than a former—but that is also dependent on the state of the individual applying it and/or receiving it; it must be within their *reach* as a *Reality.*

An individual that is not *Actualized* to a point of *confronting* the responsibility of *creating* their own *Mental Images* is not just going to "get there" because you or this book says it's a "truth." Systematic processing is meant to "steer" an individual's management of considerations in the direction of *realizing* the basic material for themselves, which is then expanded upon with training from these books and lectures.

We have emphasized, in this book and previous material, "response-mechanisms" and the "reactive imagery" that is tied to the circuitry in the Mind-System that we *are* prepared to *confront*; but what about that which seems "hidden" from view? Obviously, the subject of "memory" has been a long-time fascination of interest to the "social" and "neurological" sciences—but how does it pair up with our Systemology? We consider that individual's tend to *abandon* their past POV, particularly when it has been overrun by effects; they no longer wish to *confront* it, because they believe they literally cannot "tolerate" it—meanwhile the *Imprinting* still exists, albeit "hidden" from view. If we consider the amount of emotionally-charged incidents that an individual doesn't want to face up to along the *Spiritual Timeline*, it is no wonder that a clear memory of it all becomes difficult.

If we consider the diminishing scale by which an individual has succumbed to lower considerations, a complete "falling out" with each Universe—by some means or another—has brought the Alpha-Spirit to now only consider occupying the *Human Condition* as a POV. Even then, a tolerance for *beta-existence* usually continues to decline, more or less, with each *incarnation* within it. In short:

> An individual's *willingness* to *Be* or use potential POVs diminishes along with *Actualized Awareness*. The less an individual is *willing* to *Be* and the less they are willing to *look at* or *communicate* with, the worse off they get along in their experience of existence—and the less they are able to *see clearly* on the "backtrack" or *Spiritual Timeline*.

When we consider that "*Imprints*" are, in fact, "*Mental Images*"; that "emotional encoding" builds as a response to such "*Mental Images*" through repeated experiences that, in themselves, provide us with a certain sense of "time"—well, the more an individual doesn't want to be responsible for, the less "time" it seems they *have*, and this is demonstrable in their outer behaviors as well. Another example is the case of the "occluded childhood" that has been *"forgotten"* because of the deep levels of *"Imprinting"* taking place. The amount of "encoding" taking place thereafter during the course of one's lifetime can also greatly affect what is generally referred to as "memory."

Our systematic processing often seems to lead to some highly esoteric and mystical *realizations* concerning the Alpha-Spirit and what *Self* is "doing" with the *Human Condition*. For example, in this instance, the very fact that an individual refuses to *confront* or take responsibility for *Mental Images* is what actually constitutes their compulsive creation. In essence, an individual wants nothing to do with it, so they are stuck with it. On the surface, such things seem to defy basic reason—but *reasoning* is subject to associations and programming of the Mind; this says nothing of the way things *actually* are, and we should not be surprised when the truth of things is not *one-to-one* with the information that we have had impressed upon us from those individuals (and POVs) that are heavily conditioned by the Physical Universe and its reality agreements.

This is one reason why we systematically practice "reach and withdraw" in processing; as basic as it seems, an individual is not accustomed to *willing* the "letting go" part of life—sudden abandonment, unconsciousness, the sense of loss, the heat of a hot surface, and so forth, all arranges this for us, outside *Self-Determination*. The standard-issue *Human Condition* has very little practice in "letting go," when the implanted game objective has always been accumulation, and more accumulation—and when an individual is still not satisfied with that, they decide what will "do the trick": just a little bit more accumulation.

Applying "Route-2" methods to "Identity-Phase POV Processing" is introduced in *"Crystal Clear"*—and its reissue in *"Systemology Handbook"*—but additional breakthroughs in that technique resulted later at the Systemology Society, with experiments developed by Grade-III participants researching for Grade-IV. For example: applying *"Analytical/Recall"* to directly apply principles from our philosophy that are not already provided in a "scripted procedure." Some PCLs are provided to suggest the best of what we've found to work, but is certainly not the limit to what a *Seeker* or *Pilot* can apply based on the books—and possibly not even yet the *best* possible methods or techniques; but they work. We've simply gone with the best of what everyone at a particular level can generally understand and apply well.

PHASES: IDENTIFICATION AND SEPARATION (ROUTE-2, POV 3D)

—Recall a time when you were ___.

—Identify someone who is ___. (*use answer below*)

—Find a time when someone said you were like .

Alternatively, a *Seeker* might "spot a time" (they) "decided to be like *so-and-so.*" Sometimes the first step of increasing a *Seeker's* handling of POV is to get them to recognize—or *realize*—the one(s) they are compulsively occupying or "*looking through.*" The amount of fragmentation an individual is looking through contributes to the "communication lag" monitored in systematic processing (typically by a trained professional *Pilot*). The next step is, of course, getting an individual to *realize* that other POVs are "safe"—or to use language of PCLs: "would be acceptable" or "wouldn't mind."

Although the Standard Model typically demonstrates *"Beingness"* at the top of the scale—relative to the *Spiritual Beingness* of an Alpha-Spirit—the fact remains that an individual seems to take their sense of *Beingness* with them as the descend into the *Human Condition* to experience *Beta-Existence.* In fact, as one descends the scale into and through *beta-existence*, we find a fragmented individual will apply a great deal of *effort* in order to "*Be*" something—having forgotten the true nature of *Self* and its ultimate *Spiritual Beingness.*

> The pattern of personal *creation* in most Universes operates as we would expect for an Alpha-Spirit: a *Beingness* that can *do* things in order to *have* things —consciousness, action, substance.

But, when we hit the point of *Beta-Existence* and the "MCC" (*Master Control Center*) on the Standard Model—and all the implants on which the *Human Condition* is programmed and encoded—we find an individual working in the opposite direction: now they *have* something—at the very least, a "body," which requires protecting to survive—and they *must* "*do*" something, applying the efforts of the Physical Universe, in order to get a sense of "*Being*" something again. And that is among the clearest examples of "fragmentation" that we can easily demonstrate with our Systemology.

:: 6 ::
IMAGINATION—HANDLING SPACE AND CREATION

Our description of the "Alpha Spirit" *is* not a figurative construct or philosophical abstraction: it *is* the individual or living being as they *actually* are: a "point" or "unit" of *Awareness* (as "I-AM") extant[155] in its own *Alpha-existence* or "Spiritual Universe." All of Mardukite Zuism and Systemology is developed from this basic *a-priori* statement.

The Alpha-Spirit is the point of purest "Beingness" surpassing all other considerations. In fact, all other considerations and postulates (of Alpha-Thought) are generated by this point of *Awareness.*

When operating from a point of beta-fragmentation, carried through successive beta-incarnations, programming and encoding of the *Human Condition* is "wired" to sense, feel, associate and react according to the "Imagery" and "Imprints" displaying what is *imagined* to be "true" about the condition of *Self* and stability (safety and security) of the environment surrounding the POV.

Things *are* because *Self* considers they *are*—what we "existentially" treat as the "is" of something; it's "*is-ness*" factor. The basic characteristic of an Alpha-Spirit is *to be* an Alpha-Spirit —to "be its own beingness"—but the imposition of "other-determined" *space-time* in *beta-existence* causes the individual to "feel" or "believe" and validate with "postulates" and "considerations" that *Self* is a "physical being"; which, of course, puts the individual (their POV and perceived state of Beingness) out of "phase-alignment" with the true POV of *Self* as Alpha-Spirit.

The Alpha-Spirit does not require any "Mind-System"
as a catalyst to operate its own highest faculties
—creation, command postulates and consideration.

---

155 **extant** : in existence; existing.

The "Mind-System" apparently developed during condensation of Universes, while an Alpha-Spirit's consideration of its own sense of *Beingness*—its willingness and ability to command and be responsible for creation—also condensed and solidified into fixed patterns and energetic circuits. Failing to remain in full *Awareness* of these energetic flows and creations, "ridges" formed patterned circuitry for automated response-mechanisms and other "energetic machinery" that seems to take on more "mass" and "fragmentation" as the individual continues along their *"Spiritual Timeline."*

"Beta-Defragmentation" is a basic systematic processing goal that is accomplished by "clearing out" energetic debris and "mental masses" accumulated as fragmentation in circuits and channels of communication between the Alpha-Spirit, the "Mind-System" and specifically the "Mind–Body" connection when treated command of a *genetic vehicle* in *beta-existence*. Most of our previously released material on Systemology pertains to this subject.

—During *Beta-Defragmentation*, *Seekers* increase enough *Actualized Awareness* to "break gravity" of the heavy emotional encoding fixing them to low-level POVs and *Imprinting* from the *"Reactive Control Center"* (RCC).

—*Alpha-Defragmentation* methodology (for future *Wizard Levels*) depends on an individual effectively regaining responsibility and control over their compulsively created *beta*-POVs pertaining to a "Body" and "Mind."

When considering a *beta-existence* restricted to dense masses, symbolic objects, physical "efforts" and a necessity to destroy, fragment or transmute material of the Physical Universe in order to "create," it should come as little surprise that a *beta*-fragmented individual carries many of these same considerations for *Self* as being identified *one-to-one* with conditions of *beta-existence*. An individual finds great difficulty in exercising "freedom of the spirit" when they are tied to a mortal POV. Actual conditions for an Alpha-Spirit are independent of the Physical Universe—and any effective regimen for rehabilitating *Actualized Awareness* to a point beyond the "Mind" (or "Master Control Center") must include full *realization of Self* independent of lower-level considerations.

An Alpha-Spirit essentially has infinite potential and ability to *Create*, and it continues to exercise this quality of its nature all the way down the line—whether it knowingly commands such, or unknowingly and compulsively doing so.

In one's personal universe, there are no concerns as to "where" energy comes from in order to *Create*, because the Alpha-Spirit needs only "consider" or "postulate" for something *to be*. As similar with the "internal" experience of the Human Mind, the subjective *reality* of an individual's personal universe is as *real* to the individual as they *realize* it; and that is all the consideration necessary for *Self* to cause something to *be* what it *is*.

Although we have made comparisons to the "Will" of an individual, in actuality, there is no "Alpha-state" equivalent to the type of "material effort" one employs with "material means" in order to *act* in the "Physical Universe."

Consensual[156] beliefs concerning "fixed conservation" in *betaexistence*, or scarcity of available *energy* and *material*, increases perceived value of the solid and substantial "things" of this Universe in preference to what an individual can produce in *Imagination*. Somehow *others* convinced Alpha-Spirits that to be of *value*, the "force" and "consequence" of their *creations* must be more solid, more objective, and it had to be *experienced* to be *known*. Then, as reality agreements to personally experience *effects* of their *Creations* increased, the willingness and ability to be responsible for them diminished.

Spontaneous generation of infinite potentiality and direct

---

156 **consensual** : formed or existing simply by consent—by general or mutual agreement; permitted, approved or agreed upon by majority of opinion; knowingly agreed upon unanimously by all concerned; to be in agreement on the objective universe or a course of action therein.

flows of raw energy apparently became too overwhelming to manage properly in a (now) fragmented state. Where once the *Self* actualized a level of "god-like" *Beingness,* now it was creating something to *know* about—which meant it would have to *choose* to "forget" aspects of its own *Beingness* in order to *have* something to know about. In the balance, the Alpha-Spirit withdrew its conscious participation from "higher" existences, figuratively sealing up and locking away high-level *knowing*—creative ability and handling of direct energy-flows—and closing off communication-lines with, and responsibility for, abandoned POVs that an individual still maintains energetic ties to; for their true *Spiritual Beingness* still very much remains on the other side of the "Gates."

Δ Δ Δ Δ Δ Δ Δ

All the energy necessary for perceiving a reality—any reality experience—comes from *Self* directing its attention of *Awareness*—like a "beam"—on agreed upon patterns and archetypal matrix codes that are "seen" as *forms.* Both, "internal" thought-waves and "external" material energy patterns are only approximated as the *forms* we are implanted to recognize while using a Mind-System as an intermediary interface or catalyst. In effect, this buffers or shields *Self* from handling (or even experiencing) energies directly as they *actually* are, and instead, only to the extent that they are *realized* by "looking" at "second hand" information or potentially aberrated[157] "mirrored" reflection. This concept of a "telescopic spiritual lens" led to our phrase, and previous title, "*Crystal Clear.*"

As opposed to eternally confronting an *Infinity of Nothingness,* the Alpha-Spirit turned around the "other way" and became very interested in the business of "pictures"—which our ma-

---

157 **aberration** : departure from what is right; in chromatic light science, the failure of a mirror, lens or refracting surface to produce an exact "*one-to-one*" or "*A-for-A*" duplication between an object and its image; a deviation from, or distortion in, what is true or right or straight; in *NexGen Systemology,* a term to describe *fragmentation* as it applies to an individual, which causes them to "stray" form the *Pathway.*

terials tend to generalize as "*Mental Images*"—even if they are higher-level "facsimile copies" an individual began to collect and experience in *Alpha-Existence*. This is prior even to any formal solidification of a "Mind-System" implanted like a circuit-board to key-in various types of *Imprints* and additional *coding*. The basic semantic of "*mental images*" is simply more familiar and more broadly understood as "a subjectively experienced picture or memory."

It is intriguing that social science fields carry very little interest and true data regarding "*Mental Images*." Whether attributed to "memory" or some other phenomenon, modern "psychology" texts still treat the subject of "*Mental Images*" as "hallucinations" with little other regard for the way every individual is essentially creating their own "mockups" of *beta*-experience and treating it as reality. But this is not some "rare" phenomenon. On the contrary, a relatively small percentage of the Human population does not experience "pictures" in the mind—or the ability to "imagine" and "visualize."

There are many ways we could classify, code and systematize qualities and types of "*Mental Images*"—yet, we are beginning to treat not only the Mind-System in beta-existence, but also the *Alpha-Existence* and "higher spiritual universes" wherein we discover all of the highest qualities of the Alpha Spirit directly, all leading up to unlimited *Imagination* and *Creative Ability*:

• Will and Intention   • Aesthetics and Art
• Ethics and Organization   • Games and Novelty
• Logic and Reason   • Alpha Postulates

Δ Δ Δ Δ Δ Δ

There are two main types of "*Mental Image*":
those an individual *knows* they are creating; and
those which they *don't know*, but are still creating.

Indeed, even when they *don't know*, an individual is still actually participating in "facsimile-copying" and continuous creation thereafter—which directly correlates to the amount of "attention units" and/or *Actualized Awareness* and individual maintains in the "present." A primary difference between the two types going back to our original emphasis in Grade-III: *Self-Determinism.*

"Mental Images" themselves simply *are.* Fragmentation ensues when "labels" are assigned—and even this might not be an issue, if it weren't for the "associations" and "identifications" attached to not only the primary subject or form, but all of its *facets.* This is where the "power" of Alpha Thought (consideration) comes into play—and also why some previous spiritual philosophies warn against "forming judgments." In this light, the state of *Self-Honesty* might be most simply defined as: the ability to experience existence without judgment.

The Alpha-Spirit is an individuated *Spiritual Beingness* (I-AM) at the center of an *Awareness* point—described in our Hermetic/Mesopotamian interpretation (in *"Tablets of Destiny"*) as:

a *consciousness* that exists independently
from *action/motion* and *form/substance.*

Where we have an *Awareness* observing *forms* in *action*, we have perception of "manifestation." An individual copies and stores an *impression* of the total information perceived about the environment—and this is kept as the more permanent *"Spiritual Timeline"* or registry of an Alpha-component of the Mind-System that carries with an individual from one lifetime incarnation to another. After rigid consideration of this "memory" is cumulatively collected, an individual begins to falsely *identify* it one-to-one with *Self.*

Mental Imagery treated in our previous material is of the type referred to as an *"Imprint."* In some ways, an *Imprint* could be any experience which makes an "impression" on the recordings kept by *Self.* However, we are most concerned with those that significantly "impinge upon," "hang up" or "stick" an individual—and their attention units as a *Spiritual Awareness*—somewhere on their "*Spiritual Timeline.*"

> Heavily charged *Imprints* containing PAIN and/or LOSS add *emotional encoding* to an existing framework of *Implants*. There are also FAILURE/ERROR and INVALIDATION *Implants*.

While we have future goals at the Systemology Society for better approaching and systematically exploring the subject of a "*Spiritual Timeline*"—or "*past-lives*"—in *Grade-V*, it is appropriate that a continuing *Seeker* begins to "clear the way" for such realizations *now*, in "*Wizard Level-0.*"

Access to clearer memory of one's own "*Spiritual Timeline*" is occulted/filtered/screened/blocked/etc. by the very implanting that carries between lifetimes, composed of *Mental Image* stores and other strongly encoded emotional *Imprints* that attach to energetic circuits operated by the Alpha-Spirit.

From the vantage[158] point of the Alpha-Spirit, *all* of *beta-existence* is an "environment"—and this includes the physical makeup of a *genetic vehicle*. For this reason, we established appropriate semantics to describe the position of all potential *Points-of-View*—whether

> "interior" to *beta-existence*;
> "internal" to a *body*;
> "external" in the *Physical Universe*; or
> "exterior" in *Alpha-existence*.

For example, the entire Mind-System is maintained *interior* to beta-existence, but not *internal* to the body and not *externally* out in the Physical Universe. These classifications allow for a more systematic approach that simply "internal/external" as treated in other paradigms.

---

158 **vantage** : a point, place or position that offers an ideal POV.

The RCC is an "energetic mechanism" that is not found within physiologic anatomy of the "brain"—nor is the "Mind-System" in general. But, an Alpha-Spirit's stores of *Mental Images* and *Imprints* does have the ability to affect the body—producing various observable effects and *internal* sensations. Standard material sciences exclusively make conclusions based on observable effects taking place in the Physical Universe, with no real consideration of anything that *perturbs*[159] actions from "outside" of it.

We can see devices measure some electrical impulses that light up in the "brain" when a person moves their hand, and various manner of biochemical systems in motion "inside" the *genetic vehicle*; but what of the originating Will and Intention that directs this to occur as a *Self-determined* choice? Here we shine light on the limits of a material science methodology—which, to even break the glass ceiling on knowledge of "higher universes," the Observer would have to be simultaneously *under* the "microscope" and *looking through* it.

When an Alpha-Spirit—"7.0" on the Standard Model—could no longer tolerate or confront its basic state for whatever reason, it shifted its POV away from the *Infinity of Nothingness* into an Alpha-existence of seemingly unlimited potential.

As first described in *Grade-III*, we refer to this next lower level continuity (at "6.0") the domain of "Spiritual Universes" and "Games." This point on our Spheres of Existence Model corr-

---

159 **perturbation** : the deviation from a natural state, fixed motion, or orbit system caused by another external system; disturbing or disquieting the serenity of an existent state; inciting observable apparent action using indirect or outside actions or 'forces'; the introduction of a new element or facet that disturbs equilibrium of a standard system; the "butterfly effect"; in *NexGen Systemology*, *'perturbation'* is a necessary condition for the *ZU-line* to function as a *Standard Model* of actual *'monistic continuity'*—which is a *Lifeforce* singularity expressed along a spectrum with potential interactions at each degree from any source; the influence of a degree in one state by activities of another state that seem independent, but which are actually connected directly at some higher degree, even if not apparently observed.

elates with the personal *"Zu-line"* as the level of "Alpha Thought" (postulates, consideration and logic).

Having established the Models and a basic description of their parts, we can use our Systemology to gauge a certain logical sequence of "spiritual events" that led to considerations for *beta-existence*—though presently, much of this *Backtrack*[160] is still left to a *Seeker* to work out and discern[161] from our existing source material until additional developments for our *"Wizard Grades"* are more solidly tested and published in the future from the Systemology Society.

Δ Δ Δ Δ Δ Δ

Very early on the *Spiritual Timeline*—possibly as *Awareness* "awakened" POV in a "Home Universe" of *Alpha-Existence*—the Alpha-Spirit either "discovered" or was given a primitive demonstration of its own inherent *Creative Ability*. And this discovery or demonstration would have been among the first "recordings" made, revealing self-evidently, that an Alpha-Spirit can create (at the very least for itself) its own duplicate "facsimile-copy," "mirrored reflection" or "snapshot" of anything in its *Awareness*; including creations originated by others and even entire Universes of existence.

Systematic use of *Imagination* and *"Creativeness Processing"* is introduced within "Wizard Level-0" because it takes us one step beyond our basic goals of *Beta-Defragmentation* described in previous literature and begins to treat the nature of Alpha-

---

160 **Backtrack** : to retrace steps or go back to an early point in a sequence; an applied spiritual philosophy within *Metahuman Systemology* *"Wizard Grades"* regarding continuous existence of an individual's *"Spiritual Timeline"* through all lifetime-incarnations; a methodology of systematic processing methods developed to assist in revealing "hidden" *Mental Images* and *Imprints* from one's past and reclaim attention-energies "left behind" with them by increasing ability to manage and control personal energy mechanisms fixed to their continuous automated creation.

161 **discernment** : to perceive, distinguish and/or differentiate experience into true knowledge.

Existence, emphasizing a rehabilitation of "knowingness" (*Actualized Awareness*) responsibility and control of *Self-Creations*. Even if (or when) the Alpha-Spirit no longer wants to "look" or "acknowledge" their existence—since it is powerful enough in its command of *Beingness* and Alpha-Thought to deliberately "not-know"—more often than not, those *Imprints* and automated energetic-mechanisms (which are themselves only compacted sets of "pictures") are *still* being created and stored—*still* active to produce effects—beneath the surface of whatever level an individual is willing to knowingly handle directly.

An individual *Creates* in order to *experience*. Recording every action and form is also how an Alpha-Spirit generates its own "sense" of passage along a "Spiritual Timeline," which is also marked by significant changes of consideration and conditions of *Beingness* as *Self* fixes its POV and "personal identification" to lower states of existence and experience. This "timeline," by definition, is built up as a chronological sequence.[162] Each additional *experience* is cumulatively recorded/imprinted and stored as "new" information. An individual assigns personal meaning or significance to these encounters (energy-flows) using their own collection of *Mental Images* and previously established considerations (Alpha Thought postulates) about existence for a comparison.

Simple observance of "creation and destruction" cycles—the rise and fall of a *sine-wave*[163]—is all that is necessary to *experience* considerations of communication, movement, action/motion—the "ebb and flow" of manifest existence—across perceived distances of space-time. But eventually, when an

---

162 **chronologically** : concerning or pertaining to "time"; to treat as "units" of "time" ; to sequence a series of events or information with regard to the order it happened or originated (in time).

163 **sine-wave** : the *frequency* and amplitude of a quantified (calculable) *vibration* represented on a graph (graphically) as smooth repetitive *oscillation* of a *waveform*.

Alpha-Spirit is no longer willing *to be* responsible for its own creations and stores of *Mental Images* and the handling of "unlimited potentiality"; so the attention-energies that went into conscious *creation* of the *Mental Images* and *Imprints* are sorted by "*facet-association*" and systematized as "patterned circuits" or "tendencies."

> These energy circuits are compacted or condensed to form energetic-mechanisms continuously and compulsively *created* by *Self* and run in the background on automatic, foregoing an Alpha-Spirit knowingly applying personal attentions to manage energetic receipt, interpretation and communications on that line.

"Route-0" methodology is a systematic approach for processing toward these *realizations* about the true (and often forgotten) condition and faculties of Alpha-Spirit early on in the *Spiritual Timeline*. Unlimited abilities to *Imagine* anything into *Being*, create a copy of any form, and duplicate all POV in existence, requires maintaining exceptionally high-level *Self-Honest* responsibility and control. Failure to do so—as apparently happened—results in Alpha-Fragmentation: formation of a basic "platen" or "circuit-board" for potential *Implants*—which are the underlying network and systematic array of energetic receptors, each recording a specific type or quality of *emotionally encoded imprints* and other "heavily charged" *Mental Images* impressed by future encounters.

Alpha-Fragmentation also carries over to the "Mind-System" and naturally affects *beta-experience*. The basic pattern, the true "ability" and "nature" of *Self* is *fragmented* to support apparent circuitry of "compulsive action" and "unwillingness." An Alpha-Spirit has spent an exceptionally long *Spiritual Timeline* compulsively *creating* and collecting *Mental Images* and other *Imprints* in the name of "experiential knowledge" before even reaching *this* Physical Universe.

There are many *imprints* an individual doesn't want to confront or handle; but rather than "uncreate," "destroy" or postulate them out of existence, their creation is attributed to another "source" and hidden away from view, yet still active, remaining energetically fixed to an individual's *Spiritual Timeline.*

An Alpha-Spirit becomes "the effect of their own cause" as they lose control and relinquish[164] responsibility of their *created* and *copied* (mirrored, facsimile) *Mental Images.*

Furthermore, various "control centers" and "relay centers" on the *Zu-line*—which communicate experiential and existential data between *Self* and an environment—become automatic reactive filters that hide, occlude or occult the *actual* nature of experience with fragmentation. As an individual adds more "experience" to the "pile," more of its content is associatively cross-identified with each other associative data and assigned meaning or value. Each time, less freedom (space) remains and more rigidly finite parameters are in place for future considerations and the willingness to reach along that channel.

The actualized condition of "Knowing" is frequently referred to in Systemology literature, which may be an ambiguous concept to *Seekers* that are used to operating from a POV *interior* to a "head"—or "Mind" if you prefer. Of course, in the Alpha-Spirit's original state of *Beingness*, there is only a pure *Spiritual Awareness* of "I-AM"; but as an individual rigidly fixes POV and considerations of Personal Identity into increasingly more condensed Universe conditions, they are surrounded by greater quantities of "pictures" and "imprints" each treated more solidly "real" than the last.

As a *Spiritual Awareness* unit maintaining an optimum POV of Beingness, an Alpha-Spirit requires no *imprinted images* or *energetic masses* in order to "Know" anything. In fact, they can simply *create* whatever it is they want to "Know" or "look at" instantaneously. An individual's state of *Beta-Awareness* (or *Actualized Awareness*) decreases when more personal energy is routed to keep the *Imprints* that surrounds them "alive."

---

164 **relinquish** : to give up control, command or possession of.

Even when their own *Imprints* and *Images* are tearing them to shreds, an individual still feels as though they "*have something*" by retaining it; and of course, this "something is better than nothing" philosophy is what got an Alpha-Spirit fragmented in the first place.

In short: *Awareness* descends to lower levels of *beta-existence* as an individual *considers* themselves increasingly the *effect* of its environment; and more dependent on it for their sense of solid reality. Personal tolerance to handle energy, existence and even "look" at things also decreases. From this point, an Alpha-Spirit descends to a POV *below* conditions for any "Direct Knowingness." Communication with, and experiential knowledge of, a world-at-large is fragmented—heavily "filter-screened" by surrounding *Imprints* and circuitry that feedback[165] information from "sensors" and "automated response-mechanisms" that actually do the initial "looking."

This patterned progression extends all the way down to a complete relative absence of *Actualized Awareness* at the continuity level of the Physical Universe (or a *beta-existence*) marked at "0" on the Standard Model. In actuality, there is no workable "zero" value applied, but this "singularity"[166] point

---

165 **feedback loop** : a complete and continuous circuit flow of energy or information directed as an output from a source to a target which is altered and return back to the source as an input; in *General Systemology*—the continuous process where outputs of a system are routed back as inputs to complete a circuit or loop, which may be closed or connected to other systems/circuits; in *NexGen Systemology*—the continuous process where directed *Life* energy and *Awareness* is sent back to *Self* as experience, understanding and memory to complete an energetic circuit as a loop.

166 **singularity** : in general use, "to be singular," but our working definition suggests the opposite of individuality (contrary to most dictionaries); in upper-level sciences, a "zero-point" where a particular property or attribute is mathematically treated as "infinite" (such as the "blackhole" phenomenon), or else where apparently dissimilar qualities of all existing aspects (or individuals) share a "singular" expression, nature or quality; additionally, in *NexGen Systemology*, a hypothetical zero-point when apparent values of all parts in a Universe are equal to all other parts before it collapses; in *Transhumanism*, a hypothetical "run-

on our Model/Zu-line indicates a condition where the actualized POV is identifying with a "dead body"—and at this existential level of manifestation on our spiritual scale: inert matter *is equal to* inert matter *is equal to* inert matter.

By our logic, this is the *only* position in known existence where a POV could *actually be* at "One with the Physical Universe" in perfect agreement—and it is *not* the "place to be," leaving us with little need to further question why past methods and systems of mysticism and spiritualism sound "good on paper" but provide no stable workable "route out" that will effectively liberate a practitioner from the heavy gravity and spiritual (energetic) trappings of the *Human Condition* in *Beta-Existence*.

Δ Δ Δ Δ Δ Δ

When we consider systematic handling of *Imagination, Creative Ability, Space* and *POV*, there is the pragmatic matter of *where* an individual *is* present.

Standard-issue "identification with a body" has fooled many into validating beliefs that *Self*—an individual *Being*—must be somehow "residing in" a physical body with the fullness of their presence, *Awareness* and *Beingness*.

A Professional Pilot of our applied spiritual technology learns quickly how to gauge an individual's actual "presence" by their "communication lag" in systematic processing. Greater skills and training are still needed in this area for differentiating between: "no-lag" and automated responses generated off a "circuit" or some other mechanism.

---

away reaction" in technology, when it becomes self-aware, self-propagating, self-upgradable and self-sustainable, and replaces human effort of advancement or even makes continued human existence impossible; also, technological efforts to maintain an artificial immortality of the Human Condition on a digital mainframe.

Before semantics for "fragmentation" and "Self-Honesty" widely caught on for our Systemology, the most commonly used term to describe the aberrated state of the *Human Condition* was: STUCK. It represented a crude generalization, but the word carried a close enough sentiment to be effective during the "pre-Graded" era of our early underground development. As we approach the "Wizard Grades," it is relevant, if not necessary, for us to go back to this concept in view of critical facts revealed during the course of additional research and experimentation at the Systemology Society.

It can be interpreted as over-critical to reinforce semantics that someone is "stuck" somewhere. It is not "good practice" for our *Pilots*, so it was mostly left alone. In an apparent sense, it does seem most individuals *are* figuratively "stuck" somewhere other than the present. This is, however, one of those points where we must be pristine in our communication and context for any element of this idea to contribute something effectively workable for our applied spiritual philosophy—and the point was not satisfactorily reached until we initiated experiments with "*POV Processing.*"

As with the other numerous practical variations of "Route-0" (and suggestions of "*Pre-A.T.*" Wizard Level techniques introduced for Grade-IV) systematic treatment of POV is typically an extension of *creativeness processing.* It also serves quite effectively as a prerequisite for additional upper-route experiments and procedures, such as "*Zu-Vision*" and "*Backtrack.*" Increased realizations intended for "*POV Processing*" include:

—willingness to manage the present POV and phases;
—ability to transfer between any POV freely;
—tolerance and certainty for handling any other viewpoint;
—full realization that no POV is the existence of Self.

When someone refers to someone else as "stuck," they generally mean that they are "rigidly fixed" or "set in" some aspect. Since *Self* is not a "material body," we obviously do

not mean that the *genetic vehicle* is physically trapped—
although such an experience could also potentially lead to a
heavily charged *Imprint.*

Consider what a person is actually doing in a typical
state of fragmentation: the individual has suspended
some portion of their *Awareness* to a particular moment
in "time," *copied* its information and now compulsively
creates a *picture* of it to *look* at; and they are still
expecting to "change" that *image* or somehow *stop* the
motion that it represents. Alternatively, they may also
be fixed on a confusion or a "compulsive maybe" that is
being held in place to "be figured" out of.

Rather than take responsibility for continual creation and
ownership (*create*), properly managing it (*control*) and letting
it go (*destroy*), a person will often "blame" (attribute responsibility to) someone or something *else* for its creation and hold
onto it permanently as a "rare" or "unique" thing to "have"—
something of value they can use later to either evaluate their
present environment or to use on a circuit toward someone
else. This not only makes it more solid, but more difficult to
manage. As a compulsive creation, an individual is lending to
it their own energies for sustenance. This is handled better by
an individual who carries no *masses* with them, allowing for
unlimited *Self-directed* energy to simply *Create* whatever they
want to "see" or "know" without holding a POV in suspension
indefinitely.

Each different "personality phase" has its own circuitry
and basic collection of "things" used to associate knowledge of other "things"—which is why the standard
issue *Human Condition* doesn't really "know" anything,
it just compulsively "figures" and "thinks" about things
in relation to other things.

Herein, one also realizes that *creations* are actually a
"cycle of actions," and to manage full responsibility for
Creative Ability, an individual should be able to handle
all three parts of that cycle: *Create-Control-Destroy* (CCD)

—and technically, these are the *only* three types of directive action actually employed.

By its own semantic application, "*defragmentation*" represents the collecting of dispersed parts to reform a whole. The Alpha-Spirit is already a singular unit of pure *Beingness*, but once realization of this is fragmented, an individual lessens their *Awareness* and *Knowingness* and assumes various roles and *phases* to get a sense of "*Being*" something again. This is a consequence of *identifying* "I-AM"-*Self* with anything other than *Awareness* as an Alpha-Spirit. At first this must have provided *Self* with a "sense" of something to "*do*"—being in communication with a shared existence or reality separate from the individual's own personal "Home Universe."

Evidently, as additional considerations were compacted together, an individual simply forgot they were playing a *game*—or chose to forget, in order to have "more" *game*.

:: ٦ ::
RESPONSIBILITY FOR IMAGINATION AND THE MIND-BODY CONNECTION

Past mystical expressions and spiritual use of the term "remote" has been quite ambiguous when we began to apply upper-level considerations to our applied Systemology.

Whenever regarding a *Point-of-View* (POV) as "remote," it is important to specify "remote from *what*."

In most instances, we found the intended implication was "remote from the POV of a body"—basically to increase considerations that the individual *Awareness* as "I-AM"-*Self* could be separated from a *genetic vehicle.* Today, this truth would seem quite obvious to us; but, the only reason there is a truth here in any regard, is because:

the POV maintained from within a "body" (or "head") is *already* "remote" from the actual existence of the Alpha-Spirit that is doing the "*viewing.*"

A POV is a "point" *from which* "to view"—and there is no doubt that an individual has directed *Self-Awareness* to billions upon billions of "remote" POV along the "*Spiritual Timeline.*" If a *Seeker* had to go back and recollect every single one in order to advance through the *Gateways,* we would not get very far along on the *Pathway.*

At each major tier or gradient (or *Gate*), there is a significant quality of a certain type of "*Barrier*" that *Self* is imposing on *itself* by the nature of its own considerations and the relative "space" occupied by the energetic *masses* still carried.

Once "heavier locks" are removed—which figuratively bar the "Gate"—the "lighter" stuff seems to either dissipate automatically or will come off more freely when applying the higher *Actualized Awareness* attained at that "level." It all only seems overwhelming or unattainable when still holding a *vantage* that requires looking "upward" toward higher conditions and *realizations* that yet reached by an individual. This is how *Self-defeatism* can play in—and why relying on fragmented "associative reasoning of a Mind-System"—particularly at our "Wizard Levels"—has a tendency to get one just more "spun" into where they are already at.

Managing "points" is similar to "presence" as treated in *"Standard Procedure 2-C"* when a *Pilot* directs the *Seeker* to make contact (communicate) with the immediate environment. One reason is to get directed *Awareness* "present" and the other, which is related, it is:

to establish that the "points" in one's environment are actually "safe" to both "look at" *and* "view from."

An Alpha-Spirit does not like to *knowingly* leave its attentions on space that is considered unsafe (or containing "cues" from *facets* that are considered unsafe by fragmented associative reasoning)—but, if there is a strong enough impression, it does so *unknowingly* anyway, leaving part of its *Awareness* there to hold that *image* in suspension so as not to completely "turn its back" on something that might "get" them. They don't destroy the creation, as they should. They keep a facsimile-copy of it in existence with a big warning sign that says: "Must Never Duplicate"—but there it is, maintained continuously created with entangled energy all the while.

In order to succumb to identifying with the standard-issue *Human Condition*, an Alpha-Spirit has already dispersed a great amount of their *Actualized Awareness* with attentions simultaneously on many POV across the entire *"Spiritual Timeline."* Contrary to the apparent "sense" of it one might carry in *beta-existence*, the Alpha-Spirit is not "imbued with" or "imbuing" any less of their own *Beingness* or ability to create energy as it progresses along, but the degree of entangled *mass* compulsively created between the position of the Alpha-Spirit and its POV-experience of a *beta-existence*, causes a lot of its attentions and energetic channels to be "tied up" or otherwise "occupied" and seemingly unavailable in the present.

> Willingness—and therefore, ability—to locate and access a particular Universe collapses for an individual when all possible extant POV are intolerable or deemed unsafe.

In most instances, they key consideration is "betrayal." The certainty of what is safe to *view*, and acceptable points to *view from* reduces. The individual is willing to be responsible for fewer and fewer POV. We generally equate "ability" with "willingness" in our Systemology, because: the individual is less able when they are less willing; and less willing when they are uncertain in ability.

It may be said that an individual declines in their optimum condition the less they are willing to *look at* and be responsible for. This can also be socially manipulated if "how bad it is everywhere" is consistently reinforced or validated by others. This is also one of the means of entrapment because the implanted reaction to something be labeled "Not Safe" is not to *look*. This has even taken place during our own development of the Master Grades,[167] where most of what we discovered of value or from examining outside inspiration, came from sources that contemporary spiritual authorities would "highly *not* recommend" or even tell others "not to look at" (either blatantly or by degrading it).

Δ Δ Δ Δ Δ Δ

---

167 **"Master Grades"** : literary materials by Joshua Free (written 1995 and 2019) revised and compiled for the "Mardukite Academy of Systemology" instructional grades—"Route of Magick & Mysticism" (*Grade I, Part A*), "Route of Druidism & Dragon Legacy" (*Grade I, Part D*), "Route of Mesopotamian Mysteries" (Grade II) and "Route of Mardukite Systemology" or "Pathway to Self-Honesty" (*Grade III*).

Systematic processing—as a supplement to educational training—is a means for an individual to practice *Self-Determinism*
and alternating "viewpoints" that can effectively free up the
tendencies and considerations operating on "automatic." For
example, we use objective methods that involve "corners" or
"points" that anchor the space of a room, because they are
considered "determined" and "owned" by something separate from *Self.*

> An individual operating in *beta-existence* starts to be-
> lieve they cannot be responsible for (or create) *Space,*
> because it all seems to be already "determined" for
> them. Even the "ideas" (we are told) have all been
> thought of before and belong to someone else.

An interesting situation takes place for the standard-issue
Human Condition, when an individual considers that they
would be "nothing" or "not" if they weren't *identified* with
some "thing"—and, of course, at the Physical Universe level
of *beta-existence,* the identification is with "objects" (solid
masses). Therefore, one of the objectives of Grade-IV (*Wizard
Level-0*) is to detach an individual from a compulsive POV
from the *genetic vehicle* they "think" they are. This is systematically accomplished by introducing a "shift" into an
alternative or secondary POV and then practicing alternating
between them on one's own *Self-Determination.*

> Metaphysical practitioners of mysticism are usually
> quite familiar with the concept of an "astral body,"
> which has received most of the attention in former
> methods of freeing up and shifting POV out of the *genet-
> ic vehicle.* Our upper-level emphasis is on *"Zu-vision"* as a
> point of Awareness; not another intermediate "body."

An individual *can* assume a POV from within a *genetic vehicle,*
but when one *knows* they are doing so, they also have free
willingness and ability to shift to other POV independent of
any body. Since occupation of the *Human Condition* POV is
generally "enforced" or "implanted," the Alpha-Spirit forgets
considerations that it can be located *exterior* to this existence.

At its own point of pure spiritual *Beingness*, its existence is not actually located in a Universe anywhere, but its own original state. The whole matter of being fixed in a location is subject to reality agreements and considerations, whether we remember "making" them or not.

In practicing our techniques, it is preferable to shift to a POV that is not dependent on any type of form or body, astral or otherwise, in which to maintain existence as a "point." Tolerance for this can be increased by applying "*creativeness processing*" methods that treat "points" and "spots" in space. The reason many practitioners have worked with "astral bodies" in the past, is because it provides a "sense" that they still *have* something.

Operating as a point of pure *Awareness* can be a steep gradient to take on all at once. In "*creativeness processing*" an exception to this might be the practice of *Self-directing* an alternation of POV between shifting "into" and "out of" an *imagined body*, but the primary difference here is that it treats a *form* that the individual *knows* they are *creating*, can take a responsibility for, and then stop creating it and dissolve it when the exercise is completed.

As an entity or *Awareness*, the Alpha-Spirit has long been out of practice with the operation of its own faculties and relying on its own *Creative Ability* and perception. Considerations at the degree of the Physical Universe result in a standard-issue *Human Condition* that believes itself dependent on the "physical body" to communicate with an "external environment."

The goals of our "Wizard Grades" takes this a step further in developing tolerance and willingness for POV that are "*exterior*" to not only considerations of a *genetic vehicle*, but the fragmented circuitry of the "Mind-System" as well. If desired, such a vantage would be optimum for treating conditions of a "Mind" and "Body" when one does not feel as though they are "stuck" within them. This concept is also found at the heart of many archaic forms of *shamanism*.

The generally accepted belief that an individual *must* be occupying a POV exclusively *interior* to a Mind-Body in order to operate that *genetic vehicle* is quite false. *All* of the potential POV are actually "remote" from existence of *Self*, therefore an Alpha-Spirit could maintain a POV "just outside" the Mind-Body system and still very adequately operate it independent from an *Identity with Self*, just as one might operate a marionette puppet. This is actually preferable for many reasons, but most importantly, it more closely matches the truer state of things *just prior* to exclusive and compulsive standard-issue POV creation fixed *inside* the Mind-Body system.

Reality agreements that an individual occupies, and is fixed to, a POV "*interior*" to *beta-existence* is reinforced and validated the longer this consideration is held outside full *Self-Determinism*, and also the amount of "impact" the individual experiences from "external" or "environmental" sources while they are doing so. This is one of the only reasons that "pain" and "loss" are considerable points of solid *beta-fragmentation*: an individual considers they are *Identified* as the *genetic vehicle* and thus it associates all of its experiences as happening *to Self* as the Alpha-Spirit. Because we consider this heavily—that things in this Physical Universe are *happening to us*—significant amounts of energy are "wound up" or "entangled" with keeping "hold on" these *Imprints* across a "*Spiritual Timeline*" of many "existences."

The idea of "*Zu-Vision*" (under one label or another) is not a *new* concept, but a very very ancient one. A proper understanding of it failed to be duplicated across history, but with the rise of the "New Thought" movement in the early 1900's, the esoteric ideal of "operating as Self" or accessing "Spirit Vision" became quite prominent in many spiritual circles up to the mid-20th Century. But, attentions in the world started shifting again as World Wars ensued, the atomic bomb was created and migration to "space" within the Physical Universe began to take priority. Human civilization has been operating in the shadows of this mechanical-technological paradigm shift ever since.

Although much of the methodology is fairly simple, the premise of *"Zu-Vision"* is not introduced prior to "Wizard" work, because earlier materials focused on *Seekers* reducing energetic intensity of the "field" created by circuitry of the Mind-Body system as *"Beta-Defragmentation."* This circuitry is usually created and reinforced while an individual is "keyed-in" or "fixed to" those *interior* considerations—and this "electric field" seems to also have a "magnetic" quality to it. An individual *does* have a natural ability to "get out" on command, but there is also a tendency to "snap in" again with some force or sensation of impact. This sense of "pull" or "gravity" can accumulate and decrease willingness and ability to knowingly *Self-direct* "getting out" *again*. To correct this properly for accessing higher gradients of realization, we have *"Wizard Level-0."*

Δ Δ Δ Δ Δ Δ

Several years ago, a member of the Systemology Society suggested a basic technique inspired by an old obscure volume of German mysticism. Therein, "transference of consciousness" is described—where:

> an initiate practices imagining their POV "going inside" solid masses separate from the *genetic vehicle.*

However, the original methods all seemed to emphasize one direction of flow, and we can improve this for our practices:

> using alternation—"going in" *and* "going out"
> —with repetition and fluidity.

Experiments demonstrated better initial results could be earned by selecting large masses, which one is familiar with but that are not in the immediate vicinity—which returned us to the original suggestion of "a mountain" on which the individual is not already sitting on. This differs from other "magical" suggestions where beginners use a candle in the room or the tree they are in front of. For this practice, we still want to start with an "imagined facsimile-copy" of an actual mass in the Physical Universe (and "a mountain" works well).

Practice of "Locational POV" may be *Self-processed* or *Piloted.* If *Piloted,* a *Pilot* is not to evaluate significances or invalidate results for the experience. Whatever is happening in a *Seeker's* reality and perception *is* what is happening for them. To ensure a proper continuation of processing and to keep the *Seeker's* attention "on the mark" so to speak, a *Pilot* may follow up a "Route-0" or "*creativeness processing*" PCL series with: "Did you?" But this is mainly to be certain a *Pilot* remains in communication with a *Seeker* during subjective use of imagination; it should never be asked with skepticism; and so long as a *Seeker* says "Yes," a *Pilot* should only follow the response with an acknowledgment that the message was received, such as "Okay."

LOCATIONAL POV—ALTERNATING (ROUTE-0, BASIC 3D)

—Imagine being above (*a mountain*) looking down on it.

—Imagine your POV moving in *to* it.

\ Imagine your POV moving out *from* it.

LOCATIONAL POV—ALTERNATING (ROUTE-0, A.T.-SP 3D)

—Be near (*or above*) ___ .

—Be inside of ___ (*it*).

\ Be outside of ___ (*it*).

—Be at the center ___ (*it*).

\ Be outside ___ (*it*).

—Be on the surface ___ (*it*).

\ Be above ___ (*it*).

This may be done as practice with eyes closed and by imagining a "secondary POV" independent of the *genetic vehicle.* By establishing a new viewpoint, a *Seeker* is not as dependent on reaching for the much higher-level goal of completely separating them from the compulsive one within the "body"—the certainty of that will come with greater actualized success.

When an individual *is* practiced in commanding their POV (for *ZU-Vision, &tc.*), an extended "Actualization Tech" version (included above for reference) is applied in Wizard Grade upper-routes to direct *Actualized Awareness* to various POV in the Universe—and beyond it—on command. It is based on a popular meditation technique appearing in Eastern Mysticism concerning "journeys to other planets."

However, by effectively working with an "imagined point" and focusing attention of *Awareness* on that "secondary POV," an individual may notice that the noise and interference from the Mind-Body "field" is "quieted down" during this practice. This is because the energy that keeps the "field" *created* is supplied by the individual themselves; and an Alpha-Spirit is certainly able to maintain circuits with multiple POV simultaneously and shift its *Awareness* fluidly among them.

Once an individual has certainty on the basic technique, it may be expanded to include practice maintaining multiple POV. With the above example, a *Seeker* "anchors" the POV they are using above "the mountain" and holds it. They can begin alternating:

attention between the "imagined POV" with eyes closed and the POV maintained by the *genetic vehicle* with eyes are open

—making sure that the "secondary POV" is held stable in the imagination, so when one closes their eyes they are immediately assuming this other viewpoint.

As an additional gradient of practice, a *Seeker* can develop enough perception with this experience to simultaneously "*look*" through both POV. It will be noticed, of course, that perceptions of the *genetic vehicle* POV are considerably "louder" than a "secondary" one. All an individual needs to do, even with eyes open, is increase the attention that is directed to the "secondary POV" to keep it from completely fading out. "Alternating Locational POV" may be incorporated into an individual's regular "*Creativity Session*" regimen, since certainty on this ability can always be increased—and it quite critical for upper-level development.

With increased development with this type of work, an individual increases their willingness on what is acceptable or "safe" to *view* and the possible "points" to *view* from. When one considers that this free *Awareness* is able to do so without consequence to the body, an individual's "spiritual" reach or *realization* increases. They can begin to *look* and *know* without consideration of a *genetic vehicle* or sensory limitations of the standard-issue *Human Condition*. Although these exercises may be, themselves, imaginative practice—the gains in *Creative Ability* and higher realization are *actual*.

:: 8 ::

RESPONSIBILITY FOR IMAGINATION AND THE CREATION OF SPACE

Applying Systemology to POV management is important for rehabilitating abilities of the Alpha-Spirit in many ways—one of which being the creation and handling of *Space.* This first and foremost:

| begins with a *point* in which to consider that Space *is.* |

When the mystic says that "space extends infinitely in all directions," it assumes an epicenter[168] *point* in which to "view" *out* into "Space" *from.* We can also consider that there are specialized points—such as we treat in geometry—that define a dimensional plane of space.

| The concept of distance and time enters in when there is more than one existing *point* to consider. |

To truly *create* energy, matter and various forms, there must be space for them to exist in.

The Alpha-Spirit has forgotten its own ability to create and handle space, relying on the existence of the *genetic vehicle* and Physical Universe to *have* any sense of space. Although many commonly treat the concept of Space and Universes as a *spherical* nature—such as a mystic or magician that "casts circles" or *imagines* a "shield-like sphere" surrounding their ritual area, but our experiments show:

| —easier and more effective, in basic practice, to represent six directions of a three-dimensional space with a "cube." |

As a demonstration, this basic idea can be put into practice as an extension of the exercises given in the previous lesson-chapter. However, rather than use "a mountain" as it exists

---

168 **epicenter** : the point from which shock-waves travel.

within the actual Physical Universe, this time we want to actually *imagine* "a mountain" within one's own "Personal Universe." This is "practiced with imagination" by first *creating* the dimensions of "space" and then the masses and objects within.

An individual tends to consider the forms and experiences that are on Earth or in the cosmos—those that represent a shared common reality that can be communicated with others—as more *real* than those created and existing just for *Self.* The primary difference in "reality" between a "Personal Universe" and the "Physical Universe" is the level of common agreements—which has been explored in prior material regarding the semantics of "reality" and "agreements."

In "*creativeness processing,*" an individual *could* just close their eyes and "*Imagine*" certain forms that they perceive, which satisfy written directions for techniques (or from a *Pilot*)— but, if greater attention is given to the *creation* of *space* that the *form* exists in, than greater certainty on actual *Creative Ability* can be earned.

Eventually, "*imaginative*" work increases *realizations* so that an individual's *Awareness* can even receive *actual perception.*

So, rather than closing your eyes and essentially "recalling" an actual mountain in which to duplicate a scene, this time we want to *create* the dimensions of a *space* in our "Personal Universe" for which to *imagine* "a mountain" of our own unique design.

Even the "*creation of space*" may be practiced progressively— because it really is dependent on an individual's ability to perceive a "*point*"; something that is increasingly developed as one continues their personal "*Creativity Sessions.*" The following process applies the most basic steps to create a "cube of space." Once an individual has a sense of this, a more direct method is simply to *Imagine* the eight points to form a cube and *Create* it as a single-step. This isn't a "race" however; it is more important that an individual has absolute certainty on the *creation* of each point as fully as possible. It has taken some *Seekers* a considerable amount of time to simply achieve a total realization of even holding a single "point" still enough to perceive it solidly—and this is far more important for ongoing progress on the *Pathway* than simply "flash creating" a random series of thin imagery.

CREATION OF SPACE (ROUTE-0. PRE-A.T., BASIC 3D)

—Imagine a *point* that is independent of *beta-existence*.

—Imagine a *line* stretches to a second *point*.

—Imagine those two *points* extend *lines* upward to another two *points*.

—Imagine these four *points* connected by *lines* form a *square*.

—Imagine another set of four *points* connected as a second *square*.

—Imagine lines connecting the *squares* to form a *cube*.

—Imagine that this *cube* is pure *space*.

Once there is certainty on effective "Creation of Space," an individual can then go on to *Imagine* the creation of "a mountain" *inside* the "cube"—which is why it is important to *create* a large enough space to work in.

For effective "*creativeness processing*," an individual should make certain that the imagery *created* is not a *reactionary imprint* or *mental image* that spontaneously comes into view, for example at the mention of the word "mountain." This is ensured by "throwing away" any of the "pictures" that "come to Mind" and further, *creating* changes in whatever is *imagined*—for example, reforming and adjusting the shape and color and other *facets* until it is absolutely certain that *Self* is fully responsible for the *creation* of every detail.

As an individual considers applying exercises from the previous lesson-chapter to their uniquely imagined mountain, a realization may occur that equally applies to the structure of POV in every Universe: there is a fixed or "anchored" POV in place that maintains the *creation* of the space and form, meanwhile the "secondary POV" may still be directed "in to" and "out of" the object. The same exercises may be applied. As an additional step, the POV is alternated between the "copied beta-mountain" (from the previous chapter-lesson) and the "uniquely created mountain" (from this one). For best results, rather than simply flashing between the two scenes, use the POV to *actually look* at some detail or *facet* that is interesting, acceptable and/or safe to look at.

This type of work is mimicry of events that took place early on the *"Spiritual Timeline"*—"refresher practice" for an Alpha-Spirit that has otherwise forgotten how it once *created* and *viewed* in this manner (with full *Awareness*) prior to any existence of a "common agreement" Games-Universe shared with other Alpha-Spirits. The exercise relates the idea that:—

> The POV of a *Spiritual Being* as a unit of *Awareness*, can:
> *create* dimensional boundary points to define a space;
> *create* forms to view by condensing points within that space;
> shift its POV to be any point in a form or point within space,
> while still maintaining POV on *creation* of forms and space.

We could fill many volumes on various concepts, theories and research underlying all of this work, but with consistent practice and development, the intended *realizations* for this gradient of our Systemology should become increasingly self-evident.

Δ Δ Δ Δ Δ Δ

"Creation-of-Space" is a long-standing esoteric and mystic concept, but previous systems never truly explored its full heights; and there are, of course, numerous variations and

extensions of our basic procedures. Most importantly, we are treating *Self-determined* creation and management of *space*, so the Alpha-Spirit can *knowingly* practice and rehabilitate *Creative Ability* and responsibility for its existence.

A beginner would find in invalidating to attempt this in a *beta-existence* where reality agreements restrict one to only "borrowing external" space-time and energy-matter to *do* or even *have* anything in the Physical Universe, because the base materials and fodder, the objects and the *space* they occupy— it has already been put in place prior to the Alpha-Spirit's entry. In fact, the conservatism imposed on the physics[169] of continuity in this *beta-existence* is a reality agreement in place specifically to prevent an individual from manifesting "spontaneous generations"—which would, of course, "spoil the game."

At this juncture of development, we are most concerned with what can be managed within an individual's own "*created space*"; and even the very "*creation-of-space*" for a "Personal Universe." It is far better to train and practice our brand of "Wizardcraft" in a dimension of "personal space" independent of Physical Universe reality agreements. The previous exercises are intended to direct attention toward realizations that: the Alpha-Spirit, as a "point" of *Awareness*, can *create* space and forms within it with one POV and then experience it with another. This defies many commonly held beliefs about this *beta-existence* and yet is a simple truth in Alpha-Existence.

As in the traditional styling of former mystical texts, we tend to present basic instructions for our procedures as guidance for what may otherwise be overlooked—mainly due to the "simplicity" of the directions. The entire idea that "one step is preliminary to some other step that might produce an effect" causes a student or initiate to overlook significance of

---

169 **physics** : regarding data obtained by a material science of observable motions, forces and bodies, including their apparent interaction, in the Physical Universe (specific to this *beta-existence*).

the more "basic" step—not realizing that a more actualized certainty on a particular level, or foundation, will actually increase the potential "reach" of what follows. This commonly occurs in contemporary "magical traditions," where high-level mastery of basic rudiments (that actually determine any results) are carelessly put aside in favor of more "interesting" rituals and "elaborate" ceremonial dramatics (which carry no living power in themselves, regardless of what gestures or words are uttered).

There are many key suggestions for practice in the *Creative Ability Test (CAT)* and various techniques all throughout this present volume (and former literature). As an Academy Grade and tier on the *Pathway*—what we are most concerned with (for *Wizard Level-0*) is just how certain an individual can be in their *creating* and just how strong of a perception they can eventually have on it (relative to the solidity we perceive of the Physical Universe).

> It is important that *Awareness* is strengthened in a safe session environment and practiced within one's own Universe; no other considerations about *beta-existence* are applied.

> While establishing a greater reality on *Self* and developing personal *Creative Ability*, we are certainly not treating apparent "manifestation"—"spontaneous generation" "teleportation" "levitation"—of these *creations* for common-agreement *beta-existence*.

> Apparent reality for an individual in their Personal Universe is subject to their own level of actualization on those perceptions; as a personal experience, there is nothing to invalidate an individual and their progress.

In actual practice, an hour or more developing total certainty on *creation* of a single "point" is more significant for ongoing development than if considering a whole "cube" vaguely and only having a slight perception on its reality.

The "*point*" is an interesting fundamental encountered by the Seeker during the *Creation-of Space*; because the "*point*" represents *no-dimension* and *no-mass* and thus so closely resembles the nature of the Alpha Spirit's own existence.

It takes *two* "points" to create a line (segment) and a single "*spatial dimension.*" This makes the "point" an effective tool in systematically processing to "reach" higher states; because holding the concept of a "point" by itself runs an individual very close on having to confront "non-motion" and "non-existence" comparable to experiences on the "*Spiritual Timeline*" that an Alpha-Spirit had difficulty prior. Hence, our Systemological compass pointed to do a 180-degree turnabout on the condensation and restriction of our considerations of *Beingness.*

When we practice "*creation-of-space,*" no attention is given to other considerations or *mental imagery.* This also means—after reaching a stable condition of Beta-Defragmentation—we expect no interference of "automated" *imprints* or impinging *pings* sensed from the *genetic vehicle* while an individual is holding the *creation* of a single "point" in place within their own Personal Universe. If understood properly—in connection to training given in previous Systemology volumes—these "Route-0" methods can actually be used to carry out high-power Beta-Defragmentation processing as well.

As an individual maintains total focus on basic existence of the "point," these other automatic response circuits *will* "turn on" if not already defragmented—which is one more reason we held back this material until after an individual had potentially worked through previous books.

However, if determined enough, the personal phenomenon (fragmentation) that occurs while maintaining attention on a single "point" can simply be treated right then and there. This is effective for clearing out debris from channels that may not have defragmented fully during earlier Routes.

> Total *Actualized Awareness* and full *Creative Ability* is hindered only by "automated circuitry" and "mental machinery" that an Alpha-Spirit formerly *created* (or *copied, then compulsively creates unknowingly*) to manage control of all these functions.

Our ongoing solution is to knowingly take responsibility and control over whatever is compulsively unknowingly or reactively happening automatically. Such is the basic theory behind the exercise regimen provided as the *Creative Ability Test (CAT)*, which can more appropriately be considered our standard *Creative Ability Training*. This should make greater sense as an individual practices with a "point."

> For example, the natural tendency is to put in *"effort"* to "stop" (destroy) what is taking place outside personal control and determination; but a more effective method of regaining control is to "change" what is happening or make it happen more strongly. An individual might create their "point" with structural intent of no mass or dimension, yet it takes on characteristics on its own; perhaps of a "spot" by expanding its size, or flashing as a light rather than remaining a static point.

A static point, whether as a point "anchoring" corners of *created space* or a point within space, should be able to be fixed in a location and suspended from motion. In either case we have "other-determined" actions affecting the basic command postulate directed to hold a single "point" still. If it's faintly flicking in and out of *Awareness* or flashing, the individual can intend for it do so strongly and more boldly. If it won't remain still, the course or direction it travels can be changed. If it keeps moving in on the body, give it a little "knock" the other way back toward its intended location, rather than giving in to withdrawing your POV backward.

> Anything that impinges on a specific/fixed "postulate-of-creation" can be systematically put under control of *Self* using gradients of *change* to increase or decrease what is already happening, even if it seems

contrary to the original intent. A fast moving *image* or *point* can be more easily *changed* to go faster before there is enough certainty to slow it and hold it still.

The same degree of attention and certainty should be applied to each basic "step" to *"Creation-of-Space."* An alternative "Universes" method treats the flat two-dimensional *plane* ("square") as the base (or bottom for corner-points) of the *"cubed-space,"* rather than as a "wall"-surface that one is facing (as suggested in the basic version).

Once there is certainty on creating and viewing "out in front" (of their POV), the next applicable gradient is *creating* eight points around the individual's own POV—so as *to be* the only existential-point and *Awareness* within the "cube" of *created space* that is otherwise intended as "empty" of *creations* and *imagery.*

Responsibility is connected to *ability, knowingness, willingness* and *control*—all of which are treated at length in former volumes. *Responsibility* for *"Creation-of-Space"* increases with certainty of command and control of it; hence remaining at *"Cause"* throughout the cycle-of-creation—including discard, dissolve or destruction—when an individual intends to no longer create it and has not intended on it to persist compulsively on some automatic-circuit of creation, because we now know that *Self* contributes to that as well.

In the same style of placing attention on "corners" of space as suggested in the *Creative Ability Test (CAT)*, this can be done while remaining stationary within the *created-space.* An individual can also rotate their view to inspect the boundaries as well. To further increase certainty on the *creation* and its contents (or lack thereof), the individual can go *look* from other POV to see that it is empty and simultaneously determine for *Self* the level of control and responsibility maintained on their ability. For example, unlike the points that define the dimensions of this space, the individual's POV *can* be relocated, such as from one corner to the next and *look* inward at the space. A *realization* should become increasingly actualized that: *Self* completely owns and is totally responsible for this independently created personal space.

Δ Δ Δ Δ Δ Δ

Many of our goals for Systemology "Wizard Grades" follow an arcane pattern or sequence that we often refer to as the *"Gates"*—and there are traces of this lore throughout 6,000 years of recorded esoterica, regarding "veils" and "kabbalistic spheres" and "dimensions" and "aethyrs" of existence. In such instances, the "initiate" primarily relies on familiarity of an "astral body" while "pathworking" (or "imagining") a "predetermined mental image set" that is meant to induce or incite some new impression of *"Beingness."* This is the approximate extent to which the practical applications of *Grade-I* and most *Grade-II* material actually reach.

Even then, such techniques can only be realized as *actual* to the degree an individual is able to *actually* handle the *space* they are operating in. And if their presence is not masterfully immersed[170] in a vivid experience (due to unpracticed handling of *Imagination*), then those former methods—which arcane schools and lodges have long relied on quite heavily—do not provide an individual with much more *reality* than when simply reading them.

Standard-issue operation of the *Human Condition* is restricted by a heavily implanted Mind-System that orients the POV toward "protecting" the survival of *genetic vehicle*. All of the mental machinery presently operating with this intention interrupts our experience of a *Self-Honest* existence with an entire *imprinting* factory and *personality package* that cumulatively associates more of an individual's Universe, and more of an individual's potential action in that Universe, to low-level misemotional response-mechanisms. Eventually, the entire slate is filled up with scenes and signals that provide a sense that the individual has no space and no action remaining in the "game."

---

170 **immersion** : plunged or sunk into; wholly surrounded by.

When an individual is convinced that this is the only game around, it is quite difficult to *imagine* something else that is independently created from familiar parameters of the Physical Universe. In fact, one of the reasons mystical practitioners rely on "mental bodies" and other "mental scenery" in allegedly "astral work" is because they are still operating, to some great extent, *within* or *interior to* the Mind-System; thus they still are very heavily affected by its fragmentation and implants. Traditional practices of this sort do not necessarily free *Awareness-as-Self* (*Actualized Awareness*) beyond or *exterior* to mental circuitry, since without full control and responsibility for *Space* and *Creation*, an individual still relies on self-generated mental machinery to manage all *creating, looking* and *evaluating* on automatic.

Practicing, imagining and eventually establishing a POV in a *created-space* of one's own Personal Universe is an objective goal for *Wizard Level-0* completion; not only for its function, but also to increase on subjective certainty or personal reality that:

> *Space* can exist independent of the *Physical Universe* and experiencing existence of exterior Universes depends on an *Exterior POV* and not a *genetic vehicle* in *beta-existence*. I-AM is an *Alpha Spirit* existing independent of any body and any universe other than its original *Alpha-Existence* as a unit of *Awareness* with unlimited Creative Ability.

Actualization *follows* Realization. Only when the I-AM-*Self* (Alpha-Spirit) is certain enough that there is *somewhere to be* existing outside of this *beta-existence* can enough willingness and determinism break ties that have long fixed one's attention exclusively on existence in this Physical Universe. The range of *Actualized Awareness* under full control of the Alpha-Spirit is fairly unlimited in ability to direct its POV and locate itself in existence, but logically: an individual must first realize that a destination exists for them to actually be there.

Our methodology of "spiritual rehabilitation" still follows the same effective formulas of handling *Self-Determination* and automatic-mechanisms that brought us up to this point on the *Pathway*—they are simply applied to the conditions of each gradient or "Gateway." Here, we have illuminated the true boundaries of this Physical Universe and operation of POV-implants; we are reintroducing *Self* to handling imaginative faculties and ability to command Creative Ability, taking back control of and responsibility for mental machinery that reinforced fixed attention circuits further validating solidity of this *beta-existence*.

As we complete the selection of standard discourses intended for this volume, treating the end of a cycle or a departure of communication, there is one additional matter to call attention to—one which must be consistently treated at each level of *Personal Defragmentation*, because it is a basic implant installed and then impressed more strongly the more an Alpha-Spirit began to participate in Game-Universes: "*Loss.*" And this implant, like all of them, is an ongoing chain or branching tree of associations that is built upon the intensity and charge of a preexisting incident: "*Loss of Space*"—certainly a deeply *imprinted* experience on the "*Spiritual Timeline.*" An individual has a certain sense that a Universe can cease to have any occupied existence—in fact, we have all known the loss of at least one Universe due to violent collapse or some other type of explosive phenomenon.

There is a considerable amount of imprinting tied to a sense that we might "lose something we have" by not compulsively existing in this Physical Universe—or that it might cease to be if we weren't here to somehow reinforce and support its existence "for ourselves and our fellow citizen" because in such fragmentation, there is no other *beingness* possible.

The majority of those presently operating the *Human Condition* are here by similar circumstances—the most basic being: entrapment of an Alpha-Spirit's consideration of *Beingness* from a "higher" Universe, interior to enforced spatial dimensions of *beta-existence*, where

Awareness is fixed as a "point" locatable for that other-determined *space*, subject to being the effects of reality agreements concerning external energies and forces of the Physical Universe. As anyone can see, this is clearly just a very technical description for *a prison.*

Certainty on the *Beingness* of *Self* correlates to the level of *Actualized Awareness* available; to an individual heavily fixed in their singular *Identification* with the *Human Condition* and that it is their only means of existence, there are no considerations for any existence *exterior* to those conditions.

And that is the only reason a *Spiritual Being* would remain trapped in a *material prison* where the only one guarding the gate, *is themselves.*

With use of *Imagination* in practice of *Creative Ability*, we continue to systematically process a *Seeker* in the direction of taking control of whatever *Self* is participating in unknowingly or by some other determinism. It does require a bit of intuition for individual use; the scope of any single book is tied to specific goals and objectives, while its variations for potential application are virtually unlimited.

All our experience, thought and action
is a created product of imagination.
We can never express any thing
that we do not first imagine.
Imagine freely and often.
Live as a Free Spirit.
Create. Create.
Create.

IMAGINOMICON

— APPENDIX —

ADVANCED TECH REPORTS
and
SYSTEMOLOGY GLOSSARY

:: A ::
IMAGINATION APPLIED TO SYSTEMATIC PROCESSING
TECH REPORT FOR SYSTEMOLOGY PILOTS
GRADE-IV WIZARD-0 ROUTE-0
IMAGINOMICON EDIT

IMAGINATION is the primary subject of *Systemology Grade-IV Wizard Level-0*, as explored in *Liber-3D*. Potential application to systematic processing are unlimited, but our methodology emphasizes increased *Self-directed* "control" (*willingness, knowingness* and *ability*) of communications and creation—an Alpha-condition of "responsibility" for cause and effect.

An Alpha-Spirit occupying POV in denser Universes along the "*Spiritual Timeline*" progressively considers their own *ability* to have less direct effect on their environment—possibly fearing some "punishment" for control of this responsibility. But, this leads them to eventually stop *knowingly* creating at all, putting these faculties on automatic—until finally forgetting their *Creative Ability* altogether.

Use of *Imagination* in systematic processing allows *Seekers* to *knowingly* practice command of *Creative Ability*, the control and responsibility of being at "*Cause*"—because they *know* they are *creating* this *illusion* in their own "Personal Universe" (where it is safe to do so). There is no kickback effect or consequence enforced by the "Physical Universe" as a result.

> The two are independent of each other; and the more a *Seeker* is processed to realize this with certainty, the better their ability to handle existences of each Universe as they *are*—not simply as they are "thought" *to be* using some filter or circuit to receive fragmentary information. It is only after the *realization* is present that a *Seeker* can *actually* reassign their considerations.

Previous "Routes" of systematic processing mostly emphasized *recall* or *resurfacing* of events registered in "memory"—concerning what has actually happened. In addition to emotional qualities and other intellectual associations, these "memories" contain *facets* connected to specific types or pattern-forms of "energy-matter." The *Mental Imagery* attached to these *imprinted* experiences often carries the "*energetic charge*" of the original impression along with it. When such is stimulated as an automatic-response to some stimulus in the present environment, information from previous impressions that contain similar *facets* is also communicated as part of the reality experience.

In the beginning, the Alpha-Spirit used its *Creative Ability* for "fun" - for "art" - and its own personal amusement. Getting "lost" and identified with POV of its own *Creations* not-knowing the true nature of *Self* as I-AM, came later.

Meanwhile, here in *beta-existence*, we can employ *Imagination* in systematic processing as a means of handling "assignment of consideration" along a circuit or channel without being restricted only to "*activating events*" which have both: actually occurred *and* are within the scope of reality for a *Seeker* to effectively confront or recall directly.

Most *imprinting incidents* become heavy charged fragmentation only when an individual is not willing to directly *look*, and therefore take control and responsibility for either eliminating the creation or reassigning its value, instead of relying on mental machinery and other relays to handle perpetual creation and interpretation of the reality experience.

Concepts of "pain," "loss"—witnessing violence or death—such compulsively created *imprints* can often seem *more real* to an individual than the present environment. Of course, these events *did* happen, but the energy and attention a *Seeker* keeps entangled and suspended with their *Awareness* around each is what holds *Self* back from breaking the gravity of *beta-existence*. Even when unknowingly and compulsively maintaining creation of mental machinery and its products, the Alpha-Spirit is still *fragmenting* the wholeness of its

Awareness by doing so, hence the decline of the *Actualized Awareness* that is "present" at a given moment.

An individual puts up so much resistance to the *mental image*, hoping to stop the motion it contains, meanwhile compulsively creating it as it is; and the force they are applying against it makes it more solid and thus perceived as stronger and more difficult to handle, thus feelings of overwhelm as an effect and the abandonment of control and responsibility for treating its contents. If handled directly with systematic processing, *imprinted* information can be *defragmented* from the circuits; but this requires an ability and willingness of the *Seeker* to actually "*look*" at the *image* they are carrying around from it. Applying increased *Actualized Awareness* disintegrates the "charge" held on it—perhaps one reason that "stares" instinctively bother many beings.

| NOTE: *This tech report does not invalidate previous material.* |

Various training, exercises, techniques and processes given in *Tablets of Destiny*, *Crystal Clear* and *Metahuman Destinations* combine to establish a systematic regimen for "beta-defragmentation." We are now able to approach a new level of "beta-Actualization" by applying "*Imagination*" and "*Creativeness Processing*" to our methodology. Material for this is covered in *Liber-3D* (released as "*Imaginomicon*") in combination to these updated tech reports. Rather than a new *direction* of practice, "Route-0" is a result of new *realizations* achieved using our former work as a *ledge*. This has been the pattern of our development all along. Suggestions contained herein may be *added* to previous material; applicable to both *Self-Processing* and *Professional Piloting*.

Δ Δ Δ Δ Δ Δ

Systematic processing goals are only achieved when a *Seeker* directs actual attention to the exercises. This is referred to as "presence" in the outline for Standard Operating Procedure (#2C) for Grade-IV, where the first steps begin with increas-

ing the *Awareness* given to the present environment, especially the session. Processing is directed toward *Self*, not one
of the phases or circuits or *imprints* created by *Self*. The instructions are referred to as "commands" because they
introduce Alpha-Thought considerations for the *Seeker* to
"run" on their own "operating system"—

"command lines" are received from the text or *Pilot* until an
individual resumes *Self-determined* control of this command.
And a Seeker must actually *be* "present" *doing* the exercises.

Most individuals are operating on so much automatic
circuitry and looking through so many filters that very little
Actualized Awareness is present. Of course, *if* complete stable
"crystal clear" *Beta-Awareness* were actually present during
the first step, there would be little need for standard "*beta-
defragmentation*" exercises; and the individual could focus on
"upper-level" considerations. But, at the start, we apply a
standardized systematic method under the assumption that
some part of an individual's *Awareness* is fixed somewhere
apart from their present environment.

When an individual stops *looking*—for whatever reason—
they use mental machinery to do the "*looking*" for them.

Therefore, most "objective universe" methods of increasing
attention-on-the-present have to do *literally* with "*looking*"
"*contacting*" and "*communicating*" with the present environment. This demonstrates a enough certainty in the "safety"
of the environment for *Self* to actually apply its *Awareness*.
Properly handling the various "Point-of-Views" (POV) that
Self utilizes is an integral part of "Route-0"—

because while this "crystal lens" remains fragmented, so too
is the view taken in regard to *Imagination* and *Creative Ability*.

At the beginning of a session, a *Seeker* is directed to "look
around" at their environment and notice things, one to the

next. The environment may even appear to get "brighter" as this happens.

> So much of what an individual really believes they are
> perceiving is actually fragmented by circuits and filters
> before the information is even communicated to *Self.*

This is better demonstrated, for example, when an individual enters a new environment—and more of their attention is placed on what is around them. It does not take long for a "familiarity" to set in and then scenery perception is mostly being created on automatic—not really "looked at." The average individual is not educated to remain at "cause" over their selective directed attention. There are exercises that direct a *Seeker* to look at precise points, one to the next, as opposed to simply glancing around or lightly scanning. Many of these are actually summarized and included in the *"Creative Ability Test"* (CAT), also used as our *Creative Ability Wizard-Training Regimen.*

Techniques and training for "Wizard Level-0" are intended to increase an individual's certainty on operating as the Alpha-Spirit and using its own *"Zu-Vision"* independent of the *genetic vehicle* and *beta-existence.* The most direct technique (or PCL)—*"Be outside that body"*—is not always the most widely effective when other reality agreements and fragmented considerations are still impinging strongly on an individual. At the start, overtly direct "mystical-like" suggestions tend to invalidate an individual's existing certainty of reach.

> *Systemologist Seekers* practices exercises to increase
> the reach on *knowing* their own spiritual existence,
> rather than agreeing to carry a vague idea about it.

Additionally, "Route-0" may be applied to all previous "objective processing" methods. These are just a few ways that suggestions from former texts may be retained and returned to again at these upper-levels of practice:

They are practiced while seated with eyes closed, using "Imagination" (or assumption of an actual secondary POV) to treat the environment. An individual places their full attention on the room (or the object), then closes their eyes and uses *Imagination* to makes a facsimile-copy of it. If an exercise requires contacting or moving an object in some way, then the *Seeker* is to remain still and get a "sense" of it happening as fully as possible.

Other "objective processes" practice *Self-directing* communication with objects, masses and even walls in the environment. A *Seeker* may be directed to pick a spot on an object and touch it; then they are directed to let go. When this is carried through without lag, the *Seeker* is to get a sense of making the decision when to touch and when to let go. For "Wizard Level-0," an additional step is added to direct or project a *"beam"* with *Awareness* that is used to touch and let go. A *Seeker* may also upgrade methods of *"Presence in Space-Time"* (in *SOP-2C*), contacting the walls while sitting still and directing a POV (or using *Imagination*) to move back and forth across the room.

Δ Δ Δ Δ Δ Δ

Fragmentation is that which inhibits clear communication between Alpha-Command of *Self* and the resulting activity.

Systemology focuses on the Alpha-Spirit, which is controlling a Mind-System and a *genetic vehicle*. But what is *actual* for the Alpha-Spirit exists in the domain of Alpha-existence, not beta. When an individual is fragmented, their experience of "thought" is restricted to associative information kept in circuits of the Mind-System. It is true that creative expressions in *Beta-existence* are the result of efforts first circulated through the Mind and manifested by efforts of a physical organism—but the impulse that directs this comes from a higher source.

CREATIVE ABILITY (ROUTE-3, CIRCUIT-0, BASIC 3D)

—What have you done using imagination or creativity?

—What have you kept yourself from doing using imagination or creativity?

For many reasons, an individual often becomes less willing to be the *Cause* of things. This basic PCL can be expanded for application to other "circuits" (as described in *Metahuman Destinations*) for recovering considerations about: what you would allow others to do and keep from doing; what others have done and kept themselves from doing, &tc. As with other systematic processing, this is run until an individual has freed their considerations and willingness regarding use of imagination and creativity, with no reactive or automatic tendencies regarding the concept.

In our natural state, the I-AM-*Self* (Alpha-Spirit) can only have its own abilities reduced as a result of its own Alpha-Thought—a high-level consideration or command-level postulate on existence. We have the ability to place *Awareness* at any POV, even where our consideration for *Beingness* is less than we actually are.

Suggestions toward our own invalidation—which we "accepted as reality"—allowed implantation of considerations rigidly fixed to a POV as the standard-issue *Human Condition*. Fear of invalidation can prompt an individual to decrease their willingness and certainty on ability. Regardless of where an invalidating cue or suggestion originates from, it is only by our own acceptance and incorporation of it as a reality agreement that allows us to become its effect. The circuits introduced as "Route-3" (for *SOP-2C*) may be applied to systematically treat processing of "Invalidation."

Δ Δ Δ Δ Δ Δ

On our Standard Model, the *Zu-line* represents a continuum of "Identity" that an individual Alpha-Spirit associates with itself. But the actual existential position of an Alpha-Spirit (7.0) is an Individuated Beingness, not an identity "identified" with any "thing"; and not actually located in any *space*, but is itself a single unit or point of pure *Spiritual Awareness*—often imagined as a single island-peak from out the *Sea of Infinite Nothingness* ("8"). However, the Alpha-Spirit may directed its POV toward *creation*, *space* and *Universes*. As *Awareness* "descends" on the *Zu-line* toward *beta-existence*, an individual more strongly associates itself and its own *Beingness* with lower POV that it is operating from.

In the past, mystics and magicians emphasized control of the body by operating from the Mind; and their POV is very much entangled within the Mind-System and the "mental plane." This is particular evident in the themes and semantics of their paradigms. It is from the "mental plane" that an individual is very *Aware* of "mental fields" surrounding "mental bodies" and a whole vast network of circuits and relays composing "mental machinery."

In most cases, "New Age" practitioners remain *interior* to the Mind-System, which is a step above being fixed to the *genetic vehicle* itself; but it is still not enough to access Higher Gates of Realization, which allow the potential for direct experience of Higher Universes. Assuming the individual has successfully defragmented the emotional stores connected to the *Reactive Control Center* (RCC), this still leaves them somewhere around the *third* "Gate" or "Veil"—still to break free of the Mind.

There are many instances when the POV of an Alpha-Spirit can be pulled-in or snapped-in on the fields and mechanisms inherently part of a "body." This may take place during intense emotional stress or trauma[171] when the perspective of

---

171 **traumatic encoding** : information received when the sensory faculties of an organism are "shocked" into learning it as an "emotionally" encoded *Imprint*; a duplicated facsimile-copy or *Mental Image* of severe misfortune, violent threats, pain and coercion, which is then categorized, stored and reactively retrieved based exclusively on its

Self is fixedly tied in on the sensations of a "body"—and this strengthens the circuits of *Identity* that *Self* is located in a "body." This happens much more often when an individual is already suspended *interior* to a Mind-System, already surrounded by the associative thought and emotional encoding circuits of the *vehicle*.

The Alpha-Spirit is capable of commanding a *genetic vehicle* and its functions (mechanisms and energetic fields) while retaining its original POV *exterior* and independent of the *vehicle* they are operating and Universe they operate in.

Δ Δ Δ Δ Δ Δ Δ

Entrapment in a Mind-Body Identity is possible and later cemented by "*Implants.*" There are many implant platforms and on which various circuits operate—but at this level of work, we are mainly concerned with a realization they exist and that their installation had a tremendous impact on the POV and considerations remaining with an individual to knowingly handle. Rather than prompting by a PCL directly, the *implants* on which *programming* and *encoding* occurs, are increasingly more accessible and less sensitive after a complete and thorough application of all materials comprising Grade-III and Grade-IV Systemology. *Implants* are treated in upper-level work when they "surface" and/or when a *Seeker* is in a position of *Awareness* to confront them directly.

Many who do already have a sense of their entry into this Universe and *Human Condition* will often liken it to *falling into* or being *sucked into*, &tc.; but in all cases where we have considered the action taking place to "*Implant*" an individual with the *Human Condition* in *this* Universe, the common theme suggests that one is *outside* and then one is suddenly *inside*—and during disorientation between, *something* happens.

_____
emotional *facets*.

Depending on whether an individual is working with *this life-time* or has begun work on the *Spiritual Timeline*, the methodology employed to start opening these channels for exploration is essentially the same: treating considerations and sensations attached to "going in" or "getting in" something or somewhere.

Significant "energetic charge" is attached to "Entry into Universes" or "Implanting." Much of this caliber of work is still under research and review at the Systemology Society for inclusion in higher Wizard Grades; so one might wonder why we mention its background before closing out Grade-IV. We discovered—some might say "by accident"—that *Tech* applied for "Wizard Level-0" *can* potentially trigger actual realizations of how a *Seeker* arrived "here." Since it is often reacted to without understanding and without realizing what this phenomenon is ahead of time, the fragmented automatic-response circuits connected to these events add some difficulty in maintaining high enough Awareness to fully achieve goals set forth for Grade-IV.

> By processing the concepts of moving *inside* and *outside*, a *Seeker* is less likely to handle such with automatic circuitry.

Systematic processing using *Route-3* (and/or *Route-0*) is applied to defragment considerations for accessing "Zu-Vision," operating "*exterior*" to the physical body, or even the handling of space and creation of a "Personal Universe." So long as a POV can be "snapped in" on the Mind-Body system outside of *Self-Determination*, the individual's *Identity* is still very much entangled and associated with those mechanisms.

- Incidents when you wanted to get inside but can't
- Incidents when you were kicked out from where you wanted to be
- Incidents of being trapped inside
- Being forced inside
- Pulled in

- Pushed in
- The feeling or sense that you must get in
- The feeling or sense that you can't get in...

—all of these types of incidents potentially carry a heavily imprinted charge, which greatly reduces *Self-Awareness* and *Self-Determination* and therefore, *presence*, when left uncontrolled. You can use the above concepts for PCLs to treat circuits with *Recall* or you can *Imagine* incidents and see what *Mental Imagery* seems most correct. In either case, earning some relief in this area will assist with handling the basics of upper-level work.

> An Alpha-Spirit exists apart from all thought and creation,
> but once it *believes* it is located among them,
> it is subject to its reality agreement with
> external conditions & environmental factors.

Another heavy-impact spiritual incident that can be both "restimulated" and "detrimental" to effective progress using *Wizard Level-0* techniques is: the Collapse-of-Space and Collapse-of-Universes—and this is something that all individuals have experienced intensely at some point on the *Spiritual Timeline* at least once, with their Home Universe.

In our exercises, we depict the basic structure of a *space* or *Universe* as a "cube"—defined by eight "corners" or "points" that *anchor* the boundaries of the dimension. Just as there are experiences of one's own POV "snapping in" or "caving in" on a new plane of *space* or *mass*, so too are there times when the *space* and *energy-matter* —and the very corners of a Universe itself—"collapse in" on the individual. Heavy fragmentation charges on this experience can affect a *Seeker's* willingness to be responsible for the "*Creation-of-Space*" as found in Grade-IV exercises.

The "*hot buttons*"[172] treated in systematic processing for "Collapse-of-Universes" are quite similar to the "going in" or "interior/exterior" buttons used previously. In this instance, rather than a POV being "snapped in" to some *space* or *energy-matter*, the reverse is treated:

- Incidents of *space* collapsing in on the POV
- The world closing in; the world folding up
- Energy imploding; energy collapsing in on the POV
- Corner-points collapsing; corner-points snapping in on the POV
- Sudden "uncreation" or folding up of all form
- The environment caving in on the POV
- Pulled backward from
- Falling away from
- Sense of everything suddenly becoming unreal...

As with the case of "POV snap-ins," these "creation cave-ins" may be encouraged or prompted by external sources and other-determined events—however, much like "invalidation" and other *facets* of personal degradation that we *choose* to "accept" or *agree* to as "reality," the experience of any POV is still *Self-Determined* on some level; including "Entry into-" and "Collapse of-" Universes,

Δ Δ Δ Δ Δ Δ

After the point of pure *Awareness* (I-AM), the next point on

---

172 **hot button** : something that triggers or incites an intense emotional reaction instantaneously; in *NexGen Systemology*, a slang term denoting a highly reactive *channel*, heavily *charged* with a long chain of cumulative *emotional imprinting*, typically (but not necessarily) connected to a significant or "primary" *implant*; a non-technical label, first applied during *Grade-IV Professional Piloting "Flight School"* research sessions of Spring-Summer 2020, to indicate specific circuits, channels or terminals that cause a *Seeker* to immediately react with intense emotional responses, whether in general, directed to the *Pilot*, or even at effectiveness of processing.

the Standard Model (or *Zu-line*) treats the Personal Universe or Home Universe of an Alpha-Spirit, which is created by and subject to the *first* Alpha-Thought: to direct considerations and command postulates for any existence *to be* or *not be*. It is composed of that which an Alpha Spirit has created for and as their own consideration—

> The "Home Universe" is the *highest* of "Creative Universes"; not "shared" in agreement—the truest sense of individuality.

In actuality—though outside the realization of the average human—an individual as Alpha-Spirit (true I-AM; highest POV) is still existentially occupying the existence of their Personal "Home Universe" foremost to any other Universe or POV—however, considerations and postulates for this Home Universe began to blur with reality agreements for a fixed POV in the remaining "shared universes," in which *Self* could engage in "creative display" and eventually "games" with other "*Selves*." A reduction in *Awareness* and ability occurred when eventually:

> Alpha-Spirits substituted considerations
> for the creation of their Home Universe
> by rigidly fixing reality agreements and
> POV in place with other Universes.

The command postulates and considerations of creation and space around "6.0" on the Standard Model required no energy or force in which *to be*. The agreement to using force—energy (in Alpha-Existence) and effort (in Beta-Existence)—is a "game condition" only. At first, things could be brought into being for a Creative Universe by "Alpha Thought" alone—and in many respects, the actual considerations and commands still originate at this level. However, with condensation of Games Universes and the individual *considering* creation as more solid *energy-matter* at each one, the actions require a similar degree of *energy* to be applied *to* it—which, again, further validates the *substance* and *reality* of a particular Universe.

When POV is anchored to *beta-existence* and controlling the functions of a *genetic vehicle*, the Alpha-Spirit is still using energy beams.

These are commanded at the level of Alpha-Thought, but they are still being conducted through Will-Intention when attention is focused on *beta-existence*, whether a "body" or the "Physical Universe" in general; both are treated as environment (or setting). However, there is also the matter of the Mind-System (4.0), mental machinery and fragmented communication/energy circuits in the way of this as well, particularly when an individual is operating "interior" to the Mind-System or lower—all of which is below the *exterior* Alpha quality of "Direct Will and Intention" (5.0).

In Alpha-Existence, we chart a point of Alpha-Command (7.0)
-followed by Alpha-Thought (6.0),
-followed by Will-Intention (5.0) treating energetic action at the continuity-level of a "typical" Spiritual Universe (4.0).

The *depths* of Alpha-Existence (4.0) are fragmented to compose the *height* of (and control point for) *beta-existence*, following a similar pattern of energy as before, with the same style of harmonics, but taking place at lower-frequencies as the manifest Physical Universe. The same pattern repeats itself through the condensation of *all* Universes; only the *parameters* shift for *what* is treated as *above* and *below* the "line" for consideration as "physical" or "apparent."

For example, if establishing a POV in the "Magic Universe" (immediately preceding the present Physical Universe), one would still consider its continuity a *beta-existence* with its own relative degree of solidity (which is actually not much different than the present Physical Universe) and all else beyond that—the "*Other*"—is still treated as Alpha-Existence. For this reason, the Standard Model can be used to represent all possible states of all viewpoints for any Universe; and is far more workable than any former description of "planes," energetic bodies, or mystical cosmology.

The energy beams that an Alpha-Spirit uses for command of a Mind-Body system are treated lightly in other types of "energy work" pertaining to certain "circuits" and "flows" in the body—such as *kundalini, yoga, chakras, &tc.*—though like other forms of mysticism, the practitioner has a tendency to remain quite fixed to the mental circuitry itself, rather than a perspective *outside* of it. One can use these other methods and often get lucky in managing some kind of repair of an existing state, but seldom does it permanently treat the *encoded* and *programmed* conditions that cause an individual to continuously require these corrective actions as a response. While the methods may produce and effect, they also validate operating reactively only and putting the individual at effect.

Handling of energy beams and flows requires operating with clear channels from a point of direct consideration and command postulates in order to *Will* or *Intend* an energetic effect. It requires no actual effort, because we are not using a physical means to affect physical mass; the space-time and energy-matter of beta-existence is not part of formula. A *Seeker* often finds working directly with energy is a bit out of their "reality" to grasp at first, quite different from how they have come to consider standard operation and action in the Physical Universe.

For example, when controlling a *genetic vehicle*, the Alpha-Spirit will connect up circuitry and energy beams—running to the inside of a head, the back of the neck, all along the central nervous system or spine, the area called the Solar Plexus, and so forth. These are areas that, in the past, have been treated as "energy centers" or "light centers" that circulate specific types of energy. Yet most traditions just *assume* them to *be*, not realizing that *Self* is not only operating them, but also responsible for agreeing to and maintaining their *creation* each step of the way.

As there are essentially *seven* of these "centers" and *seven* "shells" "bodies" or "veils" that enshroud considerations of an individual occupying this Physical Universe, we have long been navigating this ascent up the *"Ladder of Light"* using the calculable systematic correlation existing between these personal *"layers"* that were added and the cosmic "Gates" we descended.

Before heavy fragmentation occurs, an Alpha-Spirit is *Aware* that they are not actually located *interior to* a Creative Universe, but is instead "reaching inside" one to operate and experience the operation. As demonstrated when practicing exercises for "Creation-of-Universes," the individual (as an *Awareness*) is completely outside the boundaries of the space, looking *in*. [This applies to everyone, not only those individuals named Timothy Leary.] The Alpha-Spirit is already *exterior* to the entire Universe as an actuality, so the best "Secondary POV" (they think) is not located behind the "body" it wants to operate and experience, but from a POV that is *inside* it. Which is, of course, how an individual gets over-identified with, and can fixedly snap into, a "body" more permanently.

The more an individual associates their *Identity* with the *genetic vehicle*, the greater energy will be applied to *protect it* and maintain its survival above all other considerations—and it is the "above all else" to the detriment of *Self-Awareness* that allows for personal fragmentation. When an Alpha-Spirit *identifies* with the "pain" or other sensations of a physical body, additional circuitry is crystallized or calcified in place, which we have called *imprints*. The "shock" snaps the POV into the body with force.

Since the Alpha-Spirit also now wants to protect itself—considering itself to share the same fate as the body—it develops all manner of shields, filters, relays and other automatic mechanisms to assist protecting the *genetic vehicle*. Given the logical conclusion of this mode of action repeated numerous times through many incarnations, the inherent sense of "betrayal" inevitable down the line is sure to put an individual out of communication with bodies and spaces throughout this *beta-existence* altogether—and another Universe collapse. Then, we'll find the considerations for the next shared-agreement Universe to sink one notch lower as a common denominator.

The Alpha-Spirit maintains an *interior* POV for the *genetic vehicle*, but realizing it is not always a "safe" place to be, sets up additional "points" to view from just outside of it. This is the area that *Awareness* will suddenly move to, using *Self-generated* response-mechanisms, during severe accidents. These points of "unconsciousness" are actually times when the POV has been expelled from the *genetic vehicle* automatically. It is also from this point that an individual's *Awareness* will suddenly "snap-in" on the body again. The very fact that these incidents result in a sudden shift of *interior* and *exterior* and *interior* (again) POV, outside of one's direct *Self-determinism*, contributes to the ongoing difficulty one has in "getting out" as a stable condition and resuming control of a body knowingly and willingly as opposed to being "stuck" inside one.

Given the manner in which we have so aptly unfolded and summarized keynotes of the map by which we arrived here, the way out should be a clearer view for a *Systemologist* that has reviewed our collective library of material. By practicing proper handling of the fundamentals, a greater understanding on primary areas of "energetic charge" and targeting the channels and terminals associated with turbulent incidents that led a *Seeker* to a point where they are now, a *Professional Pilot* will have gained the training, skills and certainty necessary to effectively assist others to redirect their course and increase their reach to fly out and beyond the boundaries of beta-existence.

:: B ::
THE APPLICATION OF CREATIVENESS PROCESSING
TECH REPORT FOR SYSTEMOLOGY PILOTS
GRADE-IV WIZARD-0 ROUTE-0
IMAGINOMICON EDIT

CREATIVENESS is perhaps the highest faculty and functional purpose of the I-AM-*Self* Alpha-Spirit in its basic state of Beingness as pure *Spiritual Awareness*. The more we increase a *Seeker's* level of *Creative Ability*, the more certain they will be in ability to control the creation of various *impressions* and *imprints*—the *Mental Imagery* and its *facets* that they have copied and continued to compulsively *create* in order to *"have"* something. Until an individual has systematically reduced encoded effects from former *"loss"*—including loss of creations and universes (see former *Imagination Tech Report*)— and practice in *Self-determining* their own "withdrawal" of attention or reach, a difficulty may arise that is common to the *Human Condition*:

| ability to let go of and disconnect from what we *have*. |

"Creativeness Processing"—for Route-0 and "Wizard Grades"— provides *Seekers* sufficient practice of their own *Creative Ability* in order to demonstrate that:

> *Self* can create whatever whenever—and everything that is experienced and recorded is being copied by *Self* and as a personal creation. We are, in essence, creating a facsimile-copy of the Physical Universe around us and treating the *Mental Imagery* of that copy within our Personal Universe. All of the perceptions are being communicated through circuitry and relays and screens; not directly.

The Universe that many individuals are fixed to when they close their eyes and *Imagine*, is very often still a duplicated facsimile of *beta-existence*; which means all their considerations for creation and ability and reality for a Personal Universe are tied exclusively to *beta-existence* as well. Systematic application of *"Creativeness Processing"* and *Imagination* assist in defragmenting these considerations and returning additional certainty to *Self* about its own true nature as a *Free Spirit.*

A *Seeker* should also begin with our previous Routes and methods of *Beta-Defragmentation* (such as in *Crystal Clear* and procedures in *Metahuman Destinations*) to reduce the heaviest charges on *imprinting* or reactive *"pictures"* prior to working intensely on increasing their perception of *Mental Imagery.* This keeps from allowing reactive *imprints* being perceived more vividly or with more "bite."

It may be the case that spiritual rehabilitation of *Creative Ability* is the master key to stable *Beta-Defragmentation;* whereas all other systematic processing essentially makes *this* more possible. For processing, the early steps of any standard procedure regarding "Presence" in environment and "Control" of the body are necessary for increasing *Awareness* enough to actually make *"creativeness processing"* effective for our purposes.

If a *Seeker* (as an *Awareness* point) is not truly "present," than all of the exercises, procedures and fancy PCLs will only be performed using some automatic response circuit. The individual, as *Self,* may still not being executing the commands at all. Most procedures for "Route-0" involve the *Seeker* in a subjective universe to work from, giving a *Pilot* only certainty on action he can actually observe. If an individual is still having difficulties with exercises and processes that *can* be observed and communicated easily, a *Pilot* should be careful investing[173] too much time toward applying "upper-routes."

Δ Δ Δ Δ Δ Δ

Increasing a *Seeker's* tolerance of POV and *Creative Ability* in-

---

173 **invest** : spend on; give or devote something to earn a result.

volves confronting *space* and "points" in *space*. Traditionally, an individual is more comfortable with *mass*, calcified *energy-matter*; and many exercises and techniques applied to "*Wizard Level-0*" are dealing with "points" and "spots" in existence, which have, in themselves, no *mass* or color or shape or feel. Of course, these "points" can be collapsed within a Universe and condensed into greater solidity—but that is not the level of solidity we are dealing with in higher existences.

"Route-0" emphasizes what *Self* is doing in regards to its own Personal Universe. In the past, we have treated other circuits of energy-flow and imprint storage regarding what *Self* has done to others, what has happened to *Self* from others, and what *Self* has observed others doing to others. All of this is stored and registered within the Mind-System. Whether it carries strong emotional encoding or not, if *Self* assigns significance and association to it, this information may contribute to what an individual carries for their considerations as Alpha-Thought. But this is entirely subject to an individual's own participation, command postulates and creation—even when information and cues are strongly suggested by external forces.

Another application of "Route-0" is found embedded in the most esoteric part of Systemology since the beginning, and that is "*Procedure 180.*" In this, *Self* is in command of its own *Beingness* from the POV of the Alpha-Spirit and not fixed to a specific dimensional anchor. We treat much of this upper work as *Imagination*, or "knowingly creating an illusion," when *Seekers* are first introduced to the "Wizard Grades," to safeguard against any invalidation of results. The "*Creative Ability Test*" (CAT) and other suggestions in the "*Imaginomicon*" (*Liber-3D*):—

> may simply be *gotten a "sense of"* until they can be *Imagined*; and they can be *Imagined* until *Actualized Awareness* is at such a level that *Self* starts to experience *actual* perceptions. *Imagination* increases *realization* and *potential* for the actual.

In order to *Be* as an *Awareness* at various "spots" and "points" in existence, and especially to be able to scan the "*Spiritual Timeline*," a *Seeker* must increase their tolerance to *look*. This means to actually apply attention to a "locational point" somewhere in *space-time*. The Alpha-Spirit has the ability to direct its POV to any location that it is willing to "see." And this should be practiced differently than the arcane mystic schools have taught.

Rather than considering a "spirit in flight," a *Seeker* should strengthen realizations that the true I-AM-*Self* POV is actually non-local point that "moves the scenery"—or rather *creates it*—around them.

A *Seeker* that works through material from earlier volumes relatively easily, but only sees "blackness" or "darkness" when applying *Imagination*, may have heavy Alpha-Fragmentation that is impinging on their handling of *space* and other concepts beyond *beta-existence*. They may require more time in practice with "*Wizard Level-0*" exercises before moving forward. Such *Seekers* may also have to practice observing "points" or "spots" in their physical environment before treating an "imaginary" or otherwise "spiritual" one.

A *Pilot* should practice with them in locating and touching "spots" in the room that are not attached or in relation to an object or *mass*.

"*Wizard Level-0*" goals should be approached gradually rather than invalidating what a *Seeker* is unable to reach at their present state. Therefore, certainty on the "abstract" can be strengthened by practicing with "objective."

Similar to techniques for "Presence" and "Control of the Body," a *Pilot* can place marks on objects and have a *Seeker* directing themselves between those, and even resuming the function of "choice" by deciding when to "touch" and "let go." The *Seeker* can practice moving the body over various spots in alternation.

When this has been satisfied, only then should a *Pilot*

have a *Seeker* "imagine" spots in their physical environment and perform the same steps. It is important that they can repeatedly indicate exactly where it is with certainty and that it is a "point" in "space" and not regarded in relation or vicinity to another object or *mass*.

A *Seeker* that is able to practice these things objectively can then apply the same methodology to their *Imagination* and use of *Creative Ability*. For whatever the reasons, the POV for Alpha-Existence is confined to "blackness" for some individuals. This is not the same as an Infinity of Nothingness, but the *Imprinting Incident* has left something so similar that it produces a fear of approaching the Gates of Infinity and standing for-and-as *Self*, the point of pure *Spiritual Awareness*.

A *Seeker* can practice placing "black points" out and getting a sense of them, even if they are not visible. Once the *Seeker* is certain enough of their existence and control of their creation, they can turn them white. As with the traditional application, any impinging or automatic phenomenon can be accelerated, changed, exaggerated or alternated until the individual has the creation under their control as intended.

Δ Δ Δ Δ Δ Δ Δ

Another element of "*creativeness processing*" became more critical the longer our experiments were treating "points" and "spots" with no *mass*. An individual was likely to not feel very well during the session, being constantly left to confront or stand before *space* and prompts toward *Nothingness*. An individual finds *energy-matter* more interesting and enticing as their *Awareness* decreases—because it gives them something to "know about." When its sole consideration was a "Personal Universe" where everything was known because everything was *Self-directed*, there was no "game" involved.

Although "games" and "energy" are what got an Alpha-Spirit into trouble early on the "*Spiritual Timeline*":

> it is difficult to increase *Actualized Awareness*
> back to its original state without also consistently
> giving the Alpha-Spirit something
> to *do* with a *purpose*—or something to *play with.*

When one is raising a young person—or even, for example, training a dog—they are likely to get into things that they shouldn't or start playing with something that is dangerous.

> If you want to take something away and
> not leave them unhappy,
> you give them something in its place.

This is not very different from an individual that has come to depend on their memory-stores of *Mental Images* that have all been assigned meaning from former events and still carry *facets* of significance into the present, altering the way in which an individual is able to experience existence. An individual would feel quite lost, disoriented and unhappy if we were to simply take all of the *imprints* away at once. It became clear to us that for a *Seeker* to "let go" willingly, they would have to be able to *create* something in its place that did not carry the same "weight" or encoded significance as their former creations.

> An individual has grown accustomed to being an
> "energy unit" rather than an "Awareness Unit."

When systematic processing is *reducing* emotional intensity, analyzing imprints to the point of their *dissolution*, and *de-fragmenting* old circuits of their "pictures" and "programs"—a *Seeker* can feel as though they are *losing*, not just the things themselves, but their sense of "game." They are no longer in a state of non-knowing, dependent on their stores of "think-ing" debris in which to "know."

However, if this is not handled systematically, a *Pilot* may find that as one "automatic circuit" is reduced, another one "turns on" with full intensity, so long as the *implanted compulsion* remains that the individual "has to have" something.

Our method is neither to "strip down bare" or "feed stuffed full"; the covert goal of *Imagination* and *Creativeness* processes is to assist a *Seeker* in being free of the implanted compulsion to "*have*" things. One of the basic steps in doing this is to simply work with "masses." We've mentioned having a *Seeker* really "*look*" at things around them in the "session room" to orient their presence—but, this is just as effective in one's usual environment, when they are already dealing with POV in this Physical Universe that are simply no longer "game enough" to be occupied; thus an individual is willing to duplicate, or repeat, less and less in each Universe.

Scenery has a tendency to fade into the background when its registry is set on automatic; it has no life or beingness given to it by *Self* until its restimulated in some way. Then, suddenly, being asked to *really* look at a tree or a hillside and notice its substance, even though one has "seen" a thousand times before, the perception is suddenly so much more vivid. This is what happens throughout the course of a "*Spiritual Timeline.*"

> An individual "sees" a tree and registers a facsimile-copy of it in their "Personal Universe"; they no longer will look at the tree, even when its present; they have the picture they generated and they will treat the recorded picture as the thing for "thought" and "consideration."

> Even when a live impression is recorded from the present external environment, an individual is still looking at an impression of the waves and particles hitting sensors and relays within a circuit, and not the actual thing that *is*.

> Theoretically, an Alpha-Spirit seeing something truly as it *is* would have the ability to dissolve its creation insta-

ntaneously. This may be more difficult to demonstrate in the *Physical Universe* of shared consensual reality agreements, yet the truth is that this is exactly why any defragmentation processing is effective in our Systemology and for an individual handling their own version of *it* as a Personal Universe.

Δ Δ Δ Δ Δ Δ

As released in *Liber-3D* (*"Imaginomicon"*) *and* these Tech Reports, *"Creativeness Processing"* refinement occurred at the Systemology Society as an upper-route alternative to "Route-2" (*Analytical Recall*). (Much as "Route-3" is an upper-route alternative to "Route-1.") Each former Route would apply to a particular set of subjects or imprint-types, but might prove more tedious when applied to later goals.

Applications of "Route-0" emphasize what *Self* is *doing*, but specifically what it can *create*—or *is* creating. The more a *Seeker* practices handling their *Creative Ability*, the greater the realizations concerning just how significantly *Self* has played a role in compulsively and unknowingly creating with various types of energetic-machinery all along. This is incredibly difficult for some individuals to accept properly; but it is among the minimum requirements for proceeding beyond *Grade-IV* and *Wizard Level-0*.

Working with energy directly has proven quite obscure to communicate for Grade-IV Systemology and its present methodology of applied spiritual philosophy; therefore, we have treated *Mental Images* for the energy that they do represent; partially like a magician uses a *symbol* in substitution for what is actual. But it is not the same. Rather than symbols, our *encoded imprints* actually do contain a reserve or entanglement of personal *Awareness* on a particular channel. Handling circuitry on that channel affects the *imprint*.

Our *Mental Images* are very personal to us and they carry a lot of personal energy within them—and each time they are restimulated from various *facets* and generated with automatic-mechanisms, the entire fragmented *Human Condition* is given more solidity—because an individual is also responsible even for the continuous creation of the machinery at work. In short: *"Creativeness Processing"* can allow a *Seeker* to regain control over their creation of *Mental Imagery* along a certain channel or representing a specific terminal that is not otherwise resolved easily using other "Routes."

In "Games Universes" and below, on the Standard Model, extending all the way through *beta-existence* (and the "Physical Universe"), we have a consideration of something very specific that does not exist in an individual's own "Home Universe," which is:

> "Scarcity-and-Abundance"—This exists as a consideration only if there is a dependency on "energy" to communicate actions and intention, rather than direct "Alpha-Thought."

This reality agreement is installed as part of *implant platform*, solidifying certain limitations and conditions placed on lower "Shared Universes"—providing a certain order-and-sequence to "forms" moved by "energy" and the creation of both. Everything gets knocked down a notch with each condensation; everything that was, becomes a "way to" something else. And this continues on.

> The perception of "scarcity" is what causes an individual to cling that much tighter to what they perceive they "have." An individual begins to *create* less on their own, the more "pictures" they copy. Failing to knowingly create, they hold onto the compulsively created *imprint* as something that is rare.

Of course, most encoded information tends to be a hindrance to experiencing and *Self-directing* that experience. It's easy to see how a very long existence across the *"Spiritual Timeline"* could have a tendency to cumulatively degrade abilities and fragment *Awareness* of an otherwise Unlimited *Spiritual Being*.

Collecting experience hinders *Awareness* for new experience. The only reason we keep it to "learn from" is because we put ourselves into a position of "not-knowing" in the first place —it was something to do; we've done it; now its one more consideration restricting what we will do next.

A *Seeker* carrying automated-images and other reactive-responses connected to "pain" is doing so because they perceive a "shortage" of such *Mental Imagery* in their "files" or ability to "create." So, it continues to be created on automatic and held in close to the POV. The information, sensory triggers, pings and other uncomfortable sensations will all continue to be generated by this reactive *Image* and encounters with its *facets* until control can be maintained over its *creation*.

As explained in Grade-III, particularly in *"Tablets of Destiny,"* a tendency to develop and depend on these primitive "survival" mechanisms is part of the evolutionary make-up of the *genetic vehicle* and only later *assumed* into the platform of *implants* that define parameters of the *Human Condition* as it is experienced by the Alpha-Spirit. But the basic truth, whether fully "defragmented" or not is that:

these are *just* response tendencies and impulse patterns; an individual doesn't *have to* "listen to" and "obey" them.

That is fundamentally what we are improving along the way. It is quite difficult for someone still working through heavy beta-defragmentation steps to come to a solid actual realization that: *they are creating this experience.* That is a lot for someone to take responsibility for all at once, especially if pushed before they are ready to handle it; the idea will certainly be rejected if it comes from another source. Therefore, the bulk of "beta-defragmentation" hangs on the amount of time it takes for an individual to come to this realization with complete certainty for themselves.

> Each "Route" is intended to "free up" enough
> *Actualized Awareness* to apply additional routes
> and higher gradients of systematic processing.

"Route-1" is mainly effective for lower-level cases that are heavily suspended in emotionally encoded *imprinting* in the present; those things which are so intrusive that no next-level "analytical" work can be effectively processed. It is used by *Pilots* when necessary and as a basic counseling methodology for *Ministers* of the Church of Mardukite Zuism. When operated beyond its intended purposes, "Route-1"—and any elements of erasure or reduction found in *dissolving fragmentation* on the channels with other Routes—not only validate reactive-mechanisms too often, but due to a perceived "energy loss," can cause other *imprinting* to become stronger and "snap in" tighter. An individual starts to "hold on" with a sense something is taken away. "Route-0" and "Circuit-0" applications of *Creativeness* and *Imagination* can resolve this when alternated in between other Routes. Prior to, and including, "*Wizard Level-0*," a *Pilot* should be very observant of the *Seeker's* condition regarding "energy loss"—alternating use of "objective" exercises with the "subjective" ones.

Δ Δ Δ Δ Δ Δ Δ

"*Creativeness Processing*" negates the automation and imprinting associated along a certain channel by replacing it with a new creation of the same type. Being of the same degree and frequency, the one essentially cancels the other out.

An individual could spend lifetimes retracing each one of their steps, each *imprint* and each facsimile-copy *Mental Image* they took on—but this would not have given us the results we were after here and now—and which we may summarize quite completely and concisely for the first time:

BETA–DEFRAGMENTATION
SYSTEMOLOGY OPERATING PROCEDURE
(VERSION 1.1 : 30 APRIL 2021)

Once a *Seeker* has completely worked through Grade-III (see *"Tablets of Destiny"* and *"Crystal Clear"*; or *"The Systemology Handbook"*) and the "hot-buttons" of Grade-IV using *"Route-3"* and SOP-2C (see *"Metahuman Destinations"*), all remaining beta-defragmentation is primarily accomplished with *"creativeness processing"* (see *"Imaginomicon"*)—this also requires imagining the creation and handling of all kinds of various terminals—possibly hundreds of different objects and masses—that have emotional encoding or associative programming restricting their "free" consideration and the *Awareness* fixed on them.

Each *Mental Image* representing a terminal is systematically handled in one's Personal Universe until the *creation, protection (preservation)* and inevitable *destruction* of it is freely treated and comfortably acceptable on all circuits of that channel. Finally, a *Seeker* reviews *all former* work, but applying *"Imagination"* to all PCL, adjusting all processing so as to not invoke any physical actions or recall pertaining to *beta-existence*.

Then, when an individual is clear of compulsive and unknowing tendencies to *create*, has fully rehabilitated *creative faculties* of a Personal Universe, and regained a commanding viewpoint as the Alpha Spirit exterior to any considerations for the Physical Universe, we consider that individual defragmented -or- *Actualized* up to a *beta-state* of *Self-Honesty*, a basic stable point, just outside the Mind-System, from which to knowingly continue to experience the Human Condition—and if so inclined, pursue a higher spirituality with the Mardukite Wizard Grades of Metahuman Systemology.

Since an individual typically has difficulty in handling *imprints* with heavy energetic charges on them—hence the purpose of the *imprint* and other mechanisms as a "buffer"—it is quite likely that they will have different reactions to being responsible for certain types of *"Mental Images."* It may be that when they *Imagine* something very clearly, and then make it more solid, that it is difficult to do anything with it other than admire—least of all, throw it away or destroy it.

Destruction is really counter-creation. Making something more solid or persistent is the continuous creation of many copies tightly compressed together. It may be that some *Seekers* would have to be prompted to create several copies of an *imagined object* before they are willing to discard or dispense with any. Needless to say, the ultimate goal here is for a *Seeker* to be able to freely create, confront and discard anything it can possibly *imagine* without an automatic tendency, associated response or any other consideration aside from: the practice of Alpha-Thought to make something *Be* what it *is.*

Ideally, *"Creativeness Processing"* for defragmentation processing requires some type of *assessment* on a *Seeker* concerning the terminals and forms that carry an energetic charge. There are ways of even using various biofeedback devices in conjunction with "word-association"—as even suggested in Carl Jung's later papers on the subject. An individual could list out all various items, as best they could, paying close attention to those that they are unwilling to create or be responsible for; also those that they have an emotional response-reaction to.

> Some *Pilots* have gone as far as to introduce PCL that query a *Seeker* alternately: "What are you willing to create?"/"What are you not willing to create?" Others have used to the keyword "confront" in place of "create." This works best primarily for more advanced *Seekers* experienced with *Piloted Procedure.* A less direct PCL would replace "are you" with "would you be."

Concerning applications to earlier materials: "Route-1" treats the heaviest incidents that are acting as the thickest blinders to maintaining present *Awareness*; "Route-2" employs "*recall*" PCLs, which can be converted to "*imagine*"; all of the "hot-button" terminals and circuits treated with "Route-3" in "*Metahuman Destinations*" can also be converted—making certain that imagined incidents and events are indeed uniquely and knowingly created, not something that the *Seeker* has a sense is a facsimile-copy from actual experience or a reactive image that simply "comes to mind" as soon as a terminal, subject or object is named.

The original "two-step maneuver" given for "Route-0" (Grade-IV, SOP-2C) appears as: a) *Imagine*; b) *Create It*—with no other commentary. In order to take what is *Imagined* and use it for "*Creativeness Processing*," the *Seeker* must have a sense that they are actually creating it and that it is not a reactive-response or being generated for them by some other mechanism that they, long ago, set up to deliver "pictures" on a "screen."

> For this, a *Pilot* can suggest any particular terminal (object, mass, &tc.) for the *Seeker* to "*Imagine*"; then this is followed up with a PCL to "make it more solid"—essentially to take what one has imagined to *be* and, by consideration, granting it *more beingness*. Until this is effective done by postulate command, a *Seeker* can start with making many copies and pushing them together to make a solid or turning up a "dial" to make it "brighter." At first, in lack of certainty on direct postulates or Alpha-Thought, a *Seeker* may be likely to rely on *imagining* a means of accomplishing the action in a way that is "in agreement" with experience of the Physical Universe.

Because an individual is constantly creating *energy-masses* that snap-in or pull-in on their POV, whether that is the *genetic vehicle* "body" or some other consideration of "*Self*," it is necessary to facilitate this on one's own determinism. However, a PCL directing this:

should *never* be a "pull" action (from inside),
but rather a "push" or "shove" (from outside).

The individual has enough "caving-in" on them when
they are fixed to a *genetic vehicle* POV; therefore, we employ methods to establish a "secondary POV" that allows
them to "push" or "shove" their *Creations* into the *genetic vehicle* from a point *exterior* to it. This is also excellent
pre-A.T. practice for *"Zu-Vision."* The *Pilot* should direct
an end-cycle to each *Creation*, alternating: "push into
that body" and then "throw away." If necessary, the
Seeker can "squish it into a ball" before the end-cycle action.

In addition to exercises selected for the *Creative Ability Test*
(*CAT*), the other processes described throughout Grade-IV
materials, and proper attainment of necessary realizations,
there is another primary "test-out" for *"Wizard Level-0."* This
was originally inspired by arcane ritual texts extending back
into nearly-prehistoric[174] Mesopotamia almost 6,000 years
ago; and the same methodology can be found in modern rites
of "ceremonial magic"—although little regard is made to it
otherwise.

These archaic scripts refer to the individual standing
within created-space while keeping a solid image on all
six sides from going away.

In some cases, a practitioner envisioned a "deity"; in
others a "star" or "symbol"—but most importantly, the
entire effectiveness depended on the *Creative Ability* and
Actualized Awareness to maintain this for the duration of
a ceremony.

While we are not as concerned with "magical" semantics for
our application of Systemology, the fact remains that the
minimum to effectively aspire beyond Wizard Level-0 is:

ability to handle *Creation-of-Space* on all sides of an indi-

---

174 **prehistoric** : a time before history is *written*; prior to c. 4000 B.C.

vidual; then on each side, to imagine an object, keep it still in place, make it more solid, make copies of it, and suspend it before proceeding to the next side.

This can be practiced alone as part of regular *Creativity Sessions*. Select an object with no energetic charge or personal significance for best results. When *Piloted*, make certain that PCLs refer to "that body" or "the body" and not "your body." For example: "In front of that body, imagine..." and then applying to each direction of "that body."

Realization goals for *Grade-IV Wizard Level-0* include: handling automatic and compulsive creation of *Mental Images*; freeing associative restrictions on *Creative Ability* and *Imagination*; detaching a *fixed POV* from the *genetic vehicle*; assuming responsibility for *Creation-of-Space* and handling *points* in *space*; and ability to maintain a stable Alpha-Spirit POV to freely experience a *Personal Universe* that is independent from, outside of and exterior to the *Physical Universe*.

BETA–DEFRAGMENTATION

SYSTEMOLOGY OPERATING PROCEDURE

(GRADE-IV WIZARD LEVEL-0 METAHUMANISM)

Once a *Seeker* has completely worked through Grade-III (see *"Tablets of Destiny"* and *"Crystal Clear"*; or *"The Systemology Handbook"*) and the "hot-buttons" of Grade-IV using "Route-3" and SOP-2C (see *"Metahuman Destinations"*), all remaining beta-defragmentation is primarily accomplished with *"creativeness processing"* (see *"Imaginomicon"*)—this also requires imagining the creation and handling of all kinds of various terminals—possibly hundreds of different objects and masses—that have emotional encoding or associative programming restricting their "free" consideration and the *Awareness* fixed on them.

Each *Mental Image* representing a terminal is systematically handled in one's Personal Universe until the *creation, protection (preservation)* and inevitable *destruction* of it is freely treated and comfortably acceptable on all circuits of that channel. Finally, a *Seeker* reviews *all former* work, but applying *"Imagination"* to all PCL, adjusting all processing so as to not invoke any physical actions or recall pertaining to *beta-existence*.

Then, when an individual is clear of compulsive and unknowing tendencies to *create*, has fully rehabilitated *creative faculties* of a Personal Universe, and regained a commanding viewpoint as the Alpha Spirit exterior to any considerations for the Physical Universe, we consider that individual defragmented -or- *Actualized* up to a *beta-state* of *Self-Honesty*, basic spiritual stability to step "outside" the Mind-System, from which to knowingly continue to experience the Human Condition—and if so inclined, pursue a higher spirituality with the Mardukite Wizard Grades of Metahuman Systemology.

Version 1.1 : 30, April 2021

NEXGEN SYSTEMOLOGICAL GLOSSARY
VERSION 4.3 - IMAGINOMICON EDIT

A-for-A (one-to-one) : an expression meaning that what we say, write, represent, think or symbolize is a direct and perfect reflection or duplication of the actual aspect or thing—that "A" is for, means and is equivalent to "A" and not "a" or "q" or "!"; in the relay of communication, the message or particle is sent and perfectly duplicate in form and meaning when received.

aberration : a departure from what is right; in chromatic light science, the failure of a mirror, lens or refracting surface to produce an exact "*one-to-one*" or "*A-for-A*" duplication between an object and its image; a deviation from, or distortion in, what is true or right or straight; in *NexGen Systemology*, a term to describe *fragmentation* as it applies to an individual, which causes them to "stray" form the *Pathway.*

abreaction : the "burn off" or "purging" or "discharge" of "unconscious" (reactive response) as applied to early 20th century German psychology, from *abreagieren*, meaning "coming down from a release or expression of a repressed or forgotten emotion; in *NexGen Systemology*, fully "resurfacing" traumatic past experiences consciously (on one's own determinism) in order to purge them of their emotional excess (or "charge"); also "*Route-1*" and "*catharsis.*"

acid-test : a metaphor refers to a chemical process of applying harsh nitric acid to a golden substance (sample) to determine its genuineness; in *NexGen Systemology*, an extreme conclusive process to determine the reality, genuineness or truth of a substance, material, particle or piece of information.

acknowledgment : a response-communication establishing that an immediately former communication was properly received, duplicated and understood; the formal acceptance and/or recognition of a communication or presence.

activating event : an incident or occurrence that automatically stimulates a conscious or unrecognized reminder or 'ping' from an earlier *imprinting incident* recorded on one's own personal timeline as an emotionally charged and encoded memory; an incident or instance when thought systems are activated to determine the consequence or significance of an activity, motion or event—often demonstrated as *Activating Event → Belief Systems → Consideration.*

actualization : to make actual, not just potential; to bring into full solid Reality; to realize fully in *Awareness* as a "thing."

affinity : the apparent and energetic *relationship* between substances or bodies; the degree of *attraction* or repulsion between things based on natural forces; the *similitude* of frequencies or waveforms; the degree of *interconnection* between systems.

agreement (reality) : unanimity of opinion of what is "thought" to be known; an accepted arrangement of how things are; things we consider as "real" or as an "is" of "reality"; a consensus of what is real as made by standard-issue (common) participants; what an individual contributes to or accepts as "real"; in *NexGen Systemology*, a synonym for "*reality.*"

alpha : the first, primary, basic, superior or beginning of some form; in *NexGen Systemology*, referring to the state of existence operating on spiritual archetypes and postulates, will and intention "exterior" to the low-level condensation and solidarity of energy and matter as the 'physical universe'.

alpha control center (ACC) : the highest relay point of *Beingness* for an individuated *Alpha-Spirit, Self* or "I-AM"; in *NexGen Systemology* —a point of spiritual separation of ZU at (7.0) from the *Infinity of Nothingness* (8.0); the truest actualization of *Identity*; the highest *Self-directed* relay of *Alpha-Self* as an *Identity-Continuum*, operating in an *alpha-existence* (or "Spiritual Universe"–AN) to *determine* "Alpha Thought" (6.0) and WILL-*Intention* (5.0) *exterior* to the "Physical Universe"–(KI); the "wave-peak" of "I" emerging as individuated consciousness from *Infinity.*

alpha-spirit : a "spiritual" *Life*-form; the "true" *Self* or I-AM; the *individual*; the spiritual (*alpha*) *Self* that is animating the (*beta*) physical body or "*genetic vehicle*" using a continuous *Lifeline* of spiritual ("*ZU*") energy; an individual spiritual (*alpha*) entity possessing no physical mass or measurable waveform (motion) in the Physical Universe as itself, so it animates the (*beta*) physical body or "*genetic vehicle*" as a catalyst to experience *Self*-determined causality in effect within the *Physical Universe*; a singular unit or point of *Spiritual Awareness* that is *Aware* that it is *Aware.*

alpha thought : the highest spiritual *Self-determination* over creation and existence exercised by an Alpha-Spirit; the Alpha range of pure *Creative Ability* based on direct postulates and considerations of *Beingness*; spiritual qualities comparable to "thought" but originating in Alpha-existence (at "6.0") independently superior to a *beta-anchored*

Mind-System, although an Alpha-Spirit may use Will ("5.0") to carry the intentions of a postulate or consideration ("6.0") to the Master Control Center ("4.0").

amplitude : the quality of being *ample*; the size or amount of energy that is demonstrated in a *wave*. In the case of audio waves, we associate amplitude with "volume." It is not a statement about the frequencies of waves, only how "loud" they are—to what extent they are or may be projected (or audible).

AN : an ancient "Sumerian" cuneiform sign for Heaven or "God"; in *Mardukite Zuism and Systemology* designating the *'spiritual zone'* (or *'Alpha Existence'*); the *Spiritual Universe*—comprised of spiritual matter and spiritual energy; a direction of motion toward spiritual *Infinity*, away from or superior to the physical (*'KI'*); the spiritual condition of existence providing for our primary *Alpha* state as an individual *Identity* or *I-AM-Self* which interacts and experiences *Awareness* of a *beta* state in the *Physical Universe* (*'KI'*) as *Life*.

anathema : a thing or person to be detested, loathed or avoided; a thing or person accursed or despised such as to wish damnation or "divine punishment" upon.

anchor (conceptual) : a stable point in space; a fixed point used to hold or stabilize a spatial existence of other points; a spatial point that fixes the parameters of dimensional orientation, such as the corner-points of a solid object in relation to other points in space; in *NexGen Systemology*, "beta-anchored" is an expression used to describe the fixed orientation of a viewpoint from Self in relation to all possible spatial points in *beta-existence* ("physical universe"), or else the existential points that fix the operation of the "body" within the space-time of *beta-existence*.

Ancient Mystery School : the original arcane source of all esoteric knowledge on Earth, concentrated between the Middle East and modern-day Turkey and Transylvania c. 6000 B.C. and then dispersing south (Mesopotamia), west (Europe) and east (Asia) from that location.

apparent : visibly exposed to sight; evident rather than actual, as presumed by Observation; readily perceived, especially by the senses.

archetype : a "first form" or ideal conceptual model of some aspect; the ultimate prototype of a form on which all other conceptions are based.

ascension : actualized *Awareness* elevated to the point of true "spiritual existence" exterior to *beta existence.* An "Ascended Master" is one who has returned to an incarnation on Earth as an inherently *Enlightened One*, demonstrable in their actions—they have the ability to *Self-direct* the "Spirit" as *Self*, just as we are treating the "Mind" and "Body" at this current grade of instruction; previously treated in *Moroii ad Vitam* as a state of Beingness after *First Death*, experienced by an *etheric body*, which is able to maintain consciousness as a personal identity continuum with the same *Self-directed* control and communication of Will-Intention that is exercised, actualized and developed deliberately during one's present incarnation.

assessment scale : an official assignment of graded/gradient numeric values.

associative knowledge : significance or meaning of a facet or aspect assigned to (or considered to have) a direct relationship with another facet; to connect or relate ideas or facets of existence with one another; a reactive-response image, emotion or conception that is suggested by (or directly accompanies) something other than itself; in traditional systems logic, an equivalency of significance or meaning between facets or sets that are grouped together, such as in $(a + b) + c = a + (b + c)$; in NexGen Systemology, erroneous associative knowledge is assignment of the same value to all facets or parts considered as related (even when they are not actually so), such as in $a = a, b = a, c = a$ and so forth without distinction.

assumption : the act of taking or gather to one's Self; taking possession of.

attention : active use of *Awareness* toward a specific aspect or thing; the act of "attending" with the presence of *Self*; a direction of focus or concentration of *Awareness* along a particular channel or conduit or toward a particular terminal node or communication termination point; the Self-directed concentration of personal energy as a combination of observation, thought-waves and consideration; focused application of *Self-Directed Awareness*.

awareness : the highest sense of-and-as Self in knowing and being as I-AM (the *Alpha-Spirit*); the extent of beingness directed as a POV experienced by Self as knowingness.

Babylonian : the ancient Mesopotamian civilization that evolved from *Sumer*; inception point for systematization of civic society and religion.

Backtrack : to retrace one's steps or go back to an early point in a sequence; an applied spiritual philosophy within *Metahuman System-ology* "*Wizard Grades*" regarding continuous existence of an individual's "*Spiritual Timeline*" through all lifetime-incarnations; a methodology of systematic processing methods developed to assist in revealing "hidden" *Mental Images* and *Imprints* from one's past and reclaim attention-energies "left behind" with them by increasing ability to manage and control personal energy mechanisms fixed to their continuous automated creation.

band : a division or group; in *NexGen Systemology*, a division or set of frequencies on the ZU-line that are tuned closely together and referred to as a group.

BAT (Beta-Awareness Test) : a method of *psychometric evaluation* developed for *Mardukite Systemology* to determine a "basic" or "average" state of personal *beta-Awareness*; first developed for the text "*Crystal Clear.*"

"bell, book & candle" : three dissimilar objects that are kept accessible during a processing session (the book is often a copy of *The Systemology Handbook* or a hardcover copy of *The Tablets of Destiny* with the dust-jacket removed if it is less distracting that way); a term meant to indicate a Pilot's "objective processing kit" of objects generally present in the session room (accessible on a shelf, table or pedestal stands); in *NexGen Systemology,* the name of an objective processing philosophy pertaining to command of personal reality; historically, a formal ritual used by the Roman Catholic church to ceremonially declare an individual "guilty of the most heinous sins" as "excommunicated (to hold no further communications with) by anathema"—whereby a *bell* is rung, a *holy book* is closed and all *candles* are snuffed out—thus we therapeutically use the same symbolism historically representing religious fragmentation for modern systematic defragmentation purposes.

beta (awareness) : all consciousness activity ("*Awareness*") in the "Physical Universe" (KI) or else *beta-existence*; *Awareness* within the range of the *genetic-body*, including material thoughts, emotional responses and physical motors; personal *Awareness* of physical energy and physical matter moving through physical space and experienced as "time"; the *Awareness* held by *Self* that is restricted to a physical organic *Lifeform* or "*genetic vehicle*" in which it experiences causality in the *Physical Universe*.

beta (existence) : all manifestation in the "Physical Universe" (KI); the "Physical" state of existence consisting of vibrations of physical energy and physical matter moving through physical space and experienced as "time"; the conditions of *Awareness* for the *Alpha-spirit* (*Self*) as a physical organic *Lifeform* or "*genetic vehicle*" in which it experiences causality in the *Physical Universe*.

beta-defragmentation : toward a state of *Self-Honesty* in regards to handling experience of the "Physical Universe" (*beta-existence*); an applied spiritual philosophy (or technology) of Self-Actualization originally described in the text "*Crystal Clear*" (*Liber-2B*), building upon theories from "*Systemology: The Original Thesis*."

biological unconsciousness : the organism independent of the sentient *Awareness* of the *Self* to direct it; states induced by severe injury and anesthesia.

biomagnetic/biofeedback : a measurable effect, such as a change in electrical resistance, that is produced by thoughts, emotions and physical behaviors which generate specific 'neurotransmitters' and biochemical reactions in the brain, body and across the skin surface.

calcified : in nature, to calcify is to harden like stone from calcium and lime deposits; in philosophic applications, refers to a state of hardened fixed bone-like inflexibility; a condition change to rigidly solid.

capable : the actual capacity for potential ability.

CAT / "Creative Ability Test" : a method of increasing personal freedom and unlimited creative potential of the Alpha-Spirit (Self) independent and exterior to conditions and reality agreements with beta-existence; a Wizard-Level training regimen first developed for the Grade-IV text "*Imaginomicon*" (*Liber-3D*).

catalog / catalogue : a systematic list of knowledge or record of data.

catalyst : something that causes action between two systems or aspects, but which itself is unaffected as a variable of this energy communication; a medium or intermediary channel.

catharsis / cathartic processing : from the Greek root meaning "pure" or "perfect"; Gnostic practices of "consolamentum" where an individual removes distorting/fragmented emotional charges and encoding from a personal energy flow/circuit connected or associated with some terminal, mass, thing, &c.; in *NexGen Systemology*, the emptying out or discharge of emotional stores; also "*abreaction*" or "*Route-1*."

chakra : an archaic Sanskrit term for "wheel" or "spinning circle" used in *Eastern* wisdom traditions, spiritual systems and mysticism; a concept retained in NexGen Systemology to indicate etheric concentrations of energy into wheel-mechanisms that process *ZU* energy at specific frequencies along the *ZU-line*, of which the *Human Condition* is reportedly attached *seven* at various degrees as connected to the Gate symbolism.

channel : a specific stream, course, current, direction or route; to form or cut a groove or ridge or otherwise guide along a specific course; a direct path; an artificial aqueduct created to connect two water bodies or water or make travel possible.

charge : to fill or furnish with a quality; to supply with energy; to lay a command upon; in *NexGen Systemology*—to imbue with intention; to overspread with emotion; application of *Self-directed (WILL)* "intention" toward an emotional manifestation in beta-existence; personal energy stores and significances entwined as fragmentation in mental images, reactive-response encoding and intellectual (and/or) programmed beliefs; in traditional mysticism, to intentionally fix an energetic resonance to meet some degree, or to bring a specific concentration of energy that is transferred to a focal point, such as an object or space.

circuit : a circular path or loop; a closed-path within a system that allows a flow; a pattern or action or wave movement that follows a specific route or potential path only; in *NexGen Systemology*, "*communication processing*" pertaining to a specific flow of energy or information; *see* also "*feedback loop.*"

Circuit-1 : in *Grade-IV* "communication processing" (introduced in *Metahuman Destinations* as *Route-3*), the flow of energy and information connected to outflow, what *Self* has expressed, projected outwardly or done.

Circuit-2 : in *Grade-IV* "communication processing" (introduced in *Metahuman Destinations* as *Route-3*), the flow of energy and information connected to inflow, what "others" have done to *Self,* what it has received inwardly or had *happen to.*

Circuit-3 : in *Grade-IV* "communication processing" (introduced in *Metahuman Destinations* as *Route-3*), the flow of energy and information connected to cross-flows, what *Self* has witnessed of others (or another) projecting or doing toward others (or another).

Circuit-0 : a more advanced concept introduced to *Grade-IV* "communication processing" (as listed on SOP-2C in *Metahuman*

Destinations for *"Pre-A.T"* or *"Route-0"* applications), which targets *'postulates'* and *'considerations'* generated and stored by *Self* for *Self* and the direction, energy or flows representing what *Self* "does" for and/or to *Self.* This circuit is treated further in *Wizard Level* work,

chronologically : concerning or pertaining to "time"; to treat as "units" of "time" ; to sequence a series of events or information with regard to the order it happened or originated (in time).

clockwork : rigidly fixed gear-like systems that operate mechanically and directly upon one another to function; a "clockwork universe theory" is a "closed-system design" popular in Newtonian Physics attributes all actions of energy-matter in space-time as reactions in accordance with a "Divine Decree" or fixed design that functions like a "clock-mechanism" and does not account for the "Observer."

codification : process of collecting, analyzing and then arranging knowledge in a standardized and more accessible systematic form, often by subject, theme or some other designation.

collapsing a wave : in *Quantum Physics*, the concept that an Observer is "collapsing" the wave-function to something "definite" by measuring it; defining or calculating a wave-function or interaction of potential interactions by an Observation; in *NexGen Systemology*, when a wave of potentiality or possibility because a finite fixed form; Consciousness or *Awareness* "collapses" a wave-function of energy-matter as a necessary "third" Principle of Apparent Manifestation (first described in *"Tablets of Destiny"*); potentiality as a wave is collapsed into an apparent *"is"*, the energy of which is freed up in systematic processing by *"flattening"* a "collapsed" wave back into its state of potentiality; also, *"wave-function collapse."*

command : in *Metahuman Systemology*, responsibility and ability of Self (I-AM) as operating from its ideal "exterior" *Point-of-View* as Alpha Spirit; to direct communication for control of the *genetic vehicle* and Mind-Body connection that is perfectly duplicated from a source-point to a receipt-point along the ZU-line.

command line : see *"processing command line"* (PCL).

communication : successful transmission of information, data, energy (&tc.) along a message line, with a reception of feedback; an energetic flow of intention to cause an effect (or duplication) at a distance; the personal energy moved or acted upon by will or else 'selective directed attention'; the 'messenger action' used to transmit and receive energy across a medium; also relay of energy, a message or signal—

or even locating a personal POV (viewpoint) for the Self—along the *ZU-line*.

communication processing : a methodology of Grade-IV Metahuman Systemology that emphasizes analysis of all Mind-System energy flows (information) transmitted and stored along circuits of a channel toward some terminal, thing or concept, particularly: what Self has out-flowed, what Self has in-flowed, and the cross-flows that Self has observed; also *"Route-3."*

compulsion : a failure to be responsible for the dynamics of control—starting, stopping or altering—on a particular channel of communication and/or regarding a particular terminal in existence; an energetic flow with the appearance of being 'stuck' on the action it is already doing or by the control of some automatic mechanism.

condense (condensation) : the transition of vapor to liquid; denoting a change in state to a more substantial or solid condition; leading to a more compact or solid form.

condition : an apparent or existing state; circumstances, situations and variable dynamics affecting the order and function of a system; a series of interconnected requirements, barriers and allowances that must be met; in "contemporary language," bringing a thing toward a specific, desired or intentional new state (such as in "conditioning"), though to minimize confusion about the word "condition" in our literature, *NexGen Systemology* treats "contemporary conditioning" concepts as imprinting, encoding and programming.

confront : to come around in front of; to be in the presence of; to stand in front of, or in the face of; to meet "face-to-face" or "face-up-to"; additionally, in *NexGen Systemology*, to fully tolerate or acceptably withstand an encounter with a particular manifestation or encounter.

consciousness : the energetic flow of *Awareness*; the Principle System of *Awareness* that is spiritual in nature, which demonstrates potential interaction with all degrees of the Physical Universe; the *Beingness* component of our existence in *Spirit*; the Principle System of *Awareness* as *Spirit* that directs action in the Mind-System.

consensual (consensus) : formed or existing simply by consent—by general or mutual agreement; permitted, approved or agreed upon by majority of opinion; knowingly agreed upon unanimously by all concerned; to be in agreement on the objective universe and/or a course of action therein.

consideration : careful analytical reflection of all aspects; deliberation; determining the significance of a "thing" in relation to similarity or dissimilarity to other "things"; evaluation of facts and importance of certain facts; thorough examination of all aspects related to, or important for, making a decision; the analysis of consequences and estimation of significance when making decisions; in *NexGen Systemology*, the postulate or Alpha-Thought that defines the state of beingness for what something "*is.*"

continuity : being a continuous whole; a complete whole or "total round of"; the balance of the equation ["–120" + "120" = "0" &*tc.*]; an apparent unbroken interconnected coherent whole; also, as applied to Universes in *NexGen Systemology*, the lowest base consideration of space-time or commonly shared level of energy-matter apparent in an existence, or else the lowest degree of solidity or condensation whereby all mass that exists is identifiable or communicable with all other mass that exists; represented as "0" on the *Standard Model* for the Physical Universe (*beta-existence*), a level of existence that is below Human emotion, comparable to the solidity of "rocks" and "walls" and "inert bodies."

continuum : a continuous enduring uninterrupted sequence or condition; observing all gradients on a *spectrum*; measuring quantitative variation with gradual transition on a spectrum without demonstrating discontinuity or separate parts.

control (systems) : Communication relayed from an operative center or organizational cluster, which incites new activity elsewhere in a system (or along the *ZU-line*).

correlate : a relationship between two or more aspects, parts or systems.

correspondence : a direct relationship or correlation; see also "*associative knowledge.*"

Cosmic History : the entire continuous *Spiritual Timeline* of all existence, starting with the *Infinity of Nothingness* and individuation of Self and its Home Universe, running through various Games Universes and ultimately leading to condensation and solidification of this Physical Universe experienced in present-time.

Cosmic Law : the "Law" of Nature (or the Physical Universe); the "Law" governing cosmic ordering; often called "Natural Law" in sciences and philosophies that attempt to codify or systematize it.

cosmology : a systematic philosophy defining origins and structure of an *apparent* Universe.

Cosmos : archaic term for the "Physical Universe"; semantically implies chaos brought into order; in *NexGen Systemology*, can also include considerations of "Universes" experienced previously as a *beta-existence*.

crash-course : a very intense or steep delivery of education over a very brief time period, usually applied to bring a student "up-to-speed" or "up-to-date" for receiving and understanding newer or cumulatively more advanced material.

creative ability test : see "*CAT*."

creativeness processing : a methodology of Grade-IV Metahuman Systemology that emphasizes personal use of Imagination, or else the creative ability of Self and freeing the considerations of the Alpha-Spirit to *Be* or *Create* anything within its Personal Universe, independent of reality agreements with beta-existence; also "*Route-0*."

Crystal Clear : the second professional publication of Mardukite Systemology, released publicly in December 2019; the second professional text in Grade-III Mardukite Systemology, released as "*Liber-2B*" and reissued in the Grade-III Master Edition "*Systemology Handbook*"; contains fundamental theory of "*Beta-Defragmentation*" and "*Route-2*" systematic processing methodology.

cuneiform : the oldest extant writing system at the inception of modern civilization in Mesopotamia; a system of wedge-shaped script inscribed on clay tablets with a reed pen, allowing advancements in record keeping and communication no longer restricted to more literal graphic representations or pictures.

cuneiform signs : the cuneiform script, as used in ancient Mesopotamia, is not represented in a linear alphabet of "letters," but by a systematic use of basic word "signs" that are combined to form more complex word "signs"—each sign represented a "sound" more than it did a letter, such as "ab," "ad", "ba", "da" &tc.

data-set : the total accumulation of knowledge used to base Reality.

dead-memories : outdated, inadequate or erroneous data.

defragmentation : the *reparation* of wholeness; collecting all dispersed parts to reform an original whole; a process of removing "*fragmentation*" in data or knowledge to provide a clear understanding; applying techniques and processes that promote a *holistic* interconnected *alpha* state, favoring observational *Awareness* of continuity in all spiritual and physical systems; in *NexGen Systemology*, a "*Seeker*" achieving an actualized state of basic "*Self-Honest Awareness*" is said to be *beta-defragmented*, whereas *Alpha-defragmentation* is the rehabilitation of the *creative ability*, managing the *Spiritual Timeline* and the POV of *Self* as Alpha-Spirit (I-AM); see also "*Beta-defragmentation*."

degree : a physical or conceptual *unit* (or point) defining the variation present relative to a *scale* above and below it; any stage or extent to which something *is* in relation to other possible positions within a *set* of "*parameters*"; a point within a specific range or spectrum; in *NexGen Systemology*, a *Seeker's* potential energy variations or fluctuations in thought, emotional reaction and physical perception are all treated as "*degrees*."

destiny : what is set down, made firm, standard, or stands fixed as a constant end; the absolute *destination* regardless of whatever course is traveled; in *NexGen Systemology*, the "*destiny*" of the "*Human Spirit*" (or "*Alpha Spirit*") is infinite existence—"*Immortality*."

differentiation : an apparent difference between aspects or concepts.

discernment : to perceive, distinguish and/or differentiate experience into true knowledge.

dissonance : discordance; out of step; out of phase; disharmonious; the "differential" between the way things are and the way things are experienced; cognitive dissonance could be demonstrated as A = abc, or C = A, the duplication of truth/communication is not A-for-A.

dross : prime material; specifically waste-matter or refuse; the discarded remains collected together.

dynamic (systems) : a principle or fixed system which demonstrates its '*variations*' in activity (or output) only in constant relation to variables or fluctuation of interrelated systems; a standard principle, function, process or system that exhibits '*variations*' and change simultaneously with all connected systems.

Eastern traditions : the evolution of the *Ancient Mystery School* east of its origins, primarily the Asian continent, or what is archaically referred to as "oriental."

echelon : a level or rung on a ladder; a rank or level of command.

emotional encoding : the substance of *imprints*; associations of sensory experience with an *imprint*; perceptions of our environment that receive an *emotional charge*, which form or reinforce facets of an *im-

print; perceptions recorded and stored as an *imprint* within the "emotional range" of energetic manifestation; the formation of an energetic store or charge on a channel that fixes emotional responses as a mechanistic automation, which is carried on in an individual's spiritual timeline or personal continuum of existence.

encompassing : to form a circle around, surround or envelop around.

energetic exchange : communicated transmission of energetically encoded "information" between fields, forces or source-points that share some degree of interconnectivity; the event of "waves" acting upon each other like a force, flowing in regard to their proximity, range, frequency and amplitude.

energy signatures : a distinctive pattern of energetic action.

enforcement : the act of compelling or putting (effort) into force; to compel or impose obedience by force; to impress strongly with applications of stress to demand agreement or validation; the lowest-level of direct control by physical effort or threat of punishment; a low-level method of control in the absence of true communication.

entanglement : tangled together; intertwined and enmeshed systems; in *NexGen Systemology*, a reference to the interrelation of all particles as waves at a higher point of connectivity than is apparent, since wave-functions only "collapse" when someone is *Observing*, or doing the measuring, evaluating, &tc.

entropy : the reduction of organized physical systems back into chaos-continuity when their integrity is measured against space over time.

epicenter : the point from which shock-waves travel.

epistemology : a school of philosophy focused on the truth of knowledge *and* knowledge of truth; theories regarding validity and truth inherent in any structure of knowledge and reason.

erroneous : inaccurate; incorrect; containing error.

esoteric : hidden; secret; knowledge understood by a select few.

evaluate : to determine, assign or fix a set value, amount or meaning.

exacting : a demanding rigid effort to draw forth from.

existence : a *state* or fact of *apparent manifestation*; the resulting combination of the Principles of Manifestation: consciousness, motion and substance; continued *survival*; that which independently exists; the *'Prime Directive'* and sole purpose of all manifestation or Reality;

the highest common intended motivation driving any *"Thing"* or *Life*.

existential : pertaining to existence, or some aspect or condition of existence.

experiential data : accumulated reference points we store as memory concerning our "experience" with Reality.

extant : in existence; existing.

exterior : outside of; on the outside; in *NexGen Systemology*, we mean specifically the POV of *Self* that is *'outside of'* the *Human Condition,* free of the physical and mental trappings of the Physical Universe; a metahuman range of consideration; see also *'Zu-Vision'*.

external : a force coming from outside; information received from outside sources; in *NexGen Systemology*, the objective *'Physical Universe'* existence, or *beta-existence*, that the Physical Body or *genetic vehicle* is essentially *anchored* to for its considerations of locational space-time as a dimension or POV.

facets : an aspect, an apparent phase; one of many faces of something; a cut surface on a gem or crystal; in *NexGen Systemology*—a single perception or aspect of a memory or *"Imprint"*; any one of many ways in which a memory is recorded; perceptions associated with a painful emotional (sensation) experience and *"imprinted"* onto a metaphoric lens through which to view future similar experiences; other secondary terminals that are associated with a particular terminal, painful event or experience of loss, and which may exhibit the same encoded significance as the activating event.

faculties : abilities of the mind (individual) inherent or developed.

fate : what is brought to light or actualized as experience; the actual *course* taken to reach an end, charted end, or final *destination*; in *NexGen Systemology*, the *'fate'* of a *'Human Spirit'* (or *'Alpha Spirit'*) is determined by the choice of course taken to experience *Life*.

feedback loop : a complete and continuous circuit flow of energy or information directed as an output from a source to a target which is altered and return back to the source as an input; in *General Systemology*—the continuous process where outputs of a system are routed back as inputs to complete a circuit or loop, which may be closed or connected to other systems/circuits; in *NexGen Systemology*—the continuous process where directed *Life* energy and *Awareness* is sent back to *Self* as experience, understanding and memory to complete an energetic circuit as a loop.

flattening a wave : see *"process-out"* for definition; also see *"collapsing a wave."*

flow : movement across (or through) a channel (or conduit); a direction of active energetic motion typically distinguished as either an *inflow*, *out-flow* or *cross-flow*.

fodder : food, esp. for cattle; the raw material used to create.

fractal : a wave-curve, geometric figure, form or pattern, with each part representative of the same characteristics as the whole; any baseline, sequence or pattern where the 'whole' is found in the 'parts' and the 'parts' contain the 'whole'; a pattern that reoccurs similarly at various scales/levels on a continuous whole; a subset of a Euclidean space explored in higher-level academic mathematics, in which fractal dimensions are found to exceed topological ones; in NexGen Systemology, a "fractal-like" description is used specifically for a pattern or form that has a reoccurring nature without regard to what level or scale it is manifest upon. Examples include the formation of crystals, tree-like patterns, the comparison of atoms to solar systems to galaxies, &tc.

fragmentation : breaking into parts and scattering the pieces; the *fractioning* of wholeness or the *fracture* of a holistic interconnected *alpha* state, favoring observational *Awareness* of perceived connectivity between parts; *discontinuity*; separation of a totality into parts; in *NexGen Systemology*, a person outside a state of *Self-Honesty* is said to be *fragmented*.

game : a strategic situation where a "player's" power of choice is employed or affected; a parameter or condition defined by purposes, freedoms and barriers (rules).

game theory : a mathematical theory of logic pertaining to strategies of maximizing gains and minimizing loses within prescribed boundaries and freedoms; a field of knowledge widely applied to human problem solving and decision-making; the application of true knowledge and logic to deduce the correct course of action given all variables and interplay of dynamic systems; logical study of decision making where "players" make choices that affect (the interests) of other "players"; an intellectual study of conflict and cooperation.

general systemology ("systematology") : a methodology of analysis and evaluation regarding the systems—their design and function; organizing systems of interrelated information-processing in order to perform a given function or pattern of functions.

genetic memory : the evolutionary, cellular and genetic (DNA) "memory" encoded into a *genetic vehicle* or *living organism* during its progression and duplication (reproduction) over millions (or billions) of years on Earth; in *NexGen Systemology*—the past-life Earth-memory carried in the genetic makeup of an organism (*genetic vehicle*) that is *independent of any* actual "spiritual memory" maintained by the *Alpha Spirit* themselves, from its own previous lifetimes on Earth and elsewhere using other *genetic vehicles* with no direct evolutionary connection to the current physical form in use.

genetic-vehicle : a physical *Life*-form; the physical (*beta*) body that is animated/controlled by the (*Alpha*) *Spirit* using a continuous *Lifeline* (ZU); a physical (*beta*) organic receptacle and catalyst for the (*Alpha*) *Self* to operate "causes" and experience "effects" within the *Physical Universe*.

gnosis : a *Greek* word meaning knowledge, but specifically "true knowledge"; the highest echelon of "true knowledge" accessible (or attained) only by mystical or spiritual faculties whereby actualized realizations are achieved independent of specialized education.

Gnostics : a name meaning "having knowledge" in Greek language (see also *gnosis*); early sect of Judeo-Christian mysticism from the 1st Century AD emphasizing true knowledge by *Self-Honest* experience of metahuman and spiritual states of beingness, emphasizing defragmentation of "illusion" and overcoming of material "deception";an esoteric proto-Systemology organization disbanded by the Roman Church as heretical.

gradient : a degree of partitioned ascent or descent along some scale, elevation or incline; "higher" and "lower" values in relation to one another.

holistic : the examination of interconnected systems as encompassing something greater than the *sum* of their "parts."

Homo Novus : literally, the "new man"; the "newly elevated man" or "known man" in ancient Rome; the man who "knows (only) through himself"; in NexGen Systemology—the next spiritual and intellectual evolution of *homo sapiens* (the "modern Human Condition"), which is signified by a demonstration of higher faculties of *Self-Actualization* and clear *Awareness*.

Homo Sapiens Sapiens : the present standard-issue Human Condition; the *hominid* species and genetic-line on Earth that received modification, programming and conditioning by the *Anunnaki* race of

Alpha-Spirits, of which early alterations contributed to various up-grades (changes) to the genetic-line, beginning approximately 450,000 years ago (*ya*) when the *Anunnaki* first appear on Earth; a species for the Human Condition on Earth that resulted from many specific *Anunnaki* "genetic" and "cultural" *interventions* at certain points of significant advancement—specifically (but not limited to) *circa* 300,000 *ya*, 200,000 *ya*, 40,000 *ya*, and 8,000 *ya*; a species of the Human Condition set for replacement by *Homo Novus*.

hot button : something that triggers or incites an intense emotional reaction instantaneously; in *NexGen Systemology*, a slang term denoting a highly reactive *channel*, heavily *charged* with a long chain of cumulative *emotional imprinting*, typically (but not necessarily) connected to a significant or "primary" *implant*; a non-technical label, first applied during *Grade-IV Professional Piloting "Flight School"* research sessions of Spring-Summer 2020, to indicate specific circuits, channels or terminals that cause a *Seeker* to immediately react with intense emotional responses, whether in general, directed to the *Pilot*, or even at effectiveness of processing.

Human Condition : a standard default state of Human experience that is generally accepted to be the extent of its potential identity (*beingness*)—currently treated as *Homo Sapiens Sapiens,* but which is scheduled for replacement by *Homo Novus*.

hypothetical : operating under the assumption a certain aspect actual "is."

identification : the association of *identity* to a thing; a label or fixed data-set associated to what a thing is; association "equals" a thing, the "equals" being key; an equality of all things in a group, for example, an "apple" identified with all other "apples"; the reduction of "I-AM"-*Self* from a *Spiritual Beingness* to an "identity" of some form.

identity : the collection of energy and matter—including memory—across a "*Spiritual Timeline*" that we consider as "I" of *Self*, but the "I" is an individual and not an identification with anything other than *Self* as *Alpha-Spirit.*

identity-system : the application of the *ZU-line* as "I"—the continuous expression of *Self* as *Awareness*; see "*Identity.*"

illuminated : to supply with light so as to make visible or comprehensible.

imagination : the ability to create *mental imagery* in one's Personal Universe at will and change or alter it as desired; the ability to create, change and dissolve mental images on command or as an act of will; to create a mental image or have associated imagery displayed (or "conjured") in the mind that may or may not be treated as real (or memory recall) and may or may not accurately duplicate objective reality; to employ *Creative Abilities* of the Spirit that are independent of reality agreements with beta-existence.

Imaginomicon : the fourth professional publication of Mardukite Systemology, released publicly in mid- 2021; the second professional text in Grade-IV Metahuman Systemology, released as *"Liber-3D"*; contains fundamental theory of *"Spiritual Ability"* and *"Route-0"* systematic processing methodology.

immersion : plunged or sunk into; wholly surrounded by.

implant : to graft or surgically insert; to establish firmly by setting into; to instill or install a direct command or consideration in consciousness (Mind-System, &tc.); a mechanical device inserted beneath the surface/skin; in *Metahuman Systemology*, an "energetic mechanism" (linked to an Alpha-Spirit) composing a circuit-network and systematic array of energetic receptors underlying and filter-screening communication channels between the Mind-System and *Self*; an energetic construct installed upon entry of a Universe; similar to a platen or matrix or circuit-board, where each part records a specific type or quality of *emotionally encoded imprints* and other "heavily charged" *Mental Images* that are "impressed" by future encounters; a basic platform on which certain *imprints* and *Mental Images* are encoded (keyed-in) and stored (often beneath the surface of "knowing" or *Awareness* for that individual, although an implanted "command" toward certain inclinations or behavioral tendencies may be visibly observable.

imprint : to strongly impress, stamp, mark (or outline) onto a softer 'impressible' substance; to mark with pressure onto a surface; in *Nex-Gen Systemology*, the term is used to indicate permanent Reality impressions marked by frequencies, energies or interactions experienced during periods of emotional distress, pain, unconsciousness, loss, enforcement, or something antagonistic to physical (personal) survival, all of which are are stored with other reactive response-mechanisms at lower-levels of *Awareness* as opposed to the active memory database and proactive processing center of the Mind; an experiential "memory-set" that may later resurface—be triggered or stimulated artificially—as Reality, of which similar responses will be engaged automatically; holographic-like imagery "stamped" onto consciousness as composed of energetic *facets* tied to the "snap-shot" of an experience.

imprinting incident : the first or original event instance communicated and *emotionally encoded* onto an individual's *"Spiritual Timeline"* (recorded memory from all lifetimes), which formed a permanent impression that is later used to mechanistically treat future contact on that channel; the first or original occurrence of some particular *facet* or mental image related to a certain type of *encoded response*, such as pain and discomfort, losses and victimization, and even the acts that we have taken against others along the Spiritual Timeline of our existence that caused them to also be *Imprinted*.

incarnation : a present, living or concrete form of some thing or idea; an individual lifetime or life-cycle from birth/creation to death/destruction independent of other lifetimes or cycles.

inception : the beginning, start, origin or outset.

incite : to urge on or cause; instigate; prove or stimulate into action.

individual : a person, lifeform, human entity or creature; a *Seeker* or potential *Seeker* is often referred to as an "individual" within Mardukite Zuism and Systemology materials.

inhibited : withheld, discouraged or repressed from some state.

intention : the directed application of Will; to intend (have "in Mind") or signify (give "significance" to) for or toward a particular purpose; in *NexGen Systemology* (from the *Standard Model*)—the spiritual activity at WILL (5.0) directed by an *Alpha Spirit* (7.0); the application of WILL as "Cause" from a higher order of Alpha Thought and consideration (6.0), which then may continue to relay communications as an "effect" in the universe.

inter-dimensional : systems that are interconnected or correlated between the Physical Universe and the Spiritual Universe—or between "dimension states" observably identified as "physical," "emotional," "psychological" and "spiritual." The only point of true interconnectivity that we can systematically determine is called *"Life"* or else the POV of *Self*.

interior : inside of; on the inside; in *NexGen Systemology*, we mean specifically the POV of *Self* that is fixed to the *'internal' Human Condition,* including the *Reactive Control Center* (RCC) and Mind-System or *Master Control Center* (MCC); within *beta-existence*.

intermediate : a distinct point between two points; actions between two points.

internal : a force coming from inside; information received from inside sources; in *NexGen Systemology*, the objective *'Physical Universe'* experience of *beta-existence* that is associated with the Physical Body or *genetic vehicle* and its POV regarding sensation and perception; from inside the body; within the body.

invalidate : decrease the level or degree or *agreement* as Reality.

invests : spends on; gives or devotes something to earn a result; endows with.

"kNow" : a creative spelling and use of semantics for "know" and "now" to indicate the state of present-time actualized "Awareness" as Self (Alpha-Spirit), developed for fun dual-meaning messages made by early Mardukite Systemologists in 2008-9, such as "live in the kNow" or "be in the kNow" and even "drown in the kNow" &tc.

knowledge : clear personal processing of informed understanding; information (data) that is actualized as effectively workable understanding; a demonstrable understanding on which we may 'set' our *Awareness*—or literally a "know-ledge."

KI : an ancient cuneiform sign designating the *'physical zone'*; the *Physical Universe*—comprised of physical matter and physical energy in action across space and observed as time; a direction of motion toward material *Continuity*, away from or subordinate to the Spiritual (*'AN'*); the physical condition of existence providing for our *beta* state of *Awareness* experienced (and interacted with) as an individual *Lifeform* from our primary Alpha state of Identity or *I-AM-Self* in the *Spiritual Universe* (*'AN'*).

kinetic : pertaining to the energy of physical motion and movement.

learned : highly educated; possessing significant knowledge.

level : a physical or conceptual *tier* (or plane) relative to a *scale* above and below it; a significant *gradient* observable as a *foundation* (or surface) built upon and subsequent to other levels of a totality or whole; a *set* of *"parameters"* with respect to other such *sets* along a *continuum*; in *NexGen Systemology*, a *Seeker's* understanding, *Awareness* as *Self* and the formal grades of material/instruction are all treated as *"levels."*

Liber-One : First published in October 2019 as *"The Tablets of Destiny: Using Ancient Wisdom to Unlock Human Potential"* by Joshua Free; republished in the complete *Grade-III* anthology, *"The Systemology Handbook."*

Liber-Two : First published in October 2020 as *"Metahuman Destina-*

tions: Piloting the Course to Homo Novus" by Joshua Free; an anthology of the *Grade-IV* "Professional Piloting Course," containing revised materials from *Liber-2C*, *Liber-2D* and (most of) *Liber-3C*.

Liber-2B : First published in December 2019 as *"Crystal Clear: The Self-Actualization Manual & Guide to Total Awareness"* by Joshua Free; republished in the complete *Grade-III* anthology, *"The Systemology Handbook."*

Liber-2C : First published in April 2020 as *"Communication and Control of Energy & Power: The Magic of Will & Intention (Volume One)"* by Joshua Free; revision republished as an integral part of the *Grade-IV* "Professional Piloting Course" in October 2020 within *"Metahuman Destinations"* (*Liber-Two*).

Liber-2D : First published in June 2020 as *"Command of the Mind-Body Connection: The Magic of Will & Intention" (Volume Two)"* by Joshua Free; revision republished as an integral part of the *Grade-IV* "Professional Piloting Course," in October 2020 within *"Metahuman Destinations"* (*Liber-Two*).

Liber-3C : First published in July 2020 as *"Now You Know: The Truth About Universes & How You Got Stuck in One"* by Joshua Free; a discourse in the *Grade-IV* Metahuman Systemology series; a revision of one part republished in October 2020 within the "Professional Course" manual, *"Metahuman Destinations"* (*Liber-Two*), a revision of the remaining part is republished in *"Imaginomicon"* (*Liber-3D*).

Liber-3D : First published in June 2021 as *"Imaginomicon: The Gateway to Higher Universes (A Grimoire for the Human Spirit)"* by Joshua Free; a manual completing the *Grade-IV* Metahuman Systemology professional series,with a treatment of "Wizard Level-0."

macrocosmic : taking examples and system demonstrations at one level and applying them as a larger demonstration of a relatively higher level or unseen dimension.

manifestation : something brought into existence.

Marduk : founder of Babylonia; patron Anunnaki "god" of Babylon.

Mardukite Zuism : a Mesopotamian-themed (Babylonian-oriented) religious philosophy and tradition applying the spiritual technology based on *Arcane Tablets* in combination with "Tech" from *NexGen Systemology*; first developed in the New Age underground by Joshua Free in 2008 and realized publicly in 2009 with the formal establishment of the *Mardukite Chamberlains.* The text *"Tablets of Destiny"* is a cross-over from Mardukite Zuism (and Mesopotamian Neopaganism) toward higher spiritual applications of Systemology.

Master-Control-Center (MCC) : a perfect computing device to the extent of the information received from "lower levels" of sensory experience/perception; the proactive communication system of the "*Mind*"; a relay point of active *Awareness* along the Identity's *ZU-line*, which is responsible for maintaining basic *Self-Honest Clarity* of *Knowingness* as a *seat of consciousness* between the *Alpha-Spirit* and the secondary "*Reactive Control Center*" of a *Lifeform* in *beta existence*; the Mind-center for an *Alpha-Spirit* to actualize cause in the *beta existence*; the analytical *Self-Determined* Mind-center of an *Alpha-Spirit used* to project *Will* toward the genetic body; the point of contact between *Spiritual Systems* and the *beta existence*; presumably the "*Third Eye*" of a being connected directly to the *I-AM-Self*, which is responsible for *determining* Reality at any time; in *NexGen Systemology*, this is plotted at (4.0) on the continuity model of the *ZU-line*.

"Master Grades" : literary materials by Joshua Free (written between 1995 and 2019) revised and compiled for the "Mardukite Academy of Systemology" instructional grades—"Route of Magick & Mysticism" (*Grade I, Part A*), "Route of Druidism & Dragon Legacy" (*Grade I, Part D*), "Route of Mesopotamian Mysteries" (Grade II) and "Route of Mardukite Systemology" or "Pathway to Self-Honesty" (*Grade III*).

MCC : see "*Master Control Center.*"

mental image : a subjectively experienced "picture" created and imagined into being by the Alpha-Spirit (or at lower levels, one of its automated mechanisms) that includes all perceptible *facets* of totally immersive scene, which may be forms originated by an individual, or a "facsimile-copy" ("snap-shot") of something seen or encountered; a duplication of wave-forms in one's Personal Universe as a "picture" that mirror an "external" Universe experience, such as an *Imprint*.

Mesopotamia : land between Tigris and Euphrates River; modern-day Iraq; the primary setting for ancient *Sumerian* and *Babylonian* traditions thousands of years ago, including activities and records of the *Anunnaki*.

metahumanism : an applied philosophy of *transhumanism* with an emphasis on "spiritual technologies" as opposed to "external" ones; a new state or evolution of the *Human Condition* achievable on planet Earth, rooted in *Self-Honesty*, whereby individuals are operating *exterior* to considerations that are fixed exclusively to the *genetic vehicle* (Human Body) and independent of the *emotional encoding* and *associative programming* typical of the present standard-issue *Human Condition.*

Metahuman Destinations : the third professional publication of Mardukite Systemology, released publicly in October 2020; the first professional text in Grade-IV Metahuman Systemology, released as *"Liber-Two"* and containing materials from *Liber-2C, Liber-2D* and *Liber-3C*; contains fundamental theory of *"Professional Piloting"* and *"Route-3"* systematic processing methodology.

methodology : a system of methods, principles and rules to compose a systematic paradigm of philosophy or science.

"Mind's Eye" : following semantics of archaic esoterica, the point where "mental pictures" (and senses) are generated that define what an individual believes they are experiencing in present time; activities or phenomenon described in archaic esoterica as the "Third-Eye" (or actualized MCC) where the *Alpha-Spirit* directly interacts with the organic *genetic vehicle* in *beta-existence*; in the semantics of basic Mardukite Zuism and Hermetic Philosophy, *Self-directed* activity on the plane of "mental consciousness" between "spiritual consciousness" of the *Alpha-Spirit* and "physical/emotional consciousness" of the *genetic vehicle*; *NexGen* 'slang' used to describe "consciousness activity" *Self-directed* by an actualized WILL.

motor functions : internal mechanisms that allow a body to move.

Nabu : the original "god of wisdom, writing and knowledge." (Babylonian)

neophyte : a beginning initiate or novice to a particular sect or methodology; novitiate or entry-level grade of training, study and practice of an esoteric order or mystical lodge (fellowship).

neurotransmitter : a chemical substance released at a physiological level (of the genetic vehicle) that bridges communication of energetic transmission between the *Mind-Body* systems, using the "nervous system" of the physical body; biochemical amino acids and peptides (neuropeptides), hormones, &tc.

NexGen Systemology : a modern tradition of applied religious philosophy and spiritual technology based on *Arcane Tablets* in combination with *"general systemology"* and *"games theory"* developed in the New Age underground by Joshua Free in 2011 as an advanced futurist extension of the *"Mardukite Chamberlains"*; also referred to as "Mardukite Systemology," "Metahuman Systemology" and "Spiritual Systemology."

objectively : concerning the "external world" and attempts to observe Reality independent of personal "subjective" factors.

occulted / to occult : hidden by or secreted away; to hide something from view; otherwise *occlude*, to shut out, shut in, or block; to *eclipse*, or leave out of view.

one-to-one : see "*A-for-A*."

optimum : the most favorable or ideal conditions for the best result; the greatest degree of result under specific conditions.

organic : as related to a physically living organism or carbon-based life form; energy-matter condensed into form as a focus or POV of Spiritual Life Energy (*ZU*) as it pertains to beta-existence of *this* Physical Universe (*KI*).

oscillation-alternation : a particular type of (or fluctuation) between two relative states, conditions or degrees; a wave-action between two degrees, such as is described in the action of the *pendulum effect*; a flux or wave-like energy in motion, across space, calculable as time; in systematic processing, alternation is the shift between two direction flows on a circuit channel, such as *inflow* and *outflow*, or between two types of processing, such as *objective* and *subjective*; alternation of a POV creates "space."

paradigm : an all-encompassing *standard* by which to view the world and *communicate* Reality; a standard model of reality-systems used by the Mind to filter, organize and interpret experience of Reality.

parameters : a defined range of possible variables within a model, spectrum or continuum; the extent of communicable reach capable within a system or across a distance; the defined or imposed limitations placed on a system or the functions within a system; the extent to which a Life or "thing" can *be*, *do* or *know* along any channel within the confines of a specific system or spectrum of existence.

paramount : the most important; "above all else."

participation : being part of the action or affecting the result.

patterns : observable cycles and tendencies.

PCL : see "*processing command line*."

personality (program) : a total composite picture that an individual "identifies" themselves with; accumulated sum of material and mental mass by which an individual experiences as their timeline; a "beta-personality" is mainly attached to the identity of a particular physical body and the total sum of its own genetic memory in combination with the data stores and pictures maintained by the Alpha Spirit; a "true personality" is the Alpha Spirit as Self completely defragmented of all erroneous limitations and barriers to consideration, belief, manifestation and intention.

perturbation : the deviation from a natural state, fixed motion, or orbit system caused by another external system; disturbing or disquieting the serenity of an existent state; inciting observable apparent action using indirect or outside actions or 'forces'; the introduction of a new element or facet that disturbs equilibrium of a standard system; the "butterfly effect"; in *NexGen Systemology*, *'perturbation'* is a necessary condition for the *ZU-line* to function as a *Standard Model* of actual *'monistic continuity'*—which is a *Lifeforce* singularity expressed along a spectrum with potential interactions at each degree from any source; the influence of a degree in one state by activities of another state that seem independent, but which are actually connected directly at some higher degree, even if not apparently observed.

phase (identification) : in *NexGen Systemology,* a pattern of personality or identity that is assumed as the POV from *Self*; personal identification with artificial "personality packages"; an individual assuming or taking characteristics of another individual (often unknowingly as a response-mechanisms); also *"phase alignment."*

phase alignment or *"in phase"* : to be in synch or mutually synchronized, in step or aligned properly with something else in order to increase the total strength value; in *NexGen Systemology*, alignment or adjustment of *Awareness* with a particular identity, space or time; perfect *defragmentation* would mean being "in phase" as *Self* fully conscious and Aware as an Alpha-Spirit *in* present *space* and *time*, free of synthetic personalities.

physics : a material science of observable motions, forces and bodies, including their apparent interaction, in the Physical Universe (specific to this *beta-existence*).

physiology : a material science of observable biological functions and mechanics of living organisms, including codification and study of identifiable parts and apparent systematic processes (specific to agreed upon makeup of the *genetic vehicle* for this *beta-existence*).

pilot : a professional steersman responsible for healthy functional operation of a ship toward a specific destination; in *NexGen Systemology*, an intensive trained individual qualified to specially apply *Systemology Processing* to assist other *Seekers* on the *Pathway*.

ping : a short, high pitched ring, chime or noise that alerts to the presence of something; in computer systems, a query sent on a network or line to another terminal in order to determine if there is a connection to it; in *NexGen Systemology*, the sudden somatic twinge or pain or discomfort that is felt as a sensation in the body when a particular terminal (lifeform, object, concept) is 'brought to mind' or contacted on a personal communication channel-circuit; the accompanying sensations and mental images that are experienced as an automatic-response to the presence of some channel or terminal.

player (game theory) : an individual that is making decisions in a game and/or is affected by decisions others are making in the game, especially if those other-determined decisions now affect the possible choices.

point-of-view (POV) : an opinion or attitude as expressed from a specific identity-phase; a specific standpoint or vantage-point; a definitive manner of consideration specific to an individual phase or identity; a place or position affording a specific view or vantage; circumstances and programming of an individual that is conducive to a particular response, consideration or belief-set (paradigm); a position (consideration) or place (location) that provides a specific view or perspective (subjective) on experience (of the objective).

postulate : to put forward as truth; to suggest or assume an existence *to be*; to provide a basis of reasoning and belief; a basic theory accepted as fact; in *NexGen Systemology*, the decisions or considerations made by the Alpha-Spirit (an Alpha-Thought) regarding the "*is-ness*" (what things "are") about energy-matter and space-time.

potentiality : the total "sum" (collective amount) of "latent" (dormant —present but not apparent) capable or possible realizations; used to describe a state or condition of what has not yet manifested, but which can be influenced and predicted based on observed patterns and, if referring to beta-existence, Cosmic Law.

POV : see "*point-of-view.*"

POV processing : a methodology of Grade-IV Metahuman Systemology emphasizing systematic processing toward realizations that improve a Seeker's willingness to manage a present POV and associated *phases*, their ability to transfer POVs freely, increased tolerance to experiences (or encounters) with any other viewpoint, and finally, an actualized realization that a POV is not one-to-one with *Beingness* of *Self*; an extension of *creativeness processing* and "Wizard Level" training that systematically handles *Awareness* of "points" and "spots" in space, from which an Alpha-Spirit may place its own viewpoint of a dimension or Universe—also a prerequisite to upper-route practices such as *"Zu-Vision"* and *"Backtrack."*

prehistoric : before human history is written; prior to c. 4000 B.C.

premise : a basis or statement of fact from which conclusions are drawn.

presence : personal orientation of Self located in space and time and handling the energy-matter present; the quality of some thing (energy/matter) being "present" in space-time.

"process-out" or **"flatten a wave"** : to reduce *emotional encoding* of an *imprint* to zero; to dissolve a *wave-form* or *thought-formed* "solid" such as a *"belief"*; to completely run a *process* to its end, thereby *flattening* any previously *"collapsed-waves"* or *fragmentation* that is obstructing the *clear channel* of *Self-Awareness*; also referred to as "processing-out"; to discharge all previously held emotionally encoded imprinting or erroneous programming and beliefs that otherwise fix the free flow (wave) to a particular pattern, solid or concrete *"is"* form.

processing, systematic : the inner-workings or "through-put" result of systems; in *NexGen Systemology,* a methodology of applied spiritual technology used toward personal Self-Actualization; methods of selective directed attention, communicated language and associative imagery that targets an increase in personal control of the human condition.

processing command line (PCL) or **command line** : a directed input; a specific command using highly selective language for *Systemology Processing*; a predetermined directive statement (cause) intended to focus concentrated attention (effect).

projecting awareness : sending out (motion) or radiating *"consciousness"* from *Self* ("I") to another POV.

protest : a response-communication objecting an enforcement or a rejection of a prior communication; an effort to cancel, rewrite or destroy the existence or "is-ness" (what something "is") of a previous creation or communication; unwillingness to be the Point-of-View of effect or (receipt-point) for a communication.

Proto-Indo-European (PIE) : in Linguistic-Semantic Sciences, a hypothetical single-source Eurasian root language (c.4500 B.C.) contributing to origins of common "word-roots" found in many European languages.

psychometric evaluation : the relative measurement of personal ability, mental (psychological/thought) faculties, and effective processing of information and external stimulus data; a scale used in "applied psychology" to evaluate and predict human behavior.

rationality / reasoning (game theory) : the extent to which a player seeks to play (make decisions, &tc.) in order to maximize the gains (or else survival) achievable within any given game conditions; the ability and willingness of an individual to reach toward conditions that promote the highest level of survival and existence and make the best choices and moves to see the desired goal manifest.

Reactive-Control-Center (RCC) : the secondary (reactive) communication system of the "*Mind*"; a relay point of *Awareness* along the Identity's *ZU-line*, which is responsible for engaging basic motors, biochemical processes and any *programmed automated responses* of a living *beta* organism; the reactive Mind-Center of a living organism relaying communications of *Awareness* between causal experience of *Physical Systems* and the "*Master Control Center*"; it presumably stores all emotional encoded imprints as fragmentation of "chakra" frequencies of *ZU* (within the range of the "*psychological/emotive systems*" of a being), which it may *react* to as Reality at any time; in *NexGen Systemology*, this is plotted at (2.0) on the continuity model of the *ZU-line*.

reality : see "*agreement.*"

realization : the clear perception of an understanding; a consideration or understanding on what is "actual"; to make "real" or give "reality" to so as to grant a property of "beingness" or "being as it is"; the state or instance of coming to an *Awareness*; in *NexGen Systemology*, "gnosis" or true knowledge achieved during *systematic processing*; achievement of a new (or "higher") cognition, true knowledge or perception of Self; a consideration of reality or assignment of meaning.

receptacle : a device or mechanism designed to contain and store a specific type of aspect or thing; a container meant to receive something.

recursive : repeating by looping back onto itself to form continuity; *ex.* the "Infinity" symbol is recursive.

relative : an apparent point, state or condition treated as distinct from others.

relinquish : to give up control, command or possession of.

repetitively : to repeat "over and over" again; or else "repetition."

responsibility : the *ability* to *respond*; the extent of mobilizing *power* and *understanding* an individual maintains as *Awareness* to enact *change*; the proactive ability to *Self-direct* and make decisions independent of an outside authority.

resurface : to return to, or bring up to, the "surface" what has been submerged; in *NexGen Systemology*—relating specifically to processes where a *Seeker* recalls blocked energy stored covertly as emotional *"imprints"* (by the RCC) so that it may be effectively defragmented from the *"ZU-line"* (by the MCC).

Route-0 : a specific methodology from *SOP-2C* denoting *"Creativeness Processing,"* as described in the text *"Imaginomicon"* (*Liber-3D*).

Route-1 : a specific methodology from *SOP-2C* denoting *"Resurfacing Processing,"* as described in the text *"Tablets of Destiny"* (*Liber-One*) as *"RR-SP"* (and reissued in *"The Systemology Handbook"*).

Route-2 : a specific methodology from *SOP-2C* denoting *"Analytical-Recall Processing,"* as described in the text *"Crystal Clear"* (*Liber-2B*) as *"AR-SP"* (and reissued in *"The Systemology Handbook"*).

Route-3 : a specific methodology from *SOP-2C* denoting *"Communication-Circuit Processing,"* as described in the text *"Metahuman Destinations"* (*Liber-Two*).

Seeker : an individual on the *Pathway to Self-Honesty*; a practitioner of *Mardukite Systemology* or *NexGen Systemology Processing* that is working toward *Spiritual Ascension*.

Self-actualization : bringing the full potential of the Human spirit into Reality; expressing full capabilities and creativeness of the *Alpha-Spirit*.

Self-determinism : the freedom to act, clear of external control or influence; the personal control of Will to direct intention.

Self-evaluation : see *"psychometric evaluation."*

Self-honesty : the basic or original *alpha* state of *being* and *knowing*; clear and present total *Awareness* of-and-as *Self*, in its most basic and true proactive expression of itself as *Spirit* or *I-AM*—free of artificial attachments, perceptive filters and other emotionally-reactive or mentally-conditioned programming imposed on the human condition by the systematized physical world; the ability to experience existence without judgment.

self-sustained : self-supported.

semantics : the *meaning* carried in *language* as the *truth* of a "thing" represented, *A-for-A*; the *effect* of language on *thought* activity in the Mind and physical behavior; language as *symbols* used to represent a concept, "thing" or "solid."

semantic-set : the implied meaning behind any groupings of words or symbols used to define a specific paradigm.

sentient : a living organism with consciousness or intelligence; a "thinking" or "reasoning" being that perceives information from the "senses."

simulacrum : an tangible likeness, image, facsimile or superficial representation that is similar to or resembles someone or something else; in *NexGen Systemology*, any *genetic vehicle* or physical body is considered a reflective "simulacrum" of, and used as a "vessel-shell" by, the *Alpha-Spirit* or *Self* (I-AM), which otherwise maintains no true finite locatable form in *beta-existence*.

sine-wave : the *frequency* and amplitude of a quantified (calculable) *vibration* represented on a graph (graphically) as smooth repetitive *oscillation* of a *waveform*; a *waveform* graphed for demonstration— otherwise represented in *NexGen Systemology* logic equations as 'Wf,' or in mathematics as the *'function of x' (fx)*; graphically representing arcs (*parameters*) of a circular *continuity* on a *continuum*; in the *Standard Model of NexGen Systemology*, the actual 'wave vibration' graphically displayed on an otherwise static *ZU-line* (of Infinity) is a *'sine-wave'*.

singularity : in general use, "to be singular," but our working definition suggests the opposite of individuality (contrary to most dictionaries); in upper-level sciences, a "zero-point" where a particular property or attribute is mathematically treated as "infinite" (such as the "black-hole" phenomenon), or else where apparently dissimilar qualities of all existing aspects (or individuals) share a "singular" expression, nature or quality; additionally, in *NexGen Systemology*, a hypothetical zero-point when apparent values of all parts in a Universe are equal to all other parts before it collapses; in *Transhumanism*, a hypothetical "runaway reaction" in technology, when it becomes self-aware, self-propagating, self-upgradable and self-sustainable, and replaces human effort of advancement or even makes continued human existence impossible; also, technological efforts to maintain an artificial immortality of the Human Condition on a digital mainframe.

slate : a hard thin flat surface material used for writing on; a chalkboard, which is a large version of the original wood-framed writing slate, named for the rock-type it was made from.

somatic : specifically pertaining to the physical body, its sensations and response actions or behaviors as separate from a "Mind-System"; also *"pings."*

SOP-2C : *Standard Operating Procedure #2C* or *Systemology Operating Procedure #2C*; a standardized procedural formula introduced in materials for *"Metahuman Destinations"* (*Liber-Two*); a regimen or outline for standard delivery of systematic processing used by *Systemology Pilots* and *Mardukite Ministers*; a procedure outline of systematic processing, which includes applications of *"Route-1," "Route-2," "Route-3"* and *"Route-0"* as taught for *Grade-IV Professional Piloting.*

space : a viewpoint or *Point-of-View* (POV) extended from any point out toward a dimension or dimensions; the consideration of a point or spot as an *anchor* or *corner* in addition to others, which collectively define parameters of a dimensional plane; the field of energy/matter mass created as a result of communication and control in action and measured as time (wave-length), such as "distance" between points (or peaks on a wave).

spectrum : a broad range or array as a continuous series or sequence; defined parts along a singular continuum.

spiritual timeline : a continuous stream of *Mental Images* or record of experiences that defines the "past" of a spiritual being (or *Alpha-Spirit*) and which includes impressions form all life-incarnations and significant spiritual events the being has encountered; also *"backtrack."*

standard issue : equally dispensed to all without consideration.

standard model : a fundamental *structure* or symbolic construct used to evaluate a complete *set* in *continuity* relative to itself and variable to all other *dynamic systems* as graphed or calculated by *logic*; in *Nex-Gen Systemology*—our existential and cosmological cabbalistic model; a *"monistic continuity model"* demonstrating *total system* interconnectivity "above" and "below" observation of any apparent *parameters*; the *ZU-line* represented as a singular vertical (y-axis) waveform in space across dimensional levels (universes) without charting any specific movement across a dimensional time-graph x-axis.

static : characterized by a fixed or stationary condition; having no apparent change, movement or fluctuation.

successively : what comes after; forward into the future.

succumb : to give way, or give in to, a relatively stronger superior force.

Sumerian : ancient civilization of *Sumer*, founded in Mesopotamia c. 5000 B.C.

surefooted : proceeding surely; not likely to stumble or fall.

symbol : a concentrated mass with associated meaning or significance.

systematization : to arrange into systems; to systematize or make systematic.

Systemology : see *"NexGen Systemology."*

Systemology Procedure 1-8-0 : advanced spiritual technology within our Systemology, which applies a methodology of systematic practice for experiencing: (1) Self-Awareness, (8) Nothingness and (0) Beingness.

systems theory : see *"general systematology"*

Tablets of Destiny : the first professional publication of Mardukite Systemology, released publicly in October 2019; the first professional text in Grade-III Mardukite Systemology, released as *"Liber-One"* and reissued in the Grade-III Master Edition *"Systemology Handbook"*; contains fundamental theory of the *"Standard Model"* and *"Route-1"* systematic processing methodology.

terminal (node) : a point, end or mass on a line; a point or connection for closing an electric circuit, such as a post on a battery terminating at each end of its own systematic function; any end point or 'termination' on a line; a point of connectivity with other points; in systems, any point which may be treated as a contact point of interaction; anything that may be distinguished as an 'is' and is therefore a 'termination point' of a system or along a flow-line which may interact with other related systems it shares a line with; a point of interaction with other points.

thought-form : apparent *manifestation* or existential *realization* of *Thought-waves* as "solids" even when only apparent in Reality-agreements of the Observer; the treatment of *Thought-waves* as permanent *imprints* obscuring *Self-Honest Clarity* of *Awareness* when reinforced by emotional experience as actualized "thought-formed solids" (*"beliefs"*) in the Mind; energetic patterns that "surround" the individual.

thought-wave or **wave-form** : a proactive *Self-directed action* or reactive-response *action* of *consciousness*; the *process* of *thinking* as demonstrated in *wave-form*; the *activity* of *Awareness* within the range of *thought vibrations/frequencies* on the existential *Life-continuum* or *ZU-line*.

threshold : a doorway, gate or entrance point; the degree to which something is to produce an effect within a certain state or condition; the point in which a condition changes from one to the next.

tier : a series of rows or levels, one stacked immediately before or atop another.

time : observation of cycles in action; motion of a particle, energy or wave across space; intervals of action related to other intervals of action as observed in Awareness; a measurable wave-length or frequency in comparison to a static state; the consideration of variations in space.

timeline : plotting out history in a linear (line) model to indicate instances (experiences) or demonstrate changes in state (space) as measured over time; a singular conception of continuation of observed time as marked by event-intervals and changes in energy and matter across space.

transhumanism : a social science and applied philosophy concerning the next evolved state of the *"Human Condition,"*; progress in two potential directions, either "spiritual" technologies advancing *Self* as an "Alpha-Spirit," or the direction of "external"-"physical" technologies that modify or eliminate characteristics of the *Body*; a theme describing contemporary application of material sciences emphasizing only "physical" and "genetic" parts of the *Human* experience, such as brain activity, cell-life extension and space travel; *NexGen Systemology* recently began distinguishing its emphasis on "spiritual technology" as *"metahumanism."*

transmit : to send forth data along some line of communication; to move a point across a distance.

traumatic encoding : information received when the sensory faculties of an organism are "shocked" into learning it as an "emotionally" encoded *Imprint*; a duplicated facsimile-copy or *Mental Image* of severe misfortune, violent threats, pain and coercion, which is then categorized, stored and reactively retrieved based exclusively on its emotional *facets*.

treat / treatment : an act, manner or method of handling or dealing with someone, something or some type of situation; to apply a specific process, procedure or mode of action toward some person, thing or subject; use of a specific substance, regimen or procedure to make an existing condition less severe; also, a written presentation that handles a subject in a specific manner.

turbulence : a quality or state of distortion or disturbance that creates irregularity of a flow or pattern; the quality or state of aberration on a line (such as ragged edges) or the emotional "turbulent feelings" attached to a particular flow or terminal node; a violent, haphazard or disharmonious commotion (such as in the ebb of gusts and lulls of wind action).

unconscious : a state when *Awareness* as *Self* is removed totally from the equation of *Life* experience, though it continues to be recorded in lower-level response mechanisms (fixed to a simulacrum or genetic vehicle) for later retrieval.

undefiled : to remain intact, untouched or unchanged; to be left in an original "virgin" state.

understanding : a clear 'A-for-A' duplication of a communication as 'knowledge', which may be comprehended and retained with its significance assigned in relation to other 'knowledge' treated as a 'significant understanding'; the "grade" or "level" that a knowledge base is collected and the manner in which the data is organized and evaluated.

validation : reinforcement of agreements or considerations as "real."

vantage : a point, place or position that offers an ideal viewpoint (POV).

vibration : effects of motion or wave-frequency as applied to any system.

viewpoint : see *"point-of-view" (POV)*.

wave-form : see *"sine-wave."*

wave-function collapse : see *"collapsing a wave."*

Western Civilization : modern contemporary culture, ideals, values and technology, particularly of Europe and North America as distinguished by growing urbanization, industrialization, and inspired by a history of rebellion to strong religious and political indoctrination.

will *or* **WILL** (5.0) : in *NexGen Systemology* (from the *Standard Model*), the Alpha-ability at "5.0" of a Spiritual Being (*Alpha Spirit*) at "7.0" to apply *intention* as "Cause" from consideration or Alpha-Thought at "6.0" that is superior to "beta-thoughts" that only manifest as reactive "effects" below "4.0" and *interior* to the *Human Condition*.

willingness : the state of conscious Self-determined ability and interest (directed attention) to *Be*, *Do* or *Have*; a Self-determined consideration to reach, face up to (*confront*) or manage some "mass" or energy; the extent to which an individual considers themselves able to participate, act or communicate along some line, to put attention or intention on the line, or to produce (create) an effect.

ziggurat : religious temples of ancient Mesopotamia; stepped-pyramids and towers used for spiritual and religious purposes by Sumerians and Babylonians, many of which are presented as seven tiers, levels or terraces representing "Seven Gates" (or "7 Veils") of existence, separating material continuity of the Earth Plane from Infinity (8).

ZU : the ancient Sumerian cuneiform sign for the archaic verb—"*to know*," "*knowingness*" or "*awareness*"; in *Mardukite Zuism and Systemology*, the active energy/matter of the "Spiritual Universe" (AN) experienced as a *Lifeforce* or *consciousness* that imbues living forms extant in the "Physical Universe" (KI); "*Spiritual Life Energy*"; energy demonstrated by the WILL of an actualized *Alpha-Spirit* in the "Spiritual Universe" (AN), which impinges its *Awareness* into the Physical Universe (KI), animating/controlling *Life* for its experience of *beta-existence* along an individual Alpha-Spirit's personal *Identity-continuum*, called a *ZU-line*.

Zu-line : a theoretical construct in *Mardukite Zuism and Systemology* demonstrating *Spiritual Life Energy* (*ZU*) as a personal individual "continuum" of Awareness interacting with all Spheres of Existence on the Standard Model of Systemology; a spectrum of potential variations and interactions of a monistic continuum or singular *Spiritual Life Energy* (*ZU*) demonstrated on the Standard Model; an energetic channel of potential POV and "locations" of Beingness, demonstrated in early Systemology materials as an individual Alpha-Spirit's personal *Identity-continuum*, potentially connecting *Awareness* (*ZU*) of *Self* with "*Infinity*" simultaneous with all points considered in existence; a symbolic demonstration of the "*Life-line*" on which *Awareness* (*ZU*) extends from the direction of the "Spiritual Universe" (AN) in its true original *alpha state* through an entire possible range of activity resulting in its *beta state* and control of a *genetic-entity* occupying the *Physical Universe* (*KI*).

Zu-Vision : the true and basic (*Alpha*) Point-of-View (perspective, POV) maintained by *Self* as *Alpha-Spirit* outside boundaries or con siderations of the *Human Condition* "Mind-Systems" and *exterior* to beta-existence reality agreements with the Physical Universe; a POV of Self *as* "a unit of Spiritual Awareness" that exists independent of a "body" and entrapment in a *Human Condition*; "spirit vision" in its truest sense.

SYS☥EMOLOGY
The Pathway to Self-Honesty

*A Basic Introduction to
Mardukite Systemology*

THE WAY INTO
THE FUTURE

Handbook for Humanity

a collection of writings by
Joshua Free
selected by James Thomas

*available in
Paperback and Hardcover*

Here are the basic answers to what has held Humanity back
from achieving its ultimate goals and unlocking the true
power of the Spirit and highest state of Knowing and Being.

"The Way Into The Future" illuminates the *Pathway*
leading to Planet Earth's true "metahuman" destiny.
With excerpts from *"Tablets of Destiny," "Crystal Clear,"*
"Systemology—Original Thesis" and *"The Power of Zu."*
You can help shine clear light on anyone's pathway!

Carefully selected by Mardukite Publications Officer,
James Thomas, this critical collection of eighteen
articles, lecture transcripts and reference chapters by
Joshua Free is sure to be not only a treasured part
of your personal library, but also the perfect
introduction for all friends, family and loved ones.

(Basic Grade-III Introductory Pocket Anthology)

SYS⚷EMOLOGY
The Pathway to Self-Honesty

CRYSTAL CLEAR

The Self-Actualization
Manual & Guide to
Total Awareness

by Joshua Free
Foreword by Kyra Kaos

Mardukite Systemology
Liber-2B

available in
Hardcover and
Paperback

Take control of your destiny and begin making your way
along the the first steps toward your spiritual evolution.

Realize new potentials of the Human Condition with
a Self-guiding handbook for Self-Processing toward
Self-Actualization on the Pathway to Self-Honesty
applying techniques and training from the original
"Mardukite Systemology Self-Defragmentation Course"
—once only available directly and privately from
the underground Systemology Society.

Discover the amazing power behind the
applied philosophy and spiritual technology
used for counseling and advisement by
Ministers of the Mardukite Zuism tradition.

Mardukite Systemology Research Library
(Grade-III, Liber-2B)

SYSTEMOLOGY
The Pathway to Self-Honesty

THE ORIGINAL UNDERGROUND CLASSICS

SYSTEMOLOGY:
THE ORIGINAL THESIS
An Introduction to
21st Century New Thought
by Joshua Free

(*Mardukite Systemology Liber-S-1X*)

A collection of the original underground discourses released to the "New Thought" division of the Mardukite Research Organization privately over a decade ago and providing the inspiration for rapid futurist spiritual technology called "Mardukite Systemology."

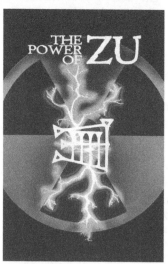

THE POWER OF ZU
A Practical Guide to
Mardukite Zuism
by Joshua Free

(*Mardukite Systemology Liber-S-1Z*)

A unique introductory course on Mardukite Zuism and Systemology, including transcripts from a 3-day lecture series given by Joshua Free in December 2019 to launch the Mardukite Academy of Systemology & Founding Church of Mardukite Zuism in time for the 2020's.

SYSTEMOLOGY
The Pathway to Self-Honesty

SYSTEMOLOGY HANDBOOK

*The ultimate operator's manual to the Human Condition
and unlocking the true power of the Spirit.*

** "Modern Mardukite Zuism" **
** "The Tablets of Destiny" **
** "Crystal Clear" **
** "The Power of ZU" **
** "Systemology—Original Thesis" **
** Human, More Than Human **
** Defragmentation **
** Patterns & Cycles **
** Transhuman Generations **

(Complete Grade-III Master Edition Anthology)

SYSTEMOLOGY
The Gateways to Infinity

METAHUMAN DESTINATIONS

Piloting the Course to Homo Novus

by Joshua Free
Foreword by David Zibert

Mardukite Systemology Liber-Two

available in hardcover

Drawing from the Arcane Tablets and nearly a year of additional research, experimentation and workshops since the introduction of applied spiritual technology and systematic processing methods, Joshua Free provides a ground-breaking Systemology manual to begin correcting—or "defragment"—conditions that have trapped viewpoints of the Spirit into programming and encoding of the Human Condition.

Experience the new revolutionary professional course in spiritual technology for Mardukite Systemologists to help "Pilot" the course of Human Evolution toward higher ideals and a way to free the Human Condition, returning ultimate command and control of *Life* back to the *Spirit*.

Mardukite Systemology Research Library
(*Grade-IV, Liber-Two*)

MARDUKITE
MASTER COURSE
Keys to the Gates of Higher Understanding

Now you can experience the Legendary "Master Course" from anywhere in the Universe, exactly as given in person by Joshua Free to the "Mardukite Academy of Systemology" in September 2020.

800+ pages of materials collected in this volume provide Seekers with full transcripts to all *48 Academy Lectures* of the legendary *"Mardukite Master Course"* combined with all course outlines, supplements and critical handouts from the original *"Instructor's Manual"*—making this the most complete definitive single-source delivery of New Age understanding and spiritual technology.

Referencing 25 years of research, development and publishing, including *"Necronomicon: The Complete Anunnaki Legacy," "The Great Magickal Arcanum," "The Systemology Handbook"* and *"Merlyn's Complete Book of Druidism."*

DRACONOMICON
The Book of Ancient Dragon Magick
25th Anniversary Collector's Edition
by Joshua Free

THE DRUID'S HANDBOOK
Ancient Magick for a New Age
20th Anniversary Collector's Edition
by Joshua Free

**ELVENOMICON
-or- SECRET TRADITIONS OF
ELVES AND FAERIES**
The Book of Elven Magick
& Druid Lore
15th Anniversary Collector's Edition
by Joshua Free

All Grade-I Route-D titles (plus more) available in the anthology:
"Merlyn's Complete Book of Druidism" by Joshua Free.

1995 · JOSHUA FREE · 2020

PUBLISHED BY THE **JOSHUA FREE** IMPRINT REPRESENTING

**The Founding Church of Mardukite Zuism
& Mardukite Academy of Systemology**

mardukite.com

CPSIA information can be obtained
at www.ICGtesting.com
Printed in the USA
LVHW080802180621
690564LV00008B/800